PIERRE

McCLELLAND & STEWART

PIERRE

Colleagues
and Friends
Talk about
the Trudeau
They Knew

Edited by

NANCY SOUTHAM

WITH A FOREWORD BY JUSTIN TRUDEAU

Hardcover edition published 2005
Trade paperback edition published 2006

Library and Archives Canada Cataloguing in Publication

Pierre : colleagues and friends talk about the Trudeau
they knew / edited by Nancy Southam.

Includes index.
ISBN 13: 978-0-7710-8168-2 (pbk.)
ISBN 10: 0-7710-8165-0 (bound)
ISBN 10: 0-7710-8168-5 (pbk.)

1. Trudeau, Pierre Elliott, 1919-2000. 2. Prime ministers – Canada – Biography.
3. Canada – Politics and government – 1968-1979. 4. Oral biography.
I. Southam, Nancy

FC626.T7P515 2004   971.064'4'092   C2004-902883-9

We acknowledge the financial support of the Government of Canada through the Book Publishing Industry Development Program and that of the Government of Ontario through the Ontario Media Development Corporation's Ontario Book Initiative. We further acknowledge the support of the Canada Council for the Arts and the Ontario Arts Council for our publishing program.

All translations from French to English were done by Jean-Paul Murray.

Epigraph on page x is taken from the poem "Directions" from *The Art of Drowning* by Billy Collins. Copyright © 1995 by Billy Collins. The verse on page 141 is from the poem "Fort Smith" by F. R. Scott.

The author has made every effort to contact the copyright holders and will be happy to amend the credit lines as necessary in subsequent editions.

Contributors' royalties for this book will be
donated to Canada World Youth and Katimavik.

Typeset in Minion by M&S, Toronto
Printed and bound in Canada

This book is printed on acid-free paper that is 100% ancient-forest friendly
(100% post-consumer recycled).

McClelland & Stewart Ltd.
75 Sherbourne Street
Toronto, Ontario
M5A 2P9
www.mcclelland.com

1 2 3 4 5   10 09 08 07 06

For The Neighbour

Contents

Still, let me know before you set out.
Come knock on my door
and I will walk with you as far as the garden
with one hand on your shoulder.
I will even watch after you and not turn back
to the house until you disappear
into the crowd of maple and ash,
heading up the hill,
piercing the ground with your stick.

Last verse, Billy Collins, "Directions"

Foreword

BY JUSTIN TRUDEAU

One of the most wonderful perks about being my father's son is that even now, twenty years after he left public life, and four years after his passing, an extraordinary number of people still stop me with huge smiles on their faces to tell me about the time they met him, or saw him, or even simply how much he touched their lives. I have always been fascinated to see how my father's image lives on within each individual in a unique way.

So when Nancy approached Sach and me with the idea for this book, I was, needless to say, intrigued. To a large extent, I know that he would have been wary of a book about him, and not about his achievements, his writings, or, at the very least, his thoughts. He always seemed mildly uncomfortable with the "cult of personality" aspect of his persona, and might have been concerned that a book on his interactions with others, on the way they perceived him, would feed that. But on the contrary, I think this collection shows how very real he was as an individual.

As well as I knew my father, there are many sides of him that I rarely saw fully in action (it's not like he brought the Constitution home to the dinner table). So from a personal standpoint, I have delighted in reading these stories. Some are emotional, some are very funny, some may be a bit of a stretch, but all show him from a different angle, revealing a different way he impacted the people around him.

A slight warning: my father was a man who, to put it mildly, tended to have a certain effect on anyone who met him. So while care has been taken to verify the stories in this book, it is natural that certain embellishments may have slipped into the tales over the years and the tellings. And that, to my mind, is as fascinating as anything else: to see how people reveal themselves through their accounts of interactions with my father.

The book you are about to discover is filled with gentle laughter, clever observations, and poignant memories of the private man who, despite himself, played a very public role in the consciousness of our nation. But perhaps it's easier for me to simply say that you are about to meet a man whose sons never had to grow out of the "my dad can kick your dad's ass" phase. And hopefully you'll understand why we all loved him so much.

Preface

Many people have asked how Pierre and I first met. The more appropriate question is: how did we *nearly* first meet? I was supposed to be introduced to him in the back garden of our family home in Vancouver, where he was spending the afternoon (little did I know) swimming in the pool and jumping on the trampoline. He was the freshly elected prime minister, a job title that on this day would mean nothing but fierce pain to me. I had just walked home from school, aged twelve, fully intent on sneaking in a few jumps on the tramp, as usual, before changing out of the dreaded school uniform. But I was briskly informed that not only was my trampoline off limits, so was the back garden and pool. Even with all the pandemonium and competition that came with being the youngest of seven children, I had never heard such a ridiculous admonition.

"But I've done nothing wrong," I bleated, "today!"

It was explained to me who he was. I shrugged (or so the story has been embellished) and said, "So what?" And then I threw a fit, and was sent to my room for the remainder of Pierre's visit. I saw him out my bedroom window, and felt something close to loathing.

So we never met then.

A decade or so later, when we did, trampolines became a running joke between us. "Trampoline" became a code word. It meant "get me out of here."

"Wonder if they have a trampoline," he'd whisper at dinner parties that bored him. "If they had a trampoline, I'd stay longer."

Even in his final few months, he never lost his sense of humour about the joke. The last time we went to his place up north, shuffling towards the house, he stopped and, waving his hand, said, "See, I have a trampoline! Want to try it?"

Getting this book done over the past two and a half years was like being permanently on a trampoline, leaping and bouncing and doing backflips after front-flips, and leaping higher again, without much repose. That is to say, beyond it being a labour of love and all the emotion that comes with that kind of covenant, this book damn near put me in the loony bin for life. Ask any number of contributors what it was like to deal with me. One contributor neatly summed up the situation (when I *really* was on deadline and their essential piece wasn't close to being finished) by referring to me as "Madame Slave Driver" in various e-mailed missives. I accepted his title graciously, telling him to stop horsing around and get his copy in.

I contacted over three hundred people around the world who knew Pierre, worked for him or against him, danced with him, heard him quote poetry or less diplomatic phrases, watched him (both the press and the RCMP), canoed with him, entertained him, or spoke with him on spiritual matters. My intention was to show the personal side of Pierre, to make him human, to let readers see what he was like as a friend, an employer, a travelling companion, and most of all – in his favoured role – as a father.

I received over two hundred responses, many of which didn't make it into this volume. One of the first pieces in was from Jimmy Carter. Then came, shortly after, submissions from a priest, a provincial premier, an old friend, and then one of his RCMP bodyguards. What struck me was not simply the intimacy and generosity of their memories, but how Pierre was revealed in (as one contributor put it so beautifully), "the softer protocol of private conversation."

What I didn't receive, until the last possible deadline, were some forty key stories I needed – almost without exception – from those people closest to him. They, like me, found the whole remembering and writing enterprise fraught with emotion. But I prodded and begged them, abused their answering machines, and bothered their consciences until they became sufficiently aware that I wasn't going to let up, that the only way to get rid of me was to get writing. Thankfully, they did. Otherwise we'd still be on the phone now, negotiating our versions of the notwithstanding clause. I'd say to them, over and over, "Notwithstanding the fact that, yes, that is true, I've not written my piece for the book either because I haven't had time . . ."

At the end of the day, I tried rigorously to live by two abiding notions. One was that it didn't matter who you are, or how famous you were, or how private your access to Pierre was. If you had something unique to say, if what you revealed was interesting, great; if not, you didn't make the cut.

The other abiding rule was much less tricky. If stuff came in that was inappropriate, too personal, or inaccurate, I asked myself this simple question: What would Pierre think?

As well, I had help from Justin and Sacha, "the boys" as we euphemistically continue to call them. Sacha (when he was not out in some war zone chasing danger) was very capable at assessing the flaws. Justin was not only a meticulous line editor in numerous readings of the manuscript, but he was a steadying and consoling voice all the way through the journey. His support, his advice, his conscience, his humour, all were delightful revelations.

Few people took Pierre on, no matter what your relationship with him was (real, perceived, or of your own making) without knowing he was a formidable intellect possessing rapid-fire retorts when your logic was shaky. He expected you to have your argument or plea well thought out. He expected that because he had demanded it of himself. Fewer people still, saw that vulnerable side of him he protected so successfully. "He made calculated forays out of his privacy," one contributor writes. Indeed, in public life and in private life, he did. I knew that vulnerable side of him. I knew him well, in many of his moods – playful, authoritarian, loving, bored, challenging, philosophical, curious, rhetorical, independent, daring. Always, daring.

None of us knew him completely. He was far too private – depending on your point of view – for that kind of nonsense or hope. So I dared myself, a year or so after he died, to do this book. Even after running the idea by the boys, one who sat with me on the roof of the Fire Station, where I live, and said well, okay, but here's who you have to get, and the other who placed me on the back of his motorcycle and drove me to dinner and back, nearly killing both of us any number of times, saying well, if it *has* to be written, you're the one to do it. Even after I had a publisher lined up, I still had a few doubts, mostly along the line of "What the hell am I thinking doing a book like this?"

So I went back to the deck of the house in Montreal, belonging to a close friend of Pierre's, which I had frequented so often that last summer of Pierre's life. It was early September 2002.

"Here's what I'm thinking about doing," I said, and told my friend, over the usual Lagavulin malt whisky.

"What do the boys think?" he asked, ever the gatekeeper. I told him.

"What do you think?" I asked.

He said a few things about the published historical record, so far, and that my approach was unique. Then there was some silence. He mentioned some details, and then several names I ought to get for the book.

Then he told a story, by way of example, of nearly losing Pierre on a canoe trip years ago. When he finished it, he was crying. Okay, I thought to myself, I will do this book.

We finished our drinks. I went home to the Fire Station, taking a wide and pensive route past Pierre's empty house, remembering those last times when he could still walk, and he would always say, "Pray for me," and, "Courage," in that order.

Then I walked up the hill and got on the trampoline, metaphorically speaking, remembering his dare: "Want to try it?"

I did and I have.

Montreal
November 2004

Chapter One

Faith

▌ ALLAN J. MacEACHEN

MP, 1953–57 and 1962–80; and Senator, 1984–96

The only written reference made by Mr. Trudeau about his religious views that I have been able to find was a short interview he gave to the United Church *Observer*. In it he was pressed to speak about whether he was "a devout Catholic." After initial parrying and dialectical probing, he gave more than the interviewer asked, by declaring, "I am a believer." Then he virtually recited, for the benefit of the United Church, the substance of the Apostle's Creed.

Another reference to religion in his public utterances was not as devotional. It was a reference that – at one particular moment – I wished he had omitted. In the 1972 general election campaign, I was visiting door-to-door in the district of Little Narrows, my Cape Breton constituency. I was accompanied by the warden of Victoria County, the late Kenneth Matheson, who was also the councillor for the Little Narrows municipal district. Both the warden and the district were staunchly Presbyterian. They took religious matters seriously. Religion was not a subject for flippant treatment.

Together, we entered the home of a church member as she was about to leave for a church meeting. She was dressed for the occasion and carried a formidable black handbag. The innate sense of hospitality characteristic of Highland stock imposed in her mind a greater duty

1

than punctual attendance at the scheduled church meeting. She invited us to sit down.

"We have always been Liberals," she said. "Not that we think we are better than the others. It just suits us to be Liberal."

That was a good beginning, except for the "better" reference, which – in the stress of an election campaign – I thought could well be omitted. Then our hostess got down to business.

"Now," she said, as she opened her purse and handed me a newspaper clipping, "your prime minister is causing me difficulties."

I read the newspaper account with increasing dismay. Now, some background is required. In the 1968 election campaign, Mr. Trudeau had highlighted the Just Society. The electorate could be forgiven for concluding that the Just Society would be ushered in forthwith, following Mr. Trudeau's election victory. This expectation had obviously been on the mind of an elector in southern Ontario, during this 1972 campaign, when heckling Mr. Trudeau.

"Mr. Trudeau," he had asked, "where is the Just Society you promised?"

Here is what Mr. Trudeau was quoted in the clipping as saying: "Ask Jesus Christ. He promised it first."

Finally, my hostess interrupted my longer-than-required gaze at the newspaper clipping that detailed this exchange.

"I regard that as blasphemy, Mr. MacEachen," she said. I had to say something other than my immediate thoughts, which were clearly in her corner, and if expressed would likely have revealed my dismay at the irreverence of the PM's comments. In addition, my concern went beyond the irreverence of the remark. The timing was awful. The electoral consequences of such flippancy might be felt in my constituency, and far and wide in Canada.

I did try, however, to reduce the anxiety by questioning the accuracy of the report. One could not always rely on such reports, I offered. It was surprising to me that such a remark would be made by the prime minister, I suggested. No doubt my effort was feeble and unconvincing. Knowing my leader as I did, deep down I feared the rapid-fire retort could indeed have happened as reported.

Years later, after we had left office, I recounted the incident in Mr. Trudeau's presence, at the launch of a book on the Trudeau legacy. He did not challenge my account. Instead Mr. Trudeau sat quietly, with a suppressed smile on his face, possibly taking some pleasure in the audacity of his remarks.

Postscript: we lost our majority in that election.

▶ HASSAN YASSIN

Head of the Saudi Arabian Information Office in Washington, D.C., 1970–80

I knew former prime minister Pierre Trudeau since 1976. While he was prime minister, I visited Ottawa many times, and he always received my friends and me very graciously. Mr. Trudeau was my guest many times in Washington, while I was head of the Saudi information office there, and we also enjoyed a number of skiing trips together in Colorado.

Pierre Trudeau's unique character, his profound understanding of others, and his deep humanity are to me best described by an occasion that has left a lasting impression on me. While he was prime minister, he visited me one summer in Marbella, at my residence in Porto Banus. He recounted to me his time as a student at the Sorbonne and a motorcycle trip he took, in 1947, around Europe and North Africa. On that trip, he had come across the village of Rhonda in the mountains of Marbella where – during the Arab occupation of Spain – a magnificent mosque had been erected, which was later converted into a church.

He asked me if I would like to visit this village with him. I agreed, and we requested special permission to visit the church with the priest that afternoon. The site and the converted mosque were as beautiful as Mr. Trudeau had promised. Upon seeing Quranic inscriptions on the walls, I innocently asked both the prime minister and the priest whether it was possible for me to pray as a Muslim in the church.

Mr. Trudeau immediately acquiesced to the idea. He then asked if I could lead a prayer as an *imam*, while he and the priest bowed in Muslim tradition. Mr. Trudeau consulted with the priest and, in this magnificent moment, the prime minister in his way contributed to uniting the two great religions of Christianity and Islam in peace and understanding.

His desire to understand other people's faith traditions – to live by consensus rather than by confrontation – was his greatest strength.

▶ B.W. POWE
Writer, teacher, author

1989: we lunched at a Chinese restaurant, not far from Trudeau's new office on René-Lévesque Boulevard.

My intentions for that meeting: to ask him to attend the Trudeau Era conference I was directing at York University in Toronto. He refused (politely), but he did ask about who was scheduled to speak, and on what subjects. I singled out a talk to be given by Michael Higgins, Vice-President and Academic Dean at St. Jerome's, at the University of Waterloo, on the influence of faith on Trudeau's thinking.

"He will be talking about the importance of religion, of your Catholic background, on your thought and approaches to political ideas," I said.

Trudeau leaned back, looked off, and said, vehemently:

"At last."

▶ MICHAEL HIGGINS
President, St. Jerome's University in Waterloo, Ontario, and first academic to directly address the role of Catholicism in the life and thought of Pierre Trudeau

*T*he second, and last, occasion when I met Trudeau – and even at that, it was somewhat distant – was in Toronto's Cathedral of St. Michael's, at a multi-anniversary celebration of Gerald Emmett Carter's years as a priest and a cardinal. The year was 1990. Trudeau had been out of office for some time, yet his presence was felt in the packed cathedral, as if he were again the electrifying new political force on the Canadian landscape that he clearly was in 1968.

Trudeau was the last person to enter the cathedral before Cardinal

Carter himself. Seated already were the prime minister, former prime ministers, the Governor General of Canada, former governors general of Canada, the Lieutenant-Governor of Ontario, former lieutenant-governors, and a cast of the Canadian corporate and political elite that dazzled even the most jaded socialite.

Unlike all the others, Trudeau had his own pew.

Sitting right behind him were RCMP officers and other security personnel. But Trudeau still had his own pew. No one else did. No prelate, political personage, international dignitary, or social eminence had such a secure and isolated footing in the cathedral.

During the course of the celebrations, I had occasion to glance in Trudeau's direction, and I noted that – even though his presence threatened the centrality of the presiding prelate – Trudeau appeared collected, serene, and prayerful.

Several years earlier, in 1983, I had seen Trudeau in another prayerful setting. I was in Montreal preparing a segment for CBC Radio's *Ideas* program, entitled "Monasticism as Rebellion." As part of the historical and theological treatment of the monastic tradition in civilization, I wanted to deal with some twentieth-century monastic voices, one of whom was the late Dom John Main, the internationally famous abbot who had set up the Benedictine Priory in Montreal.

John Main had died the year before, but I was able to interview his successor, Dom Laurence Freeman, and spend a couple of days with the Benedictine community and its wide range of followers – from all levels of society – who attended their liturgical offices. I was told by Dom Laurence that both Charles Taylor and Trudeau were regular worshippers and meditators at the priory.

On one occasion, during the midday office, I saw Trudeau. He was seated comfortably in the lotus position, back upright against a wall, meditating, as if it were second nature to him, tranquil, alone, and focused.

In the past five years, there have been two university conferences, one at Toronto's York University, called "The Trudeau Era," the other at St. Jerome's University/University of Waterloo, on Trudeau's faith and spirituality. At both gatherings, I have had the opportunity to reflect on the roots of Trudeau's spirituality – and, further, to reflect on the various

schools that informed his prayer life and on the theological and philosophical traditions that were determinative in his own ethical thinking,
as well as to examine the various ways in which he appropriated important religious insights from faiths outside his own.

It was, indeed, a rare privilege to observe him in two quite discrete
liturgical settings.

▶ LAURENCE FREEMAN, OSB
*Former prior of the Benedictine monastery on Pine Avenue near
Trudeau's Montreal home*

*I*n 1977, I came from London to Montreal with John Main, at the invitation of the archbishop, to establish a small Benedictine community of
monks and lay people dedicated to the practice and teaching of meditation in the Christian tradition. In 1980, we were given, by the McConnell
family, their large mansion on Pine Avenue. We were told soon after that
Pierre Trudeau had just bought the Ernest Cormier–designed house a
few hundred metres away, and so would be our neighbour.

Since our work was teaching meditation, we had several meditation
periods each day with our monastic hours, and we also integrated a half-
hour period of silence into each Mass. We were not a parish, but many
people who enjoyed our more contemplative liturgy would join us, especially on Sunday mornings.

One Sunday. after Mass, as people were milling round in the hall
outside the meditation room and putting on their shoes, I overheard a
brief exchange. A woman was saying to a man who had his back to me,
"Did anyone ever tell you that you look remarkably like Pierre Trudeau?"

The man replied, "As a matter of fact, yes, many people do." When
the man turned toward me, I realized it *was* Pierre Trudeau. He looked
at me – with a twinkle in his eye – introduced himself as our new neighbour, and thanked me for the Mass and meditation.

That sort of thing must happen to famous people all the time. But in
retrospect, after getting to know him – though I would like to have
known him better – that exchange suggests something particular about

him: his enjoyment, perhaps, of being recognized, but also his delight in self-concealment.

The reflections that follow are simply evocations of old memories, insignificant in themselves, but – like all memories – they acquire value over time as they seem to reveal, through ordinary details, more significant truths about a personality, at least for the one remembering. I offer them in gratitude and respect for a remarkable public man whom I got to know a little in his private self.

After he had resigned as prime minister in 1984, he began to come to the monastery fairly regularly. Some friends had introduced him to us, and he probably felt at home meeting other old friends such as Charles Taylor, the McGill philosopher, who also came regularly with their families. Pierre and I met from time to time at lunch or in the late afternoon after he had walked back up the hill from his office downtown. We enjoyed long, wide-ranging conversations.

The first time he invited me to his house, one summer afternoon, we sat on the balcony looking over the city that had been his childhood – and had become my adopted – home. We drank Cuban beer from a case that the consulate across the street had sent him. As we talked, I was struck by how relaxed he was, and how easily he divested himself of any public persona. I asked him how he found retirement, and he said he was enjoying life. He seemed genuinely relieved to be out of politics. In the immediate aftermath of retirement, he said he had received many invitations to speak or to support various causes.

It was clear he was guarding himself and his privacy, and was not missing the limelight. There was a note of contempt in his voice when he described one invitation to give a twenty-minute keynote address to the AGM of an American multinational for an astronomical fee. He had declined, he said, because "all they really wanted was a performing clown." To the impression of relaxed openness, I added another: fierce self-respect.

This self-respect was an aspect of (what I came to feel) his unusual degree of sensitivity and even vulnerability. Early on in our friendship we talked about his faith, for I wondered privately whether it was truly personal or just conditioned. He picked up my intent and responded in a kind of off-hand way, but with a strong, self-defining certainty, that he believed that "Jesus is the Son of God." His way of expressing this summary formula of faith struck me. It was very clear. And it had clearly been considered and adopted after serious reflection. It established a stable position in his religious and spiritual universe with which he was comfortable and secure.

Our conversations, whether over beer or lunch or sometimes in my room at the monastery, ranged widely around this common centre of faith. We spoke about liberalism, individualism, current politics; original thinkers like E.F. Schumacher (whom Pierre told me he had invited to Ottawa too late, just before Schumacher died); the rights of law and its tendency to conflict with justice; as well as more specifically theological issues. He had an informed and quick interest in contemporary theology, but little interest in the institutional politics of the church – which, no doubt, after his career, he found small game.

His intellectual interests were the fruit, he claimed, of his prepolitical life. He said he advised aspiring young politicians to do their reading and thinking before they started their careers, because they would have no time for these pursuits afterwards. It seemed clear to me, however, that – in his political career, at least – he had never lost the habit of thinking and theorizing openly, even while in the office of prime minister. In fact, he admitted that he had been criticized for running his cabinet too much like a seminar.

I don't know much about his political career, but he seemed to me one of those rare politicians who remember why they entered politics long after establishing a career. He retained a passionate concern for ideals, even in the frenzy of political decision-making. This made him interesting to people outside the political village. It also, perhaps, added to his natural air of aloofness and detachment, and his note of intellectual superiority, when dealing with the oversimplifications of the mass media. A sense of perspective was the fruit of this balance between idealism and practicality. While we were talking once about Quebec independence, I was surprised to hear him add at the end of his remarks, with a philosophical shrug, that after all, in the broadest historical perspective, such an outcome would not be the end of the world, and that life and society would, as always, adapt.

The year that we invited Charles Taylor to lead the John Main Seminar over a number of days in the monastery, Trudeau came faithfully to every session. Taylor was speaking with great passion, but sometimes at a high altitude, about the themes that later formed his great work *Sources of the Self*, but with a specific interest in the question of modern Christian identity. Trudeau sat engrossed throughout, silent, avoiding eye contact, ignoring the initial interest created by his presence, but grabbing Taylor after the lecture for a private conversation about his ideas.

One bitterly cold day in February, we met for lunch at the Mount Royal Club on Sherbrooke Street. He arrived on foot, breathing hard into the cold air and wrapped in his heavy fur coat and hat. I was glad, as a new Canadian who could not share others' enthusiasm for "making friends with the winter," that Pierre seemed – at least momentarily – to find it all as excessive and impossible as I did. He apologized for bringing me to the club, which he described as rather stuffy and very establishment, but convenient. As we disrobed in the coatroom, a group of very establishment-looking mandarins came to greet him, obsequiously calling him "Mr. Prime Minister," and recalling previous meetings and mutual acquaintances. Pierre responded courteously but silently to the old men, listening smilingly to their reminiscences until they left. Then he apologized for not introducing me to them. As he confessed, he had had no idea who they were.

Pierre was very interested in our work of teaching meditation, and he saw it rightly as a renewal at the root of the church and Christian life. He understood both its contemporary radicality and how it was rooted in tradition. He saw how religion, when open to this depth of the contemplative dimension, naturally entered into friendship and dialogue with sister faiths without fear or prejudice. I think he also understood that our work was at times pioneering, and he was pleased to offer what help he could in advancing it.

When I told him that we had been invited to introduce meditation at the head office of Alcan, the Montreal-based aluminum company, he expressed interest. Such an invitation was itself quite an achievement. The challenge remained to reach as broad a constituency of the company as possible. I asked Pierre if he would like to come to the first meeting, as a sign of support, and he readily agreed. When the managing director and board of directors heard that he was coming, the meditation program became a company priority.

They invited Pierre and me to lunch, during which he acted as an ideal patron of our community, though I felt he enjoyed the fact that his relationship to the monastery was something of an unexplained mystery to them. There was not much spiritual conversation at the lunch but, a week or so later, at the first meditation session, the CEO and several board members joined Pierre and me, along with junior executives, secretaries, doormen, and sales reps, in meditation. The program at Alcan was well launched and had enduring results, with no small thanks to our quiet patron.

Pierre was, of course, a private personality and guarded his privacy. However he was not inaccessible and did not hide behind a public persona as so many famous personalities do, even unconsciously. To have done that would, for him, I think, have represented the worst kind of loss of self. I felt he made calculated forays out of his privacy and revealed aspects of himself to those he liked or trusted. Whether he ever managed to share everything of himself with anyone I have no idea. But I suspect he would have found it difficult, though his obvious passion as a father must have been redemptive for him as a person.

We often spoke about prayer and faith, but on one occasion we went into it at some depth. We discussed the meaning of meditation, a form of imageless and non-conceptual prayer that involves a radical surrender of the ego. Pierre had no difficulty with an intellectual understanding of meditation in this way. But he remarked, in a factual tone of voice, that he was a person who lived, both emotionally and intellectually, under intense self-control. And – whether it was a comment or a confession I am not sure – he added that he knew he could not give up that lifelong habit of control.

I do not know how his last phase of life affected this intense habit of self-control, because I moved from Montreal and saw him only on occasional return visits. But I remain impressed – as I was at the time he made this comment – by the clarity, the honesty, the simplicity of his self-understanding, and – at least at that moment – his transparency.

▶ JOSEPH-AURÈLE PLOURDE
Archbishop emeritus of Ottawa

*I*n 1968, Mr. Trudeau and I both received honorary doctorates from the University of Moncton. At the banquet following the academic celebrations, I was asked to say a few words. As I had not seen Mr. Trudeau for some time, I began by saying, "I'm glad to be in Moncton, because it gives me the opportunity to see the prime minister of Canada."

Mr. Trudeau was asked to speak after me and, in his opening remarks, he said, "The archbishop of Ottawa indicated that he does not see me often in Ottawa. However, I go to his cathedral every Sunday, but he is never there."

He was right, of course, because on Sundays I went from one church to another, to meet as many people from the diocese as possible.

▶ ROBERT MANNING, SJ
President, Weston Jesuit School of Theology in Cambridge, Massachusetts

*I*n November of 1996, I went to Montreal for the weekend to convince Nancy Southam to continue her theological studies at the Jesuit divinity school in Cambridge, Massachusetts, of which I am president. As a Jesuit priest, I am reasonably skilled in rhetoric – and even debate – and I, like others, rather enjoy getting my own way (which I did, as far as Nancy's theological studies were concerned, but that's another story). Nancy had arranged a dinner Saturday night at her home, "the Fire Station," with a mysterious third person, who went only by the name of "The Neighbour."

Dinner was to be very informal (no jackets and ties, and certainly no Roman collars), with good wine and a simple menu, all preceded by a Mass with The Neighbour, which I would celebrate. Thus, the only fact I knew about The Neighbour was that the neighbour was Catholic. Only later in the afternoon were other details offered about The Neighbour: "he" was schooled by the Jesuits, "he" was a man of profound faith, "he" was very private and shy, and "he" would thoroughly pick my brain about fundamental theological matters; tenets of faith, hope, and mercy; what the Jesuits were teaching now; and who might be the leading Catholic theologians speaking out today; along with suggestions – of course – for further reading. And yes, he was very attracted by the possibility of a prayerful liturgy in the living room of the Fire Station.

"Relax," Nancy said to me about her neighbour. "You'll be way over your head in no time!"

As if all that didn't make me uneasy enough, she then revealed The Neighbour's identity. My reaction was swift and straightforward: it was one of utter disbelief. But, once convinced, I knew I was truly way over my head, for, even as an American, I knew of the former prime minister's towering reputation.

That evening with Pierre, as *he* insisted I call him, was thoroughly humbling for me. He was very moved by the quiet simplicity of the Mass. He graciously read one of the readings. And afterwards, over several hours of cheap pizza and expensive Italian wines, he asked questions and made comments that revealed him as a shy man of deep faith.

To my astonishment and delight, Mr. Trudeau made me feel utterly at ease in his presence, as if *he* were just another parishioner from the flock, from the neighbourhood, who needed some clarification in his prayer life. The only confusing narrative throughout that lovely evening was the occasional – but ongoing – dispute among the three of us over what to call whom.

Nancy calls me "Manning." I call her "Southam." As I said, The Neighbour convinced me to call him "Pierre" (and with difficulty I finally warmed to that, and did so). The problem was that Mr. Trudeau – I mean Pierre – refused to call me by either of my given names and continuously referred to me as "Father." It was marvellously complicated and even God must have been amused.

"Father," Pierre said to me, "in Saint Ignatius's *Spiritual Exercises*, I'd be interested to know what you think about how Ignatius arrived at his distinction between consolation and desolation in prayer."

"Father, when you read and reflected on Augustine's *Confessions*, and when you re-read it now, what one line or thought intrigues you most?"

"Help!" I thought. "I really am over my head here!"

"Father, what is the current relationship between the Jesuits and the Vatican? I've always admired the Jesuit order for being the thorn in the Vatican's side."

"Troublemakers," Southam, the Anglican, interjected. "That's the word you're looking for, Pierre, in your question to *Bob Manning*."

Pierre calling me "Father" upset Southam, because she wanted the evening to be informal and without pretence, to avoid titles, positions, and labels. But he wouldn't let up, and even I was troubled and confused by his insistence on my title.

I walked The Neighbour home that graced night, a few hundred feet downhill from the Fire Station, the first snow of winter falling on our shoulders and memories. Pierre invited me in to see his famous art deco home. I declined, a decision I will forever regret, for I never saw him again, even though there was some consolation in helping to locate a French-Canadian Jesuit priest for him in the last few weeks of his life.

Weeks later, after that evening, I was stunned on reflection to comprehend why Pierre called me "Father." It had nothing to do with me at all. His insistence had everything to do, instead, with the fact I was a priest and a Jesuit. Pierre was incapable of relating to me in any other way, so deep was his respect for the history of his own faith, for the Catholic protocols in which he was raised. Pierre was a Roman Catholic believer from another era; he came from a time of automatic respect for priests that sadly, but properly, no longer exists between many Catholics and their priests.

I learned a lot more about what humility means when I hung out with Pierre Trudeau that afternoon and evening. And I learned a lot more about what faith means from the intensity of faith that Pierre demonstrated during Mass in the Fire Station living room. He was amazed we could celebrate Mass there. I am still amazed it meant so much to him.

RON GRAHAM
Author, journalist, and editor of The Essential Trudeau

*I*t was a perfectly beautiful summer's day in the last week of August 1990, and I was scheduled to have lunch with Pierre Trudeau in Montreal. From the time of his retirement as prime minister until his final illness, it was my good fortune to meet with him two or three times a year – more when I was later engaged as the off-camera interviewer for the English version of his television memoirs and as editor of his last book, *The Essential Trudeau*. Often, by coincidence, we would meet at pivotal moments in the history of Canada, such as a few hours before his famous speech denouncing the Charlottetown Accord in 1992, or the day after the separatists' near-victory in Quebec's 1995 referendum.

Certainly there was no lack of things to talk about at this particular lunch in 1990. The Meech Lake Accord had collapsed the previous June, not least because of Mr. Trudeau's opposition; a quarter of a million Québécois had subsequently taken to the streets to celebrate Saint-Jean-Baptiste Day – and thirty years of quiet revolution – with chants of "*On veut un pays!*"; Lucien Bouchard had quit Brian Mulroney's cabinet and founded the Bloc Québécois, which won its first election victory in mid-August; Jean Chrétien had taken over as leader of the federal Liberal Party to widespread doubts and abuse; Premier Robert Bourassa had launched the provincial Liberals down a new nationalist course by establishing the Commission on the Political and Constitutional Future of Quebec; and the Mohawks had blocked bridges and roads around Montreal all summer to protest a bloody police attack and a land dispute in Oka.

Traffic jams aside, my immediate concern driving into town from my cabin in the Eastern Townships in time to get to the offices of Heenan Blaikie by noon was what to do with my one-year-old son, James, who had been left in my care while my wife was away. At first, having exhausted all the alternatives, I telephoned Mr. Trudeau and offered to postpone our lunch to another date. No need, he said, why not just bring James along? But that required certain logistical considerations. It ruled out, for example, going to one of the fancy Chinese or Italian restaurants we usually preferred. Indian food would be too spicy. The University Club was no place for a child. Ben's Delicatessen, the most practical location for dealing with my son's rather rambunctious eating style, lacked quiet, privacy, and a high chair. So I popped into Alexandre's, the elegant bistro on Peel Street, to reserve a corner booth and a baby seat.

Walking along a street with Pierre Trudeau was a good-natured version of running the gauntlet. Passersby pointed, whispered, or did double takes. Friends stopped to shake hands. Admirers asked for an autograph or a snapshot. Taxi drivers honked; truck drivers waved; occasionally a journalist or a press photographer lay in ambush near his office building's front entrance. (For several years after leaving office, I noticed, Mr. Trudeau used to nod myopically to his left and right, even when he wasn't being recognized, mostly because of habit, but partly because he didn't want to offend anyone whose greeting he might have missed.) Very rarely, no more than a couple of times in a decade by his own count, did anyone hurl an epithet his way and, as Montrealers became more accustomed to seeing him on his way to work or home, they grew less excited at every sighting.

Yet nothing in my experience matched the frisson I felt that day walking into Alexandre's with a tanned and open-collared Pierre Trudeau at my side and a blond-haired, blue-eyed boy in my arms. For an instant there was the kind of silence that's said to indicate a passage of angels in the room. The diners stopped eating, waiters stood still, and the crowd stared in our direction. Once we were seated, the two beautiful young women at the next table immediately entered into a competition on whom to bestow the warmest, most dazzling smile: on the sexy septuagenarian in the seersucker suit or the gorgeous baby.

Lunch with Pierre Trudeau was usually like feasting at the table of the gods, so wide-ranging was his knowledge, so diverse his experience, so penetrating his analysis, and so precise was his thinking. That didn't mean his company was always easy. If you said something he thought was wrong or expressed yourself in a sloppy fashion, you were quietly but forcefully challenged. Humour and gossip, though not unknown, never carried most people very far. And he was remarkably unperturbed by silence. Once, I remember, I decided to see how long we could sit through a meal without saying anything before he would feel stirred to speak. We were well into the soup course before I couldn't stand it any longer and gave up the experiment as hopeless.

This silence, which bespoke an inner calm and self-containment, helped account for the fact that so many people, friends and foes alike, bestowed upon him a magical, mystical, or spiritual power: the charismatic Wise Man with a shaman's mask for a face and Satan's 666 on his Mercedes' licence plates. There's no doubt that he was, at heart, a liberal Catholic intellectual, who could be absolutist and even authoritarian in his defence of freedom and democracy, or that he was a man of deep faith in God, arrived at through reason and conscience. He was also, I would argue, a Superior Man in the Chinese sense of the term, someone who had rigorously disciplined his mind, body, and spirit toward the goals of individual excellence and social duty. Yet the better I got to know him, the more I saw how exaggerated this power had become in other people's eyes.

A very close friend of his, for example, once told me that Mr. Trudeau's travels as a young man had been a kind of spiritual pilgrimage, during which he studied Zoroastrianism, Zen, and other esoteric teachings. But when I put the question to Mr. Trudeau himself, he insisted that his journeys had been primarily "sociological," concerned above all with learning about different societies and how they worked. Far from being in search of some greater truth, he already seemed to have found it – and found it early – in Augustine, Aquinas, and Pascal. Even then, unlike many of his contemporaries, he never felt (as far as I could ascertain) any vocation as a student to become a priest, any interest as an essayist to write about theological issues, or any attraction in his old age toward mysticism. His religion thus seemed merely one facet of an unusually multi-faceted personality.

Indeed, aside from his intimidating logic and an indisputable strength of character, I felt that much of his personal power was the power of the Withholding Parent, a psychological, cultural, and generational mode of behaviour with which I was familiar because of my own father. The less he revealed of himself through words or expression, the more he aroused the childlike insecurities of others: "Am I boring him? Am I smart enough? Am I amusing enough? Am I good enough? Am I disciplined enough? Am I worthy enough?" And into his silence many people projected the judgment of an omniscient seer who can penetrate our souls and behold our every weakness.

However, I had learned something early in our relationship that served me well, both as a friend and a journalist. Whenever Mr. Trudeau felt attacked by the tone or content of a question, his competitive instinct was to lash back with answers that may have made quotable quotes in the newspapers, devastating ripostes in the House of Commons, or electrifying moments on television, but they weren't particularly informative or precisely true. Similarly, I once saw him rudely dismiss a query about the state of Soviet–American relations from a charming woman during a dinner party because, as appeared obvious to everyone at the table, she was much less interested in eliciting his opinion than in soliciting his attention. On the other hand, whenever he felt that a question – even the same question – was motivated by a sincere and sympathetic curiosity, he tended to respond with patience, depth, and extraordinary candour.

What I discovered was a shy and inwardly humble person who never claimed to have a hold on wisdom. He didn't know how history would judge him as a political leader – let alone how God would judge him as a human being – and, though he had difficulty understanding why everyone else in the world couldn't set and attain the same high standards he had set and attained for himself, he didn't spend much time criticizing the foibles and frailties of others. Moreover, he saw his own verbal and emotional reticence, whether his inability to engage with ordinary people or his hesitation to express his feelings to those he loved the most, not as a virtue but as a fault.

By his own admission, Mr. Trudeau had erected impenetrable barriers early in his life. In order to live up to his father's expectations, he transformed himself from a puny crybaby into a combative scholar-athlete, and then suppressed the shock of his father's premature death so that no one and nothing would ever be able to hurt him again. He concealed the disappointments and humiliations surrounding the breakup of his marriage behind a stoic dignity that must have been excruciating for so proud and tender a soul. And in his last years, his refusal to speak in public stemmed from his fear that he was, as he once put it to me, "going gaga."

As God – or fate, karma, chance, call it what you will – would have it, the death of his son Michel pierced Mr. Trudeau in the one place where he was totally vulnerable. Already weakened by age and illness, he tottered like a bewildered and tragic Job in the ruins of his methodically constructed defences. At one of our last lunches together, just a few days after Michel's memorial service, he appeared physically and psychologically defeated, shrunken by grief and despair, and his silence now seemed a surrender to a suffering beyond words.

"So how are Justin and Sacha doing?" I finally asked, not knowing whether he needed to talk about his loss or was tired of being asked.

"Better than I am," he replied. Then he began to speak about his crisis of faith. He couldn't find a "reason" why God had taken his son instead of himself – an old man who had lived a full life and was ready to die. And, because his faith had been built on reason, he was plunged into anguish and doubt. I didn't know what his confessors or spiritual directors were counselling him at the time, but it seemed both cruelty and nonsense to suggest that this was all part of a divine plan whose very purpose had been to test his faith. Instead, we talked about the idea at the core of every authentic religious or spiritual teaching, which is that the attainment of wisdom ultimately requires just such a shattering of the self. You have to blow up the walls of ignorance and slay the delusions of ego. You have to fall on your knees and cry out for help. Only then – not through the enlightenment of reason, but through a dark night of the soul – can the universal truth be known.

Over the years, as long as I initiated the conversation and respected his confidences while he was alive, I found I could talk to this legendarily private man about everything under the sun. But on that sunny day in 1990, over lunch at Alexandre's, it was difficult to talk to him about anything. James, having wrestled himself free from the bonds of the baby seat, was bouncing on the leather banquette, banging the wall with a spoon, and pulling apart the flower arrangement that rested on a shelf above our heads. He soon knocked over his water, scattering shards of glass across the table, and smeared pasta all over his face, hands, and place setting. There was also an unmistakable odour coming from his diaper.

Meanwhile, in the midst of my considered analysis of the Meech Lake crisis, I looked up to see Mr. Trudeau casting what might be described as a lustful glance at both the women beside us. A few moments later, when his steak arrived, he asked if he could possibly borrow the salt and pepper shakers from my son, who was in the midst of deploying them as Batman and Robin in his attack on an evil luncheon roll.

It was best, I quickly decided, to cut my losses and run. Mr. Trudeau must have agreed, under the circumstances, because he didn't insist on lingering for his customary chocolate dessert or coffee. He did insist, however, on paying the bill. Somehow we had fallen into a pattern of taking turns with the tab for our lunches, and contrary to his reputation as a tightwad, he was meticulous in paying his fair share. On this occasion I did detect a slight hint of grievance in the droll way he added, after surveying the mess and damage, "I suppose I'll have to leave an extra large tip."

Such was my eagerness to get away that the three of us were half a block up Peel Street before I realized I had left my camera and James's baby blanket on the restaurant seat.

"Here," I said to Mr. Trudeau in my confusion, "you hold James a second while I run back to get them." And I took off before either he or my son could protest being flung into each other's arms. An instant later I returned, camera and baby blanket in hand, but not fast enough to have prevented a small and very curious crowd from gathering around the spectacle of Pierre Trudeau standing on the corner of Peel and de Maisonneuve, in the middle of the day, holding a baby.

Pierre holds his frisky lunch companion, James Graham, in August 1990.

Relax, I consoled myself, he's been the doting dad of three boys. He must be used to this. But as I drew closer, he looked at me, more with concern than displeasure, and bleated, "Is your son going to shit on my suit?"

I lifted the camera that I had in my hand, and the three of us began to laugh. To this day I'm not quite sure why, but I think it had something to do with the comic side of life, the joy of a sunny afternoon, and the complicated love between fathers and sons.

▷ NANCY SOUTHAM
Neighbour and friend

When Pierre was in London attending his final G7 economic summit meeting in June 1984, I rang him up at Claridge's Hotel to invite him to Mass the following morning at the neighbourhood Jesuit church, Farm Street. Ted Johnson, then Pierre's executive assistant, took the call, checked with his boss, and rang back, saying that summit business prevented the prime minister from accepting the rather unique invitation. Ted added the PM would call before he left London.

I walked to Farm Street for communion, on a beautiful sunny morning, wondering why G7 meetings didn't factor in summiteers' faith habits. Also – it ought to be admitted – I reflected (while sitting in the dark, empty church) on how many times a woman had asked the PM out on a date – to Mass. Pierre did ring back to say goodbye. It strikes me now that, in the sixteen years that followed and all the years we'd known each other, there was only one time he *really* said goodbye – but, by then, in this world, we both knew it was for keeps.

Pierre and I did manage to attend church services together in several locations around the world after he retired from politics. Going to church was never part of the official program for these trips (mostly arranged by our diplomatic missions, even though Pierre insisted he was travelling as a private citizen). We just said "How about it?" and went.

I am reminded of a dripping wet, sweltering walk we took to the Catholic cathedral in – of all places – Ho Chi Minh City, in December

1990. We arrived there with our clothes stuck to our bodies, and had to stand at the back, so packed were the pews and aisles by attractive young Vietnamese families, with perfectly well-behaved babies on their arms.

A few years later, on a trip to South Africa, we went to a small Catholic church in Johannesburg, where we both remarked – while strolling through the large parking lot – on the number of white parishioners who were parking so many brand new Mercedes and BMWs.

On that trip to South Africa (accompanied by Senator Jack Austin and his wife, Natalie Freeman), Pierre met separately with then-President F.W. de Klerk and the newly released Nelson Mandela. The meeting with de Klerk was rather desolating, because he clearly knew he was finished. While he appeared outwardly jolly and happy, de Klerk chain-smoked Lexington cigarettes looking as if he was still sitting with a number of Afrikaners' knives shoved in his back because of his decision to release Mandela. (Later, they both received the Nobel Peace Prize.) Pierre was typically graceful in his remarks, gently reminding de Klerk that human beings were much larger than their job titles and, anyway, what de Klerk had done was nothing less than a political lesson in humility for the world.

Pierre was more than humbled to meet Mandela, and, while Mandela appeared slightly ill at ease, with too many handlers around him, wearing a grey suit that didn't fit, it was Pierre who waved off the "Prime Minister, sir" stuff and said, simply, that it was a pivotal moment in his life, to be in Mandela's presence.

While there were many other occasions during which I noticed his shyness and humility, I never again (until his son Michel died) witnessed Pierre so meek, as that morning in Nelson Mandela's makeshift office. When the meeting was over, and the photographs were taken, I asked Pierre if he minded if I requested an autograph from Mr. Mandela (one doesn't do that sort of thing), and Pierre was not only in favour but said, "Get one for me too!"

But it was tea with Anglican Archbishop Desmond Tutu that, I believe, really moved Pierre to a deeper spiritual sense of South Africa's dilemma. Tutu, remember, almost single-handedly woke up the international community in the 1980s to the need for Mandela's release from Robbin Island (and won a Nobel Peace Prize for his persistent provocations).

The archbishop, a tiny, infectiously alive man, met us by opening the huge door of his large white nineteenth-century colonial manse, sat us down, offered up tea, and then quickly got down to business. He began by telling a narrative that, he said, would give us an idea of how bad things were.

Tutu knew a man whose small "illegal" home was being torn down by the "authorities." The man, apparently accepting this, asked the authorities if he could be given permission to take apart his own house, by himself. They allowed him to do so, and so he did, plank by plank. The following morning, the authorities returned. The house was gone, all the wood and corrugated bits were neatly stacked up in piles. The authorities found the man hanging by a rope from the only tree on his small "illegal" plot.

I remember Pierre looking over at me as I sat on the couch, playing with the cushion beside me, tears running down my cheeks, when Tutu finished this story. But Tutu wasn't finished. He had just got our attention, and he knew it. He paused for a few seconds. I briefly looked over at Pierre. His eyes were riveted on the Archbishop. His face was ashen.

"You see," Tutu continued, just warming up – but looking directly at Pierre, "what they must do is apologize, make that gesture to the majority here, and then get on with what needs to be done. It's not going to be fabulous work from here on in, but they have to do it, make that apology. They have to say 'sorry.'" The point, and the reason we were in South Africa, had been made eloquently: the country needed to go through ferocious changes of heart, peacefully.

Pierre was completely taken by Tutu's straight talk, his wit, and his ability to tell a story with passion *and* reason. That really struck Pierre. Tutu was obviously delighted to meet Pierre, that graced afternoon, even if he was more "shy guest" than "star wattage." It was a role reversal that Tutu (wearing bright purple socks) picked up on early, and which – if one thinks about their historic meeting – says lodestars about them both. After that "courtesy call," sitting in the back seat of the car on the drive back to the hotel, neither one of us attempted to utter a word.

It occurs to me now that, even before I began my formal theological studies (with the Jesuits in the mid-1990s), Pierre and I had always talked freely about our faith. I remember one new-moon night on Namibia's Skeleton Coast. We were camped – along with others – next to the Kunene River that bordered war-ravaged Angola, and after dinner we didn't so much go for a walk, as was the habit, as let the path from the mess tent lead the way. That was easy to do because the wide reach of sky above us was filled with so many stars. Looking up at them made us both unsteady. We ought to have sat down on the cooling desert sand, but we didn't. I suppose we were both stunned at the display and couldn't move. After a long silence, taking it all in, I asked Pierre, "Where is heaven?"

He was looking up at the sky and, after an endless silence, he answered.

"*Le silence éternel de ces espaces infinis m'effraie.*" (The eternal silence of these infinite spaces frightens me.)

The line, from Pascal, was not an unexpected response, even from him, standing in a desert in the middle of nowhere. It simply added to my confusion.

I asked him to repeat it. It took him some time to utter it again. It made perfect sense at that moment, for the simple reason that we both were searching for that part of our faith that wasn't wobbly, the part of our faith that required shoring up, and ballast, for that grace to end the incessant questions of where a dead loved one might be. At that moment, Pascal made way more sense than the Apostle's Creed.

The next morning, Pierre admitted the Pascal quote kept him awake most of the night. I had fallen dead sound asleep, with wild nightmares about my family being kidnapped and killed.

"Did you recognize any of the kidnappers?" Pierre asked. I told him, laughingly, I didn't.

"Well," he said deadpan, "that's no help."

I often think of that Pascal quote Pierre paused to utter under the stars. That safari was God-infested on so many levels. Aside from the skies at night we were surrounded by yellow and pink-hued sand dunes that constantly moved, allowing themselves to be reshaped northeastward by the prevailing wind, allowing themselves to be living creations, continually adapting.

One windy afternoon, the Land Rover heaved us up upon a pale pink dune. In bare feet we stood at its crest.

"Step back from your footprints," I said.

"Why?" he asked, as he always did when the reason wasn't clear.

"They shall be gone in less than a minute."

He stepped back in silence. The feral memory of his presence on the sand dune was quickly erased.

"Amazing," he whispered. "The way it should be."

The concept of heaven was always part of our conversations, as were other theological matters, such as how we prayed, our images of God, how difficult it was for the mind to grasp the immensity of God, whether one needed to go to church to receive forgiveness, the tension of God's designs for us that often clash with our own (God-given) free will, and the importance of reading the Bible – or books of it – again and again. (It would be the Book of Job that Pierre focused on in his last few years.)

When I finally took my theological studies seriously, Pierre was the only companion I had – or needed, given his own search – who was willing to hear out my arguments and confusions. I nearly lost him early on, one stormy night at home in the Fire Station, when I realized I had lost what shred of faith I had (which one inevitably does, when taking the studies seriously). I was arguing that, if I was asked to believe in the God I was currently studying in a class on the Old Testament, I had every right to lose my faith. Pierre was worried about *anyone* losing their faith, coming, as he did, from another era of faith and belief, where questioning God wasn't done.

"Anyway," I concluded, in a moment of vivid doubt, "I want nothing to do with God, given God is so clearly capable of being an overpowering shit."

Pierre didn't drop the pale blue napkin he was twirling around his finger, though it might have been easier. The dining room became utterly silent, only occasionally punctuated by his body moving in the creaking pine chair. I knew I had offended Pierre's sense of decorum, his sense of appropriate language in speaking about God, and I didn't care. I wanted to shock him into what it was like to lose one's faith, because I knew that, until that moment, Pierre had never seriously questioned God, not even about his own father's sudden death.

He allowed I had reached a wounded memory. Then, he quoted a passage from the Bible to the effect we will never have any idea what plans God has for us. The evening ended peacefully, in a truce, thank God.

I believe he indulged me and my questioning of heaven because he found it difficult to admit to, or articulate, occasional weakenings of his own faith. (This was years before Michel's tragic death, which for a time completely shredded Pierre's faith.) Yet he clearly was trying to keep his faith bearings contemporary. Though the Catholic-educated eldest son from another era, Pierre's beliefs had enough depth to be re-figured. In his last few months, he knew well the Old Testament story of waiting for that gentle wind of God to blow through the heart of the strong-minded man who once waited for thunder and floods and general seven-point-something earthquakes.

The concept of heaven was raised again on a rambunctious trip to the former (and seemingly entire) East Indies in the late summer of 1994. The night before that insane journey full of death rituals of Hindu, Moslem, and Animism faiths, Pierre and I quietly tested our lacklustre faiths, in a Jacuzzi in Jakarta.

There were sirens going off in the humid evening air, and the constant hum of traffic wafted up, yet the moon was evident and we eyeballed it. The question of heaven is raised, though now it is rephrased.

"Do you *believe* in heaven?"

"Are you getting all Bolshevik on me now?" he asks, moving around the Jacuzzi with a slight smile, his eyes very pale blue in the thin light.

No, no, I say, defensively. "I always wonder about heaven when I stare at the moon too long."

He knows this. A long silence.

"You mean do I believe in the *afterlife*?' he offers finally, using the old Jesuit trick of answering a question with another question.

"Yes, whatever," I say to him, before submerging into the warm water for the thirty seconds I figure he will need to come up with a reasoned answer.

"Yes," he said . . . pause . . . "I believe we get all the afterlife we deserve."

I remember Justin (whom I hardly knew then) answering the phone, and the front door of 1418 Pine Avenue, in those keenly heartbreaking nights and days that followed Michel's death. Pierre was in his study. Descending the nineteen steps of the twirling marble staircase, I found him standing at the bottom, dressed in his old beige safari pants and favoured sweat-shirt. In the midst of a hug, he said, "Thank you for coming." Well, all the strength I thought I had for him evaporated, then and there.

We sat on the sofa. He wanted to focus on where I had been when I heard about "The Gardener" (our code name for Michel when he spent a couple of early summers at the Fire Station "gardening" and weeding), and where I'd just arrived from. Other friends' safaris, then, were easier to question than the unimagined journey he knew he was now facing, and the reason there were tears falling down his cheeks.

"Well," I said, "I didn't get a speeding ticket getting to your door, but that's only because I flew home and walked down." That got a needed laugh out of him.

Then I asked him a couple of questions, along the same lines, and the answers poured out of him, the sheer grief evident in his weary face. Then he said, after about five minutes, what struck him most, indeed worried him most, was the RCMP officer who was assigned to come to his door to wake him up and tell him Mich was in "an accident."

"You know that man had great courage, and I think they knew more than they told me that morning. I admire the way the RCMP handled me that first visit."

We talked a little about planning Mich's memorial service, how grief makes you so absolutely exhausted, and about Pierre's prayer life.

"I don't so much pray now, as *think* about God," he said.

"Perhaps God knows you have no prayers now."

That made sense to him, though he felt guilty, caught as he was for the first time in his life between reason and passion. But there was some-thing else bothering him that night in all the fray and phones ringing. Sacha was insistent in going out west to the site of the avalanche, to the mountain and the lake to find his brother's body, and Pierre was beyond worried to have another son leave him. He wanted both Sach and Justin around, in their home, close by. He wanted help, because he was inca-pable of being the stern father he always was, he admitted, at this moment. So Sach and I had the first of a few battles. Sach went out west.

Two weeks after The Gardener's memorial service, Pierre and the remaining boys had returned from his friend Peter Green's seafront acreage in Bermuda, where he slept a lot, he said, and wandered the beach unceasingly. I happened to be at Pierre's law office, Heenan Blaikie, and rang him up and said, "How about it, we walk up the hill together; I'll be in the reception."

So I waited, reading the *Globe and Mail* business section. Then, suddenly, I heard this loud tapping on the glass wall that separates the HB reception from the offices, and I jumped two inches out of my chair, literally. It was Pierre being frisky and, after a warm and gentle greeting, he suggested the only reason I came to his law firm was to read free newspapers. I said maybe so, but I'd walk you home more often if your law firm's lawyers were free too. For a while there, delight and humour were evident in the air and in the elevator down to street level.

So I walked The Neighbour home, past the Russian Consulate, where a movie was being filmed, and he mentioned – almost longingly – how he'd enjoyed many debutante dances there years ago, when it had been a private home. Then we walked up the 103 steps to Pine Avenue – which he got to the top of first.

At his front door I showed him the moon. We stood there for a couple of minutes, and then I started to say goodbye and he said, "No, no, please come in," fumbling with his keys. I didn't want to. I wasn't up to being strong for him. "No, please, have dinner with me."

So we went into the vast drawing room. His jaw was shaking, but his hands were steady, and we sat in the darkened room, staring at the moon. Pierre was spiritually bereft, but I wasn't up to Jesuit spiritual direction, so we just sat quietly until he went and changed his suit for the safari pants and sweatshirt.

At dinner, we tried talking about how he would respond to the thousands of letters and cards he had received, so far, about Mich's death. He was reading every one and was determined to respond to all of them. He had made three piles: letters, flowers, and Mass cards. He was amazed, he said, at how kind and moving the letters were.

We talked a little about his prayer life, which was complicated by his insistence on trying to reason through God's taking Mich at such a young age, when he, an old man of seventy-eight, ought to have died instead. I said, How about if you try and give up on that analysis, that it wasn't God who decided Mich's fate, that it might be Mich who was testing his own free will and fate? Try and imagine that God is also mourning, not only Mich's death, but the way God sees you now.

While he rinsed the dishes, I looked again at the Japanese watercolour on the kitchen wall that had been there for years. It is a landscape of a steep mountainside in blue, with a small building at the top. At the bottom was the line from Matthew 25:36, "I was in prison," it said in French, "and you visited me." I didn't tell Pierre that night, though I wish now I had, that the image and the quote reminded me of Mich and God that fateful day.

Pierre lost his faith over his son's death. What father wouldn't?

The real crisis for him, I believe, was he couldn't pray to a God he felt was "responsible" for Mich's death, a God who now, indeed, looked like an overpowering shit. Even when he was dissuaded of that notion, he still was mad at God, a feeling he'd not experienced in some sixty years, since his father's death, and that threw him into prayer turmoil. He knew God was somewhere, but he couldn't yell at God.

"Why not me?" he kept saying, quietly, over and over.

So I assigned him some homework: the Book of Job.

I told him to read it and notice where he and Job were alike in their pleadings and rantings to a seemingly rough God, whom they couldn't locate. Pierre read Job and – over the course of the following two years – he and I often discussed different ways of interpreting what is easily the most difficult book in the Old Testament. My trump card was an interpretation (not mine) that suggested God was not absent but was listening to Job *in silence*. The point being that Job kept listening to his three (so-called) friends, who insisted Job must have done something wrong in God's "eyes" to have everything he loved and cared for disappear – most of all his faith – reducing him to sackcloth and angst.

Job couldn't find God, nor could Pierre. Neither one of them gave a damn about the sackcloth bits. It was the silence that rendered them empty. It was only later, maybe a year in Pierre's case, that he was able to comprehend the image of a silent but *present* God. In his prayers, which he had faithfully done most mornings and evenings, I encouraged Pierre to *yell* at God, to let it rip, to not hold back. After all, I said, it won't be the first time abuse has been hurled at God by broken-down and faithless believers.

Pierre did regain his faith before he died, clearly and certainly. What his close friends noticed after Mich's death, and the media tried to promote, was the idea that Pierre couldn't recover from this grandest of wounds to a loving father. It was partly that, but in reality he went through a crisis of faith. The experience wrecked him, certainly, but made his faith much more vibrant and stronger.

A month after Mich's death, Pierre and I went to his house up north for the weekend. The last time he'd been there with Mich and Makwa, his dog, had been six weeks or so before. There's a small bridge on the road into his land that fords a small stream, and he stopped the vehicle. We could hear a dog barking in the distance. A memory haunted him.

"This is where Michel would let Makwa out to run the rest of the way."

I don't know who wept more that weekend, but I remember being early out of the starting gates when we first walked into the house and I looked at that tidy row, in diminishing sizes, of four pairs of hiking boots lined up by the front door. He didn't notice those early, fresh tears, but did when he asked if I'd come with him up to Mich's room "just to see if it is tidy."

After dinner that night, having consumed a bottle of strong Barolo, we sat on the living-room sofa, facing the two Haida "wearing" blankets, one of a raven and one of a frog, nailed up on the wall, high above his private lake Pierre had named "Jusami," after his three sons. Above the Haidas hung the famous Joyce Wieland piece, "*La raison avant la passion*."

I sensed what was coming, because our heads were tilted up at this vast tableau of his life, and he took my hand into his. Pierre couldn't reconcile the imagery on the wall.

"Michel was the raven," Pierre offered.

"Who was the frog?" I asked.

Without a pause, he said, "The rest of us."

We fell into memory and the clear agony of Pierre's loss of faith. No matter how well you knew him or loved him or were there for him, nothing ever prepared one for being a witness to a shrunken, ship-wrecked Pierre Elliott Trudeau. His powerful intellect and steady faith had always carried the moment. Now he was in tears. And because I had some experience in sudden (and young) family deaths, and was studying theology, he – staring at the raven "wearing blanket" – wanted to know how one *survived*, kept breathing, kept praying. It was a long evening, full of sorrow and, eventually . . . hope.

All the conversations we'd had over the years about heaven were nothing compared to that weekend. We agreed, tearfully, that the love we have for the dead – and their love for us – remains, continues, vibrantly within us.

We left the dishes in the sink that night, and I excused myself and went outside to have a Marlboro, even though Pierre said he didn't mind the smoke, in fact missed it, because Mich used to smoke.

I went out on the dark deck – bracing myself against the pilings – that overlooks the silent lake that reminded me of that other one in British Columbia. There was no moon. Trying unsuccessfully to locate the Big Dipper in the wide sky, to collect my bearings, I recited the Pascal line.

Suddenly a huge shooting star arched north to northwest and burned out. The memory of it remains now, as it did the following morning, when Pierre and I walked along the lake edge to the beaver dam that blocked a stream, and he badly wounded his thumb, while breaking down the dam.

Chapter Two

Inside the PMO

▌ JIM COUTTS
Principal secretary, 1974–81, and friend

*W*hen I was Pierre Trudeau's political adviser and principal secretary, people often asked me what he was like during the "off" hours as a friend. I usually avoided the question by invoking the code that precluded gossip from "the palace." Another accurate response would have been that there was nothing to tell – he and I were not friends.

If I saw very little of the prime minister outside the workday, that was the way I wanted it, and certainly the only way he would have had it. In later years, however, I would discover that his working relationships were perhaps not quite that simple, as things seldom were with him. I valued Pierre's businesslike approach to work because of several youthful lessons I had learned. Working for a leader meant not getting too close to him, not confusing his life with your life.

Managing my first federal campaign in Alberta's MacLeod riding in 1953, I was invited to meet Prime Minister Louis St. Laurent during his election stop at the Palliser Hotel in Calgary. The scramble of southern Alberta Grits – and even of his own Ottawa entourage – to show each other, or perhaps themselves, that they counted in the intimate circle of friendship, was a rather distasteful spectacle. The jockeying for position also seemed politically counterproductive.

Coutts and his boss working on campaign stuff.

That brief experience probably helped explain why getting personally close to the leader was one of my last desires when I joined Lester B. Pearson's new government in 1963 as his personal secretary, scheduling his appointments and nearly always travelling with him and his wife, Maryon, to family as well as official events. I was to see both of them socially, particularly Maryon, until the end of their lives. But despite Mr. Pearson's famously warm and casual outward style, he was in fact quite ruthless in cutting off those who became dependent on him. I observed too many "old friends" from his diplomatic days embittered when they arrived in Ottawa expecting to "hang out" with the Pearsons and found they had confused an earlier working relationship with intimate friendship.

While a protective wall typifies most presidents and prime ministers, this was doubly true in the case of Pierre Elliott Trudeau. Like other people, of course, he had a few intimate, often lifelong, friends. But he was also a rare man who actually enjoyed solitude, who more often relaxed alone than in the company of others. As well, Trudeau had come to politics only in his forties, and one of his greatest fears was that anyone holding a Liberal membership card, or House of Commons seat, would feel entitled to social access to him.

Pierre's reservation was not misplaced. Most career politicians take great pleasure in making voters – or party workers whom they rarely see – feel that somehow they are personal friends ("The leader genuinely regrets he can't make it this weekend"). He may never grace your back-yard barbecue, but the feeling is left that one day, you never know, perhaps he will. By contrast, Pierre made it crystal clear that he just didn't go to barbecues and certainly wouldn't be going to yours.

At perhaps a deeper level, he was utterly unlike many successful politicians. More than just gregarious, many of them have an almost addictive need for their fix of aides, colleagues, and friends around them constantly, whether in the office, at home, or on the road, recounting the old stories, drinking the same drinks, talking late into the night, con-stantly performing the same old rituals.

That was decidedly not Pierre Trudeau.

Pierre carefully preserved his own space. He was not, as it were, a mate-y pal.

And so it was at work, from the very first morning I joined him in launching the 1974 federal election campaign to restore the Liberal majority his government had lost two years before. He had asked me to become the national campaign chairman, but I suggested Senator Keith Davey would be better at that task.

"If you like, I'll run your national tour and travel with you," I offered. He agreed, suggesting we meet at breakfast, in the Royal York hotel suite where he was staying, following the Toronto kickoff rally for Ontario candidates and party organizers.

Pierre's invitation to breakfast turned out to be an invitation for me to talk while he ate *his* breakfast. The old-fashioned hotel table rolled in with its heavy CPR cutlery and linen and silver lids over toast – and one poached egg, clearly set for one.

"What did you think of last night's meeting?" he asked, as I sat down at the unset side of the table.

"I suppose it was all right . . ." I began.

"You're not going to be much use if you simply tell me what you think I want to hear."

"Okay," I said, seeing he wanted to get right to work. "It was pretty awful. Your tone was wrong. The message – if there was one – was confused. You looked tired and lacked energy. The opposite of all we want to convey. If you continue like this, you'll lose the election badly."

"So what do we do about it?"

Thus began a working relationship that lasted for seven years. Pierre was always considerate, almost always congenial, and increasingly trustful as time went on. He was also determined to preserve a private life outside politics.

A man of rigorous routine, he arrived at the office at 8:45 a.m., left between 5:30 and 6:00 p.m., and went off-duty without fail during weekends. I can recall only three occasions over seven years when he called me outside of these rather rigid hours. He occasionally had working lunches at 24 Sussex Drive (by this time even I was allowed to eat) but, except on state occasions, dinner was strictly reserved for personal time.

The man I called "Prime Minister" until 1984 became "Pierre" when he left politics and moved back to Montreal. Then something quite unexpected happened. Over most of the next sixteen years, when he wasn't travelling or otherwise tied up, Pierre and I would meet socially during my occasional trips to Montreal. Usually, there was a long lunch at a restaurant he chose (he seemed to make a lifetime career of finding interesting places to eat).

What surprised me at first was that he now began to refer to both our current relationship and our past professional association in quite warm personal terms. ("Remember when we were working on the Constitution and had that difficult phone call with Blakeney?") In these later years, I also began to see or hear from others about his gestures of friendship or thoughtfulness, often unexpected, toward those he had worked with in the past, inside or outside politics. There were visits to their sickbeds, time taken to counsel or just commiserate during their troubled personal passages or, more pleasantly, visits, trips, or lengthy letters exchanged to pursue a mutual interest.

What now seems clear is that, even beyond his small circle of intimates, Pierre was not quite the lone wolf or isolated intellectual of his image at work, or during physical pursuits. In fact, he formed and maintained over time a certain number of emotionally warm relationships with one-time colleagues and partners with whom he had shared the intense adventures, causes, and varied journeys of his remarkable life.

Whether travelling in China, editing essays, scuba diving over coral reefs, or repatriating a constitution, he and they had shared an experience or a goal that Pierre had valued, in a way that engendered his quiet respect, affection – and in some cases, perhaps even gratitude. I don't know whether that should be called friendship, but it seems as good a word as any.

▶ ALBERT BRETON
Special economic adviser, 1970–79

*T*hough I had met him in the 1950s, I only got to know Pierre Trudeau well in the 1960s when we were both teaching at the University of Montreal. We lunched together more or less every week, generally alone but sometimes with friends. We talked about Canadian and Quebec politics, about this or that problem at the university, and a lot about federalism and the content and significance of the *Federalist Papers* (which he would quote from memory), and which he encouraged me to read. I first learned about federalism from him during these lunches.

In the 1970s, when I was working in the PMO as Special Adviser, we continued these conversations. We never used the words *competitive federalism* (which I began using in the mid-1980s), but he knew that federalism was competitive. Trudeau had a clear view of what the interests of the federal government were, and what were those of the provinces. And he was therefore taken aback when provincial premiers seemed not to be particularly concerned with the interests of their constituents – less, he thought, than they were in purely federal matters. "Why are they doing this?" he would ask rhetorically, in disbelief.

But I learned more than a way of thinking about federalism from Pierre Trudeau. Over the years, I came to understand what he valued most in other human beings. He did not surround himself with people who agreed with him. He was strong and he enjoyed confronting different points of view. What was most important to him, it seemed to me, was intelligence and loyalty.

One February in the 1970s, when Raymond Barre, who was then prime minister of France, came to Canada, Trudeau offered a special luncheon for Barre at Harrington Lake. Barre and Trudeau had different views on a number of subjects, which they discussed vigorously, and they often agreed to disagree. After the meal, Barre excused himself for a minute, and we all got up from the table. When Barre had gone, Trudeau came to me and, putting his index finger to his forehead, said, "*Ça tourne bien là-dedans.*" ("He's got it up there.") That was the ultimate compliment.

Trudeau very seldom made comments to me about the people with whom he worked. However, once during the years of the minority government, annoyed with one of his ministers, he said, "People, one day, will learn that he is not intelligent." That, in turn, was the greatest snub.

If he valued intelligence, he may have valued loyalty even more. He wanted those in his entourage at work to be loyal to him, and he was himself loyal to those in that entourage. Nothing demonstrates this more clearly than the wage-and-price-control episode. In October 1975, after the previous year's election campaign that had been fought almost exclusively on the promise that there would be no wage-and-price controls, cabinet – pressured by the officials of the Department of Finance and the Bank of Canada, who had lost their cool and their economics – decided that there would be wage-and-price controls after all.

After the decision was made, Trudeau announced it to the country. I was in Ottawa during all of that debate, returning to Toronto only to give my lectures at the university. I sent a steady stream of memos to Trudeau that were answers to questions he would ask me through Michael Pitfield, the Clerk of the Privy Council. Of all the members of cabinet, Trudeau was the last to "agree" to wage-and-price controls. Though it is widely believed and asserted that he was the champion of controls, Trudeau never made public that he opposed them to the very end. Why? I believe he was being loyal to his cabinet colleagues and to the bureaucrats around them. His silence went beyond cabinet solidarity, as there were innumerable ways that he could have indicated that he was not a wage-and-price-control person.

On a Friday night in December 1975, the airport in Ottawa was closed to commercial aviation because of a snowstorm. I wanted badly to return home to my family in Toronto, but it looked as if I would have to stay in Ottawa. Then, unexpectedly, I got a telephone call from Cécile Viau, in Trudeau's office, offering me a seat on the PM's plane. Trudeau was going to Toronto for a ceremony.

On the plane, when the conversation turned to the question of wage-and-price controls, Trudeau (who was eating his Nth chocolate to assuage his sweet tooth) simply said, "They [the controls] will cost me the next election." He was right.

The strong value he put on loyalty also meant that he did not take lightly what he judged to be a manifestation of disloyalty. After the October Crisis of 1970, he came to Toronto to meet and talk with a fairly large group of intellectuals and opinion makers at the home of Eleanor and Ramsay Cook. I was there. I do not believe that Pierre wanted to justify his actions. On the basis of the evidence available to him and to his cabinet – and directly or indirectly supported by people like Claude Ryan (who, it must be remembered, wanted the creation of a "*gouvernement de salut public*") and Frank Scott (who was one of the shrewdest observers of the Quebec scene) – Trudeau had invoked the War Measures Act.

At that meeting, he was roundly condemned by many of those present, who, in his mind, did not know what was going on in Quebec. Their refusal to have a dialogue, to try to understand why he had done what he had done, was not forgotten. He was always ready to listen and to modify his views if he was shown he had to. He could not stomach those who refused or were unable to do the same.

▶ JERRY YANOVER
Parliamentary affairs adviser, 1969–84

*I*n the early seventies, I often dropped into the office of Joyce Fairbairn, Trudeau's legislative adviser, after Question Period to discuss how that day's show had gone, and to talk about ongoing legislative matters. (At that time, I worked in Government House Leader Allan MacEachen's office.) On occasion, the prime minister would also walk into Joyce's office to raise some issue with her. Instinctively, I would stand up and – equally instinctively – the prime minister would wave his hands and say, "You don't have to stand up."

About the fifth time this scene repeated itself, he snapped, "Damn it! I told you to sit down!"

My reflexes were, thereafter, cured.

▶ JOYCE FAIRBAIRN
Senior legislative adviser, 1970–84; communications adviser, 1982–84; and long-time friend

M y friendship with Pierre Elliott Trudeau began in 1965 over a boiled egg and toast and milk in the fifth-floor cafeteria in the Centre Block on Parliament Hill. A small, crowded little place, it was nonetheless a haven for parliamentarians and journalists like myself, to get a good start on the day at a time when meals on the "Hill" were heavily subsidized, a fact that attracted those of us on low wages. It would also have appealed to the somewhat frugal nature of the new member of Parliament for Mount Royal. For Pierre, who then lived just a block away in the Château Laurier Hotel, this was a good place to begin the day.

At that point, many of us knew very little about him. He had arrived on the Hill following the 1965 election. Prime Minister Lester B. Pearson had worked hard to recruit two prominent Quebeckers – Jean Marchand and Gérard Pelletier – as prospective ministers in the federal cabinet, but they insisted that they would only come as a trio, with Pierre Elliott Trudeau. He was well known in his province and in academe, but was a bit of a mystery in the hallowed halls of Parliament Hill and the rest of Canada.

His reputation for being somewhat eccentric – or "ornery" as we Albertans would say – took root because of his initial casual attitude toward wearing apparel. In a House of Commons filled with suits and ties and socks and laced shoes, he showed a shocking tendency toward sports jackets, cravats, and sandals – sometimes worn without socks. And he occasionally zoomed around the Hill in his silver Mercedes.

When he and I ended up across from each other at the far end of that communal breakfast table, he did not particularly want to talk about the overnight news (having not yet seen or read it). I was curious as to what kind of fellow he really was, behind his seemingly contrary nature, his academic degrees, and his public activism in Quebec. As a young Albertan and relative newcomer to the Hill myself, I was eager to understand better his province and its current history, which had not been highlighted in my own education or experience.

Over a lengthy succession of boiled eggs, I drew an impression of a man who knew a lot and said very little compared to the light political conversation enjoyed by most on the Hill. If he had a strong view, he conveyed it directly and concisely. He was wary of his new profession, but clearly had the intellect and spirit to take it on. From the very beginning I sensed a shyness in him that was hooked on to an element of kindness that I came to know well over the years of work and friendship. That shyness unfortunately sometimes came through in public as remoteness or lack of interest or even arrogance.

However, the one trait that especially delighted me during the fourteen years I worked with him as an adviser was his sense of humour. Yes, he had a sharp and clever wit, which is both useful and dangerous in politics. But there was a lot of laughter in Pierre, which genuinely softened tensions in difficult moments and often gave me opportunities not to take him too seriously, particularly when he was being unreasonably stubborn.

One of my favourite anecdotes occurred in August 1979, at a very low point in his political life. The Liberal government had been defeated in the election of that year and, without access to an Ottawa home because of repairs being required at the Opposition residence of Stornoway, Pierre put all his possessions in storage. He went up north into the wilderness canoeing with his "canoe gang," and then he and Justin, Sacha, and Michel went camping and visiting friends in eastern Canada, while some of us held the fort in Ottawa, working away at putting our Opposition strategy together. It was a rather dismal summer, and a highlight for me and my husband, Mike Gillan, was adopting a new dog, who, in spite of having been badly abused, was a feisty, engaging little terrier with a lot of whiskers.

Canadian Press

The ratty beard he was so
"hugely comfortable" with
in the summer of 1979.

When Pierre and the boys returned to Ottawa, the city – and indeed the country – was in mourning over the death of former prime minister John Diefenbaker. Pierre was scheduled to meet the media for his comments prior to the state funeral. Contrary to public perception, he truly admired Mr. Diefenbaker, in spite of their formidable verbal jousts in the House of Commons.

As he was doing the press conference, I received a call from colleagues in the office who were in a high state of agitation, having just seen our boss. Over the summer he had not shaved, and apparently it was not a pretty sight, although *he* was hugely comfortable with his appearance. When it was suggested that, of course, he would shave it all off, he declined with some spirit. I was told the ball was now in my court.

Pierre came to see me following the press conference to thank me for the tie I had rushed over to him for the occasion. He entered my office, chin first. It truly was the most ratty beard I had ever seen – a quixotic mix of grey, red, white, brown. He looked at me sternly, but I said nothing. We went over some pending issues, and finally he asked if I had anything else to say to him.

"Not really," I replied, looking at him carefully. "You know, you look just like my new dog Bert, and he is pretty cute, too." He glared, turned on his heel, and left. The next day, a solemn, bearded-but-well-groomed, respectful Pierre Trudeau walked in the procession to honour his distinguished predecessor. Then the beard disappeared. Not another word was said, but from that day forward his private nickname around our Centre Block office was "Bert."

A few weeks later, he and the boys came to a picnic at the summer home of the family of his old cabinet colleague and dear friend, Bud Drury, at Lake Anne in the Laurentians, where I was visiting. Pierre and I were watching the children dashing up and down the beach and, all of a sudden, a little brown dog came racing up to us, ears up, tail wagging, full of joy.

Pierre looked at him closely, patted him on the head, and asked, "Is this Bert?" When I nodded, he laughed and remarked, "He really is a good-looking fellow!"

▶ RALPH COLEMAN
Assistant press secretary and chief advanceman, 1974–79;
press secretary, 1980–84

*I*t was November 15, 1976, election night in Quebec. The Parti Québécois had just stunned the country by winning a majority government with an election platform that promised to hold a referendum on separation. Being an assistant press secretary to the prime minister at the time, I phoned in to the office at around 9 p.m. to see what was going on and learned that Prime Minister Trudeau was going to speak to the news media later that same night. The PMO staff were all busily preparing. I went immediately to work.

That night we were a glum lot. Today, two referendums later and after learning to live with the threat of separation through several PQ governments, it is difficult to describe the sense of impending doom that permeated the entire country that chilly November evening. The same glumness permeated the staff in the Langevin Block, the building on Wellington Street across from Parliament Hill, where most of the PMO staff are located. As we struggled to prepare the material for the prime minister – who would be coming in for a briefing with the staff prior to meeting the news media – we felt that the country was slipping into crisis before our very eyes and would not be the same again.

At last, the prime minister arrived. Upon seeing our faces, he immediately took charge of the situation.

"Hey, why all the gloomy faces?" he asked. "The sun will still rise in the morning!"

This had a tremendously calming effect on all of us. If he was worried himself, he didn't show it. He exuded self-confidence. His tone suggested that, together, we could master this situation. The effect on us was, well, if he's not worried, then maybe we shouldn't be.

In the ensuing days, weeks, and months, Mr. Trudeau would have a similar calming effect on the entire nation through his policy actions, speeches, interviews, and news conferences. And he would ultimately make a decisive, winning impact on the 1980 referendum with his carefully chosen speeches and promises. But, before he could calm the nation, he had to calm and focus his staff. And he did that, the very night the PQ first came to power.

In nine years in the PMO, I never saw Pierre Elliott Trudeau lose his temper. He was the kind of person who rarely showed emotion to any extreme. He never praised you or slapped you on the back when something went right; nor did he throw a temper tantrum when something went wrong. This sometimes made it difficult for staff to know how he was feeling, but you learned to look for clues.

In the early 1980s, I was Mr. Trudeau's chief advanceman, responsible for all logistical arrangements for his events and official travels. The prime minister had just given a lunchtime speech at a hotel in downtown Vancouver. The lectern from which he spoke was one of those portable ones, placed on the table directly in front of him at the correct moment, and was supplied by the hotel.

I noticed during his speech that he was having difficulty reading from his speaking notes. (The text was always typed in block-capital, oversized letters, double-spaced so it could be read more easily – and without reading glasses, which are a pain for public speakers.) Nevertheless, he was squinting, and he used his glasses at several points in the speech. I knew then and there that we had a problem.

After the event, several of us found ourselves on the elevator with him, so I asked him if he had had difficulty with something about the lectern. He answered very calmly, and with no hint of irritation, that he had found it too short for his height and poorly lit. He had difficulty seeing the text in the dim light.

Then came the clue that he was *indeed* angry. Besides me, the staff in the elevator included a political assistant responsible for British Columbia, a speechwriter, press officer Pat Gossage, and the prime minister's executive assistant, Ted Johnson. There were five of us. The prime minister looked around the elevator at each of us. "With all the staff I have to organize these trips," he said very calmly, "you would think that I could have a decent lectern from which to read my speeches."

That was it, a simple, flat statement. No further comment was made. If anyone else had overheard the conversation, they would have thought it was all matter-of-fact observation; there was no emotion at all. But we all knew we had just been dramatically chastised, big time!

We vowed that this problem would never occur again. Since hotel lecterns vary in size, shape, and condition across the country, we decided that the best solution was to build our own, specific to his height and eyesight and properly lit. The lectern would then travel with the prime minister, so that no matter where he was speaking he would not have the problems he had had in the Vancouver speech.

It was only after it was built that we also decided to put the Canadian Coat of Arms on the front of it, which is also the symbol used for the office of the prime minister. The PM's critics would later accuse him of trying to be "presidential," since the U.S. president uses a personal lectern that travels with him, and also has the official seal of the president on the front. But we knew that the travelling "presidential" lectern really was born from a low-key comment made to us by the prime minister in a Vancouver hotel elevator – because we never wanted to feel that wrath again.

▶ PIERRE O'NEIL
Press secretary, 1973–75

*I*t was dusk on a January day in 1973 when I was introduced in the Prime Minister's Office as press secretary, following the Liberal Party's near defeat of October 1972. Mr. Trudeau's principal secretary, Martin O'Connell, had called many times seeking suggestions for a bilingual journalist familiar with Canadian public affairs to replace Peter Roberts as press secretary. Roméo LeBlanc, a former press secretary to Mr. Pearson, as well as Mr. Trudeau, had also called.

I had finally been offered the job, but was reluctant to accept it, as I thought, not unlike a number of observers of the political scene, that Mr. Trudeau might not wish to stay too long as the head of a minority government. Indeed, since the near-defeat of October 1972, when the Liberals realized that the land was *not* so strong, the press kept portraying the prime minister as someone who appeared to have lost his stamina and was wearing sackcloth and ashes. I had asked to discuss this with Mr. Trudeau before I considered leaving journalism for a job that might last only a few months.

The prime minister was working at his desk, the lights dimmed, creating an intimate atmosphere among the oak panels and the beige furniture of his office. After greetings and some small talk about previous encounters, I confided my predicament: my doubts about the length of his stay in the job, given the changed circumstances.

I was taken aback when he asked whether I had ever read the story of the battle of Austerlitz. I had, but then he began testing my recollection of Napoleon's strategy during the campaign leading up to the battle. I couldn't remember the details, so Mr. Trudeau instructed me.

He quoted Napoleon as saying that the outcome of a battle is only understandable in the light of the campaign that leads up to it. He recalled how Napoleon had left Boulogne, how he had taken Ulm without firing a shot, how his lines of communication were overextended, his troops exhausted, and how the Prussians and Russians kept evading.

And so, in the vicinity of Austerlitz, Napoleon feigned fear and weakness, pretended to seek peace, arranged a meeting with General Gourlouki – an envoy of Tsar Alexander – who set an outrageous list of conditions for peace that caused the French emperor to grow white with rage.

All the while, Napoleon and his troops had overshot the Pratzen plateau. That is where he had already decided to wage battle, and he made that decision known to his generals. Eventually, he let the enemy set up on the plateau and occupied lesser positions, causing the coalition to anticipate easy victory over a downcast and demoralized French army. As they say, the rest is history!

I understood then that the prime minister was going to adapt to politics a fruitful military strategy, which he believed would bring him victory in the end – and it did, a little over a year later. On the way there, the staff kept suggesting the prime minister get away from Parliament and the concentration of press in the National Press Gallery, that he hit the road, go out and meet the people. Inevitably, he would respond, "An army general doesn't come out when the terrain is soft and morale is low."

When the government was defeated in May 1974 by the NDP's reluctance to vote confidence on the budget, and a general election was called, the prime minister came out fighting. His first meeting of the campaign took place in NDP leader David Lewis's constituency, and Lewis was eventually beaten like a rug, bringing to an end the career of a likeable and wonderful parliamentarian.

The prime minister's strategy of appearing as a very different leader from the days of Trudeaumania had paid off, and the Liberals' appetite for victory had been whetted once more. Again, they formed a majority.

Some weeks after I joined the Prime Minister's Office, I was attending a meeting with about fourteen members of the staff. As we looked at the orders of day in the House and Mr. Trudeau's schedule, a discussion arose about a speech that Opposition Leader Robert Stanfield was to deliver that evening in the Commons, relating to the Official Languages Act.

I sat quietly without uttering a word, as it was one of the first large staff meetings I had attended.

At the conclusion of these deliberations, it was suggested that I immediately take the following message to the prime minister: he should sit in the session out of courtesy for the Leader of the Opposition, and in recognition of the symbolic importance, both for the Liberal Party and himself, of that piece of legislation. With some trepidation – for I knew the mission would be tricky since the prime minister guarded his evenings with his family fiercely – I trotted from the East Block to the prime minister's parliamentary office.

On arrival, I delivered the message on behalf of the staff. Mr. Trudeau was busy at his desk. He rose from his chair quickly but not brusquely, and stood behind it, leaning his elbows on the chair back. He looked me straight in the eye with some intensity.

"Pierre," he said, "will you please inform your friends and colleagues of the staff that being a politician is not unlike practising a profession and, like any professional, a politician is entitled to leisure time, to go back to a wife and family after working hours. This is what I intend to do tonight, and therefore I will not sit in the Commons to listen to the Leader of the Opposition's speech."

As a political-science student at Laval University, I knew about Mackenzie King's life dedicated to politics. I had watched and written on Maurice Duplessis, who considered politics as almost a religious calling. Later, I had whistle-stopped across the country covering John Diefenbaker, for whom politics seemed to be altogether his work, recreation, and sole hobby. But here was a focused leader with a different set of values, a different outlook on politics as a profession.

▶ BOB MURDOCH
Executive assistant, 1973–78

The most precious asset of any government is prime ministerial time. Seven times twenty-four is not enough time to meet the needs of cabinet, caucus, government, the party, correspondence, policy, or domestic and foreign travel. In Pierre Trudeau's case, added to his prime ministerial demands were the requirements of a young family, and those of a very private person who needed time alone to think. It made the life of his executive assistant, or time manager (which I was for five years, beginning in September 1973), an extremely challenging one, and one for which there was no real training. I was reminded of this shortly after taking the job. I had a very long list of appointments that had been requested, and which I presented to him in a rather unstructured way. Under his icy stare I started to burble, gradually becoming less and less coherent. Finally, the prime minister said, "Bob, did you come in here to shoot the shit or tell me something?"

Devastated, I returned to my office ready to resign, but was persuaded not to by my predecessor, Torrance Wylie, who was still providing some on-the-job training. He gave me three important pieces of advice: first, that the world *outside* our office, with its many competing demands, was extremely chaotic. My job was to create a cocoon of calm within which the prime minister could function. Second, that to build trust with Mr. Trudeau I had to defend his personal needs against the competing demands of his job. My unintelligible presentation had violated both these rules. So Torrance gave me a third one: he explained that it was sometimes easier to communicate with the prime minister in writing. At that moment the "itinerary memo" was born. It would be submitted to him Friday evening and returned Monday morning with a tick, a "no," or "discuss" beside the various points.

Pierre Trudeau was extremely protective of his family and private time – particularly weekends, which were devoted to a lot of outdoor time with the boys. This often conflicted with his role as party leader, for party functions usually took place on weekends. A weekend at Harrington Lake with the boys would always beat a barbecue with the party faithful in Estevan, Saskatchewan, or Corner Brook, Newfoundland. Although in principle he accepted the need to attend these events, he could still be a formidable negotiator as each specific request arose. Early on I was losing more battles on this subject than I was winning. I'd say, "Prime Minister, you have to do this event," and he'd say, "No, I don't want to." I'd say, "But, Sir, you have to," and he'd say, "No, I won't."

An executive assistant pretty much knows the PM's schedule, every minute of every day. To get some leverage, I proposed a system to him. I would budget his time (including the private portion) annually and then break it down on a weekly basis. I got him and the staff to agree on the time allocations, and then I kept track, almost on a minute-to-minute basis. For example, I'd show him that he'd spent only 261 minutes on a

© Rod MacIvor

The boys guarding
their Papa's office and
prime ministerial time.

particular week on Liberal Party matters, which was 4.03 per cent less than we'd agreed. I think this system appealed to his rational and logical mind. Although not perfect, it became a great negotiating tool, and I started to win more than I lost.

Although Pierre Trudeau was extremely intelligent, I believe the quality that set him apart from others was his extraordinary self-discipline. Having a young family and running a government is an impossible task. He succeeded by being very disciplined, arriving every morning at 9:00 a.m., but, more importantly – crisis or not – leaving at 6:30 p.m. sharp to be home with Margaret and the boys. He always went home with two briefcases of government documents that he dealt with after dinner. As I was his last meeting every night, and lived near 24 Sussex, I would ride home with him and clear my agenda on the way, thus saving precious time.

Only once did this efficient use of time get interrupted. Every night, in snow, rain, or sunshine, as we drove along Sussex Drive, a middle-aged lady would literally jump out from the curb and vigorously wave to the prime minister. One evening (much to our police escort's consternation) he told Dave, his driver, to stop the car, and he invited her into the limousine. For five minutes she gazed at him in rapt admiration. The PM smiled at her and neither one of them spoke, and I certainly didn't say a word. On reaching 24 Sussex, Pierre got out; Dave dropped me at home, and then returned the lady to her habitual spot – where she reappeared the next day.

▶ ROGER ROLLAND
Special adviser, speechwriter, 1968–74, and friend

*F*rom 1968 to 1974, I worked as a French speechwriter for the Prime Minister's Office. In 1968, the University of Moncton awarded the prime minister an honorary doctorate and invited him to the graduation ceremony. The invitation was accepted and I had to write a speech for the occasion. Since the honorary degree was in literature, I reckoned that literary references were necessary, and so I sketched a parallel between Corneille's *Le Cid* and Shakespeare's *Romeo and Juliet*. I concluded by entreating New Brunswick francophones not to allow themselves to be victims of their elders' quarrels, as was the case in Corneille and Shakespeare.

Once the draft speech was completed, I sent copies to the Prime Minister's Office, as well as to Marc Lalonde, the PM's principal secretary, and to Roméo LeBlanc, the press secretary, as was the custom. A few days later, I was to go to Pierre Trudeau's office for a first reading of the speech. But about an hour before the meeting, Roméo LeBlanc phoned me.

"Have you lost your mind?" he blared out. "I'm from New Brunswick. I know people in the Moncton area very well, and your speech will bore them to death. How can Corneille and Shakespeare relate to farmers and fishermen? It's totally inappropriate."

In vain, I tried to convince Roméo that the prime minister was being awarded an honorary degree within the confines of a university, and that the speech had to be equal to the situation. Voices were raised, and the discussion became more and more intense, so much so that I was in a foul mood when I got to Pierre Trudeau's office.

Still tense and worked up, I started reading the speech out loud, with everyone following on their own copy. On page 4, the prime minister

noted a point that had already been made on page 2: "Why this repetition?" he asked.

I answered firmly that, for such or such a reason, the repetition was
necessary. A little farther down, Trudeau made another comment, which
I immediately dismissed. I continued reading. On the following page, he
wondered about the relevance of a certain sentence. Still with the same
off-handedness, I told him that the sentence was totally appropriate.
Trudeau then stopped, took off his glasses, shrugged and, in the most
ingenuous manner, said, "It's no use being prime minister if you can no
longer make suggestions!"

Marc Lalonde and Roméo LeBlanc burst out laughing. As for me, I
suddenly and contritely realized that this speech wasn't mine, but was
well and truly that of the prime minister.

That's how, with a hint of humour, Pierre Trudeau often exercised
his authority.

▶ MARC LALONDE
Principal secretary, 1968–72, and cabinet minister, 1972–84

*E*conomically, the winter of 1971 was a miserable time; for months and
months, the Canadian economy had been stuck in stagflation: high
inflation and high unemployment. Trudeaumania had more or less disappeared, and even the weather did not want to cooperate. Whatever the
government did, nothing seemed to work.

No doubt inspired by a desire to get out of that depressing atmosphere, Trudeau suggested that he and I go skiing in the French Alps for
a few days, an invitation that I obviously did not turn down but, bearing
in mind the general economic and political environment in the country,
it was understood that the whole thing had to remain out of the news.
Very few people were made aware of our plans, and Roméo LeBlanc
(then press secretary to the prime minister) was left in charge of ensur-
ing that the press did not get an inkling of what we were up to. Every day,
I was to call Roméo to keep abreast of developments in Ottawa and to
pass on any instructions from Trudeau.

We discreetly flew to Courchevel, where we spent three or four glorious days skiing under the direction of a giant of a ski instructor, who took us on all kinds of expeditions. We then decided to proceed by car to Geneva to take our plane back to Canada. However, the French regional tourism organization, which had been made aware of Trudeau's presence, invited us to stop over at a couple of ski stations that had recently been opened. Since we had a few days to spare, we decided to accept the invitation.

One of the stations we visited was Les Arcs, a brand-new village built on top of a hill, which was reachable only by cable car. Upon our arrival, we were told that there was a small film festival going on, and that we were invited to attend the event that evening with a few French film personalities. We had a pleasant evening and ended up dining with Johnny Halliday and his wife, as well as with Henri Charrière, a former prisoner at Île du Diable, who, after several futile attempts, had been one of the very few (if not the only one) who had finally succeeded in escaping from that horrible penal colony off the coast of French Guyana. He had been pardoned and had written a book about his adventure, which was on the bestseller list for months in France (a very successful American film, *Papillon*, was subsequently made of it). There was very little press covering the festival, and no mention was made of Trudeau's presence – which suited us fine.

The next day, as we were again ready to go skiing, Trudeau received a message that Brigitte Bardot, who happened to be spending a few days in one of the local villas in the company of a young boyfriend, wished to have the pleasure of shaking hands with Trudeau. Naturally, Trudeau did not feel like turning down such a flattering request. So we proceeded outside and waited for Miss Bardot for a few minutes. She soon appeared, shook hands, and exchanged a few words with Trudeau. A photographer had accompanied her and took a few pictures, but we did not pay attention to him and, soon, the two of us disappeared to the hills for a few runs, before leaving for another station.

Two days later, when I phoned Roméo for news, I heard him roaring over the phone: "What the heck are you two guys doing over there with Brigitte Bardot? How stupid can you be?"

Coming from Roméo, who used to be a pretty cool cat, I was somewhat dumbfounded. I asked whether he had got up on the wrong side of the bed that morning, and started to explain to him the innocent and fortuitous character of the encounter. He abruptly interrupted, told me to go and buy a copy of *Paris-Match*, and banged down the phone.

I rushed to the next magazine stand and there, on the cover of *Paris-Match*, was Trudeau in conversation with La Bardot – with Marc Lalonde way back, looking enviously at the two of them! Needless to say, the picture also made the front page of practically every newspaper in Canada, with the inevitable comments about how, while Canadians were freezing and the economy was in the dumps, Trudeau was frolicking with Brigitte Bardot in the French Alps. As expected, Trudeau shrugged it off, but I can report that there was no cheering crowd of voters – or even of staffers – waiting for us at the Ottawa airport when we returned.

Being a member of Trudeau's staff was never boring.

▶ MONIQUE BÉGIN
MP, 1972–80, and then cabinet minister, 1977–84

When I left politics in September 1984 and started teaching at Notre Dame University, in South Bend, Indiana, Father Ted Hesburgh, the renowned university president and a great admirer of Trudeau (which is the reason why I got the job in the first place!) loved to invite his two campus "politicians" for dinner: John Gilligan, the former Democrat governor of Ohio, and myself. One evening he asked me what it was like to work with Trudeau. How did he function? How often would I meet with him every week? And so on. Father Hesburgh was passionate about knowing all the details.

At first, I could not even understand what he was after. Then I decided to tell him the way it was. In eight years as Trudeau's minister, I told Father Ted, I had exactly two appointments with "the Boss" (as some of us had nicknamed him).

The first time was when I was Minister of National Revenue, and I was accompanied by (the late) Sid Hobbart, my Taxation Deputy Minister. We had to inform the prime minister, personally, of some international tax wrongdoings involving VIPs. It must have been in 1977.

The second time was at my own initiative. It was 1983, and, as Health and Welfare Minister, I had been managing the Canada Health Act, a very public and controversial dossier. Nothing was moving on the file any more. I had done it all: bilateral visits to my provincial counterparts; numerous federal-provincial conferences; public speeches; radio hot-line shows; television interviews; meetings with newspaper editorial boards.

I had met constitutional experts, organized medicine, organized nursing, and other health-care professionals. There were threats of a national doctors' strike; threats from the provinces to take my bill to the Supreme Court, but, worse than all that, I found myself in and out of Priorities and Planning (the Executive of Cabinet chaired by the PM) meetings, as if I had become part of the furniture, with no action and no decision in sight.

So, I privately asked to meet Trudeau in his office. I went alone. He was not good at small talk, and nor was I, so I started the conversation a bit abruptly, asking him politely if he was "for" or "against" the Canada Health Act. He looked at me, a bit puzzled, and, very much à la Trudeau, replied: "The first Royal Assent that I signed as Prime Minister in 1968 was for the Medical Care Act [completing our national medicare]." He did not say more on that point. I immediately understood that his last Royal Assent would be "my" Act.

Each of those meetings with The Boss had lasted – at the most – thirty minutes. As I explained to Father Ted, such was a very special prime minister, who normally considered people – including his ministers – as fully responsible adults who, when put in charge of a responsibility, would of necessity discharge it to the best of their ability.

This is how I understand his admission, in one of his media profiles, about "not really wanting to become a leader." Besides constitutional reform and the Charter of Rights, he was interested in the general (very general) orientations of his government. But the workings of each ministry did not really captivate him. For example, when he appointed me, either to Revenue, or to Health and Welfare, he never discussed any issue or topic, because, I believe, he would not have known what to tell me his wishes were in the matter. We were not on his radar screen.

I spoke of two meetings with the prime minister in eight years. In fact there was a third one. But it was not very private. Again, it was

Canada Health Act time, and the future seemed completely blocked. So, one day, at Question Period, after he was freed from the questioning from the Opposition leaders, I took my courage, walked to his seat, bent down near his desk, and rapidly asked him his opinion on what strategy to follow. He gave me, as usual, his undivided attention.

"Boss," I said, "I just don't know where it's going anymore with medicare!"

"Who are the players, and where do they stand on the Canada Health Act?" he asked.

"The ten provinces are opposed, not just their ministers of health, but their ministers of finance, and their premiers! All of organized medicine is opposed. All the official elites are opposed."

"Where is the population in all of this?"

"In favour of the bill."

"That's a sure win," was his stern answer.

He was right of course. He was always the strategist, mastering the political culture of our country. And he always had a strong sense of basic human values and the common good.

▶ PATRICK GOSSAGE
Assistant press secretary and then press secretary, 1976–82

*N*ames. How you address people. How you are addressed. These were perhaps trivial issues, but nevertheless telling in the relationships between a leader like Pierre Trudeau and those who worked for him. They were an important part of a menu of peculiarities that in some ways defined the man.

Trudeau was famously unable to attach the right names to the right people. For at least two or three months after joining the PMO, I was "Peter," intoned with great authority and confidence when he addressed me. One is understandably reticent about correcting the Prime Minister of Canada on small matters such as who you are!

Others were more sensitive about the experience. After the end of the 1979 losing federal campaign, Trudeau was persuaded to dine with some of the journalists who had followed him assiduously for six weeks. Among the guests was one George Radwanski, then (much less infamous than recently) a scribe at the *Financial Times*, but more notably a journalist who was proud to have authored a biography of Trudeau. He had been granted several hours of interview time – unusual access, to say the least – and he was quite puffed up about it. He was also pleased to be seated next to his subject at this dinner. But he was quickly and visibly deflated when, to the delight of the rest of the table, Trudeau addressed him loudly by the wrong name!

Trudeau himself had many names when he signed notes, letters, or memos. There was a hierarchy here, and how he signed established your place in it. "PE Trudeau" without punctuation and with a wonderful swirled P melded with a dramatic E was the machine signing (and real signature) for all correspondence of a formal nature. The machine itself was well-guarded and only a select few knew how to operate it. It was, in fact, a huge wheel with smooth indents that moved a real fountain pen as it slowly turned. Watching it be fed and laboriously sign a soon-to-be-treasured photo was quite a sight.

Trudeau signed all but the most routine letters (fiftieth anniversaries, ninety-fifth birthdays, etc.) with the same PE Trudeau. This was reduced to the dreaded scrawled PET in marginal notes on your memos that returned with grammar corrected!

If it was a signature for a more friendly communication, it was Pierre E Trudeau. If you were really close (although this was seldom used), you might get the ultra-intimate Pierre Trudeau! Sometimes at the bottom of a note to a friend would be Pierre E T. No punctuation. And of course, the true intimates did get Pierre.

Learning the ropes in the pressure-cooker atmosphere of the Trudeau Prime Minister's Office really had a lot to do with learning about his preferences – how to roll with them, or fit in around them, or just accept them.

Here are a few: he required orange juice and cookies in all hotel rooms; he had to have a red rose for his lapel when on the road; he demanded proper lighting and a glass of water on his podium; he required proper servicing for his beloved and temperamental Rolex, which was done regularly at a special shop in Toronto.

There were other idiosyncrasies: his intolerance for idle chat in the confines of a car or airplane related to his continuous and absolute focus on the work at hand; his impatience with aides overstepping their areas of expertise was again a way of focusing and simplifying his decision-making; and his demands for logical rigour when someone was proposing a course of action put the onus on the person doing the suggesting, where it should be, to make their case. Rolling with all this was part of making one's own relations with a huge and impatient intellect as smooth and effective as possible.

I finally became "Patrick" after a few months.

▶ MICHAEL LANGILL
Correspondence assistant in the PMO, 1976–79. From 1980 to 1984,
he was special assistant to PM with various duties, including
the one described here.

Shortly after Mr. Trudeau's famous "Welcome to the 1980s" victory speech at the Château Laurier Hotel, I became one of the many special assistants in his office. I was under the impression that my main job was to be the junior speechwriter, but soon learned that the "junior" anything in a political office gets dragooned into all kinds of projects that have little or nothing to do with what they may have thought their job was supposed to be. Such was the case when an associate from Marshall McLuhan's institute at the University of Toronto came in to interview Mr. Trudeau about the great man, who had recently suffered a stroke and had been in a coma for some time.

Mr. Trudeau's press secretary, Pat Gossage, asked me to prepare a briefing note with suggestions for Mr. Trudeau on what to say about Marshall McLuhan, send the note up to the prime minister, and then sit in on the interview. All this was to take place within the next hour.

Of course, I knew who Marshall McLuhan was (I mean, beyond his brief appearance in *Annie Hall*). But putting something useful about him down on paper for the prime minister was another matter. In the short time I had, I strained mightily, but couldn't come up with much, except for one brilliant thought. Perhaps the prime minister could say something amusing, or at least mildly amusing. I suggested a line from the American comedian Arte Johnson from *Laugh-In*. "Marshall McLuhan, how are ya doin'?" Not exactly knee-slapping stuff, but at least maybe an icebreaker. I still don't know why I thought it was a good idea. Mr. Trudeau's senior English speechwriter, the late Jim Moore, once told me that a collection of Mr. Trudeau's humour would fill only a very thin book that would have to have lots of pictures.

As we went up to the prime minister's office for the interview, I started to think about how inappropriate the line was. McLuhan is the most famous Canadian thinker ever. He is now in a coma. He is going to die soon. He might be dead already. And I'm telling the prime minister to make jokes. Bad ones at that. Oh, God! Maybe the briefing note got lost in the mailroom.

The McLuhan associate, his *very* pretty young assistant, and I were led into the inner sanctum. As introductions were being made, the pretty young assistant, not sure where to place the tape recorder, looked at me and at Mr. Trudeau and said something like "Where should I sit with this?"

To which Mr. Trudeau replied with a smile, first to me, "What do you think, Michael?" then to her, "You could sit over there, or over here, or you could come sit on my lap." The assistant actually took a half-step in his direction before blushing beet red and sitting down on a chair beside his big desk.

The desk was clean except for one thing: my briefing note, sitting there, face up, for all the world to see. I can only vaguely remember the discussion, which seemed to go on for days. All I could think of was that stupid joke. What would the prime minister think? I knew what he would think. He would think I was an idiot. He didn't once look at the note, and he didn't (surprise, surprise) use the Arte Johnson line either.

Mercifully, the interview eventually ended, and the three of us got up to leave. As I ushered the other two out, Mr. Trudeau called me back to his desk. He handed me the briefing note.

"You might want to keep this," was all he said. I mumbled something like "Thank you, sir," and bolted out the door, straight to the shredding machine. And from then on, I kept my brilliant thoughts on prime-ministerial humour to myself.

Well, mostly.

Several weeks after the incident at Salmon Arm, British Columbia, in which the prime minister was accused of giving the middle finger to some of the residents from his train window, some enterprising people in the town sent the prime minister a box of T-shirts. The design on the T-shirt was the silhouette of a fist with the middle finger pointing up. Included was a request that the prime minister have his picture taken with one on, or beside someone with one on – preferably one or all of his sons.

The T-shirt's caption read "Pierre says we're number 1." I thought it was hilarious, so I drafted a note telling Mr. Trudeau what a great idea this would be. It would show that he had a sense of humour, that there were no hard feelings, etc., and such sentiments certainly would not hurt us in a province where Liberal fortunes were seldom very good.

I should have remembered what Jim Moore told me. I never received a reply.

▶ JOYCE FAIRBAIRN
Senior legislative adviser, 1970–84, communications adviser, 1982–84, and long-time friend

My last visual memory of Pierre Trudeau as prime minister of Canada on Parliament Hill occurred on the morning of June 29, 1984.

It was his final day, and we thought it might be a good idea if the boys came to Parliament Hill and saw him at work in the House of Commons. I took them into the Speaker's Gallery, which looks directly over to the prime minister's seat on the government side of the chamber. Rather than a subdued occasion, it was a feisty and testy performance on both sides during the daily Question Period. The boys were not much in tune with the substance, but they were quietly eager to cheer on their dad. Justin, twelve, and Sacha, ten, cleverly diverted eight-year-old Michel from shouting out to his Papa, by distracting him with the listening device that switched between both official languages. Whatever emotion the fifteenth prime minister of Canada might have been feeling during his final moments in the House, the boys were engaged and cheerful.

Jean-Marc Carisse

Joyce (with shoes) and "Bert" years after the Peace Tower climb.

After the farewell tributes wound down, we went back to the Prime Minister's Office. Pierre was in good spirits and asked them what they would like to do, offering lunch in the parliamentary restaurant. They turned him down.

"Let's go up to the top of the Peace Tower," they shouted. Pierre was not sure that was a good idea, but when I asked if he had ever been up there, and the answer was no, he lost his case.

Off we went to the elevator that takes thousands of visitors up to the top of the tower each year. It is a small elevator, and there was a good-sized lineup of tourists waiting for their turn. The commissionaire politely asked them to stand back for the prime minister but, when Pierre saw the line, he quickly inquired if there was another way up, so that he would not displace anyone. He was pointed toward a door with a narrow staircase that is rarely used, and he cheerfully rounded us all up for the climb.

It was an adventure for the boys, and they charged up the stairs after him, shouting with laughter as the sound bounced off the walls. Well behind, I huffed and puffed my way up in a pair of high heels, which I quickly removed, wondering if I was going to make it up there at all.

At the top, the view was breathtaking, stretching over the Gatineau Hills on the Quebec side, where the boys had spent their young years

Saying goodbye to public life at Liberal Party tribute in June 1984.

skiing and hiking and then swimming and boating at the Harrington Lake residence provided for our prime ministers. They peered through the railings to look at the Ottawa River in both directions as far as the eye could see. Pierre pointed out their house, and the nearby church. Then they looked down on the beautiful lawns of Parliament Hill, surrounded by the whole City of Ottawa, and (the boys) waved vigorously at the people on the ground.

It was a beautiful, hot, sunny day and the boys clustered around their dad, tugging at his arms, asking questions faster than he could answer them, and laughing at the sheer excitement of climbing the tower. Pierre grinned back at me and said, "Good idea."

It was a great way to end a historic nineteen years in public service. And that is the memory that will stay in my mind forever, because, for Pierre, as he left the Hill on that afternoon in June, those three special boys were the greatest achievement of his life.

▶ TIM PORTEOUS
Friend since 1957; speechwriter in PMO, 1968–70;
executive assistant, 1970–73

Joseph Philippe Pierre Yves Elliott Trudeau. The name was certainly distinctive, but not always helpful.

It was Gwen Clark Whittall who, in 1988, proposed a reunion dinner to celebrate the twentieth anniversary of Pierre Trudeau's selection as Liberal Party leader and prime minister. A committee appointed itself to organize the evening. The invitation list would include Pierre as guest of honour, all members of the Trudeau leadership campaign, and many who had worked with him while he was prime minister.

Trivial Pursuit, a popular-culture quiz game, had been invented by two Montrealers in the early 1980s and had rapidly become an international success. As a member of the organizing committee, I suggested that the entertainment should include our own version of Trivial Pursuit, with questions related to the leadership race. We called it Trivial Pierresuit.

The most coveted souvenirs of the leadership race were the striking posters with the high-contrast portrait of Pierre. They had been commissioned by Alison Gordon and Jennifer Rae and then rejected by the campaign executive as too radical visually. Undaunted, Alison and Jennifer ordered several thousand, and they became the much-admired and imitated icon of the campaign. (Because Pierre won the leader-ship, the media had portrayed his campaign as carefully planned and highly organized. In reality, much of it, including the posters, was spontaneous and improvised.) For our one and only prize at the reunion dinner, we found one of the posters and had it signed by Pierre and framed.

On April 6, 1988, about 150 of us gathered in the Confederation Room of the parliament buildings. The mood was festive and nostalgic. As soon as the guests were seated, the rules of the game were explained. The quiz sheets were to be filled out and collected before dessert.

I had expected that the quiz would provide a brief distraction for a few history buffs. Looking out over the crowd of ambitious achievers, however, I realized that almost everybody was hunched over a quiz sheet, concentrating on each question and competing fiercely.

We had intended that Pierre, as guest of honour, would present his poster portrait to the winner of the game. It never occurred to us that he would want to participate in the contest himself. But his competitive instincts had been aroused, and there he was, filling out his own sheet. Since many of the questions were about him, he would make a formida-ble competitor.

Having thought up the questions, and knowing the answers, I imag-ined the quiz would be quite easy for many guests, but memory is an unreliable counsellor and the test turned out to be tougher than I antic-ipated. Most of the contestants stumbled over Question One:

1. Prior to the leadership race, which provincial premier said, "If he ever decides to move to my province there is place for him in my cabinet"?
    *   W.A.C. Bennett
    *   Ross Thatcher
    *   Joey Smallwood

Everyone knew that Thatcher and Smallwood had been Liberal pre-miers who supported Trudeau, while Bennett, a Social Krediter, had opposed him. Pierre was among the small minority who identified Bennett as his would-be employer.

By contrast, Question Three was a giveaway:

3. Before deciding to run, Trudeau spoke to Gordon Robertson (Clerk of the Privy Council) about the job. What did he ask him?
    • What is the structure of the Privy Council Office?
    • What are the arrangements for briefing a new PM?
    • What time does the PM start work in the morning?

Anyone who had worked with Pierre was aware of his aversion to early rising. Everybody got this one right.

Question Five referred to Pierre's appearance on Radio-Canada's late-night comedy program *Les Couche-tard*:

5. On *Les Couche-tard*, Trudeau was asked by Clémence Desrochers who was his favourite author. What did he reply?
    • Charles Baudelaire
    • Niccolo Machiavelli
    • Marshall McLuhan

Pierre's reply displayed the streak of mischief that frequently got him into trouble, but was one of the characteristics that made him unique among our politicians.

To most people, Niccolo Machiavelli represents the epitome of cynical and unscrupulous politics. For a candidate for prime minister to claim, on national television, that Machiavelli was his favourite author was provocative, if not reckless. I doubt if any other politician would have given such an answer, even on a comedy show.

On his quiz sheet, Pierre first checked "Machiavelli" and then crossed it out and checked "Baudelaire," who was, in fact, one of his favourite poets (but not the right answer).

The final question caused a minor dust-up:

15. The Victory Party, organized by the Liberal Federation, took place at the Skyline Hotel. Who paid for it?
    • The Liberal Party Finance Committee
    • The Trudeau Campaign
    • The Skyline Hotel

One of the guests at the reunion dinner was Robert Campeau, former owner of the Skyline Hotel. He loudly insisted that he had paid for the victory party through his hotel. Pierre, who probably had no idea who had paid for the party, was persuaded to check "The Skyline Hotel." However, the record shows that, in accordance with the ground rules of the leadership convention, the Trudeau Campaign paid for the party (and could well afford to do so).

When the answers to the fifteen regular questions were tallied, Pierre was tied for first place with only four wrong answers, but the contest was not over. There was a bonus question.

Bonus Question: What is Pierre Trudeau's full name?

Joseph _____ Pierre _____ _____ Trudeau

On his quiz sheet, Pierre had written:

Joseph <u>Yves</u> Pierre <u>Elliott</u> <u>?</u> Trudeau

12- What was Trudeau's code name on the convention intercom?
Quel était le nom de code de Trudeau sur l'interphone du Congrès?

⊗ Victor   ◯ Sussex   ◯ Camelot

13- Qui étai(en)t l'(les) artiste(s) invité(s) lors de la réception du vendredi soir au Château Laurier?
Who entertained at the Friday night party at the Chateau Laurier?

◯ Liona Boyd   ⊗ Ian and Sylvia   ◯ Lighthouse

14- On the final ballot, by how many votes did Trudeau beat Winters?
Par combien de votes Trudeau a-t-il battu Bob Winters au dernier tour?

◯ 195   ⊗ 243   ◯ 249

15- La fête de la victoire, organisée par la Fédération libérale s'est déroulée à l'hôtel Skyline. Qui a payé la note?
The Victory Party, organized by the Liberal Federation, took place at the Skyline Hotel. Who paid for it?

◯ La Commission des finances du PLC/The LPC Finance Committee

◯ La Campagne Trudeau/The Trudeau Campaign

⊗ L'hôtel Skyline/The Skyline Hotel

Bonus question/Question bonus

What is Pierre Trudeau's full name? Quel est le nom complet de Pierre Trudeau?

Joseph _Yves_ Pierre _Elliott_ _?_ Trudeau
Philippe _Yves_ _Elliott_

Tim Porteous Collection

Tim Porteous and Pierre with contest winner Ted Johnson.

Amazingly, he had failed to earn the bonus by filling out only two blanks, both incorrectly. The other contestant with only four wrong answers was Ted Johnson, one of my successors as executive assistant to Pierre. He had correctly filled out Pierre's full name, winning the bonus and the competition. He was a popular winner. Pierre was delighted to present the poster to such a deserving and knowledgeable competitor.

Chapter Three

On the Road

▶ GABRIEL FILION
Painter and school friend

I met Pierre E. Trudeau in 1939–40 at Jean-de-Brébeuf College, which was run by Jesuit priests. During the 1940 school year, I was studying painting under Paul-Émile Borduas at the École du meuble on Kimberly Street.

At age twenty, due to my family background, I had a nervous breakdown, and that's when the Trudeau family took me under its wing. At the time, they lived at 84 McCullough Street. Grace Trudeau paid the doctors who treated me and often sent me to fancy boarding houses in the Laurentians. This is how I got to know the family really well: the eldest sister, Suzette, Pierre, and Charles, who was in my class at college. The servants, Martin and Melyssa, were also very nice. Mrs. Trudeau, however, was the one who lavished maternal attention on me.

It's at this time, in the summer, that I went on two trips with Pierre Trudeau. We did the first one on a motorcycle, travelling some five thousand kilometres through New Brunswick, Nova Scotia, and Prince Edward Island, sleeping in barns at night, and sometimes in churches, or in houses that were being built. Most often, however, we slept in the countryside, pitching our tent in the fields or in the forest. We ate in small restaurants, and Pierre always paid the bill, since I had no money. The trip was filled with long moments of silence and reflection. At times, we had friendly discussions; Pierre was already talking about a united

Canada, while I, being the descendant of *coureurs de bois*, already imagined an independent Quebec.

I also went on a second trip with Pierre Trudeau that summer: the trip made by François Paradis in the book *Maria Chapdelaine*, which is to say, from La Tuque to Roberval, along the Croche River, walking 110 miles through the forest. On the second day of the trip, I injured my right leg with a blow from an axe. I didn't want us to return to Montreal, so we decided to continue on. Every day, Pierre tended to my injured leg, and we managed to complete the journey to Roberval.

I never saw Pierre Trudeau again after that trip. Each of us took the road we were meant to follow: he, toward Canada; me, toward Quebec.

▶ HARRISON McCAIN
Founding chairman of McCain Foods Limited, Florenceville,
New Brunswick

I once heard Pierre Trudeau say in public, "Harrison McCain was the first political supporter I had."

When Mr. Trudeau was in his first campaign, he visited my brother Wallace and me in Florenceville. We took him around the various church halls and Legion halls, where we had invited the local people to come and hear him speak. On the way to one hall, I briefed him on what to expect.

"The place we are going is notoriously Conservative, and the ladies who will be in there won't be very sympathetic to a Liberal candidate, so you should be forewarned."

When we got inside, there was a crowd, mostly ladies, sitting around the perimeter of the hall, scowling. Mr. Trudeau spoke from the centre of the room. Here were his first words to them:

"I suppose you ladies don't know that I am the Minister of Justice for Canada, and I suppose you don't realize I know that – besides quilting – you are playing cards for money in the basement of this building. If I weren't in such a good mood today I would do something about that, because it's illegal."

The ladies were stunned, but then broke into loud laughter.

▶ TIM PORTEOUS
Friend since 1957; speechwriter in PMO, 1968–70;
executive assistant, 1970–73

*P*ierre Trudeau was a man of many parts, but he was at his best as a travelling companion. In his company, you felt and shared his energy, his curiosity, his sense of humour, and his enjoyment of adventure. But he could also be exasperating.

Among my most vivid memories is an incident that took place during a state visit to India in 1971. As executive assistant, one of my main jobs was to keep the prime minister on schedule. Since our hosts had enthusiastically crammed far too many events into the official program, and Pierre was determined to participate fully in all of them, this was virtually impossible.

It was late morning on a hot, dusty day on the outskirts of New Delhi, and we had already fallen behind our timetable. Before we attended a state banquet at lunchtime, we had been invited to tour a village that housed a large number of Gandhi-inspired craftspeople. At the entrance to the village was a man with a camel – definitely not part of the program. In sign language, he invited Pierre to mount his camel.

"Prime Minister, Prime Minister, we will be late for Mrs. Gandhi's lunch!" I cried dutifully, but ineffectively.

"But I have never ridden a camel," Pierre pointed out, as he climbed aboard.

We set off down the main street of the village, Pierre waving to the inhabitants and I trotting along behind with as much dignity as I could muster. Then the camel picked up speed, breaking into a gallop, with me desperately sprinting to keep up. We covered a lot of ground in what is probably record time for a prime minister on a camel.

At the end of the village, the camel was brought to a halt and Pierre vaulted off, landing at my feet. He pointed to his watch. "See, we are back on schedule!" he crowed.

Not on the schedule but so what?

▶ VICTOR IRVING
RCMP officer in charge of PM's security detail, 1969–71

*I*n June 1971, HM the Queen and Prince Philip came to Victoria, and Margaret and Pierre were there to welcome them. We drove in an unmarked police car to the waterfront to meet them on the Royal yacht *Britannia*. A number of vehicles were lined up on the dock to transport the royal party, the Trudeaus, and other VIPs, to Government House.

Pierre noticed the Queen and Prince Philip had an open Rolls-Royce, while he was allocated a black limousine. He then asked me if I might find a convertible instead. As luck would have it, I spotted a yellow Pontiac Firebird sports car parked in the dock master's reserved parking spot. I was able to convince the dock master that the prime minister needed his car for a while.

During the parade, the loudest cheers from the crowds lining the streets were for the newlyweds in the yellow Firebird, even though there was little room for the four of us squished into the small car, compared to the Queen's Rolls-Royce.

▶ JERRY GRAFSTEIN
Friend since 1957; policy and media adviser, 1972–84

*I*n 1972, Pierre Trudeau was not very happy with me. While for years we had been members of a circle who regularly exchanged intellectual fusillades, I had played a leading role in John Turner's leadership campaign in 1968. When Turner stayed on until the last ballot, Trudeau was not pleased.

As for me, I shared the Pearson Liberals' unease about Mr. Trudeau, because of his earlier broadsides at Mr. Pearson before he ran as a Liberal in 1965, and especially his decision to drop the Election Writ in 1968 before Parliament could pay tribute to Mr. Pearson. Mrs. Pearson was miffed at him, to say the least – less about Trudeau's earlier criticisms and more about his treatment of Mr. Pearson since becoming prime minister, especially since Mr. Pearson and his aides had quietly given

Trudeau special scope and opportunities for his leadership aspirations.

After the outburst of "Trudeaumania" in 1968, Trudeau's 1972 national campaign, heralded as an "Encounter with Canadians," and bearing the campaign slogan "The Land Is Strong," had begun to flounder and fall flat. Public adoration of Mr. Trudeau's charisma and charm had changed to public chagrin. Liberals were sinking in the polls. The Toronto Liberals, whom Mr. Trudeau had failed to cultivate after his sweeping 1968 victory, sat back. A Conservative government was looming.

Several weeks after the launch of the disastrous 1972 campaign, I received a call from the PMO, inviting me to meet with the prime minister on his next campaign swing through Toronto. The Conservatives, under the brilliant direction of the "Big Blue Machine" in Toronto, were steadily gaining momentum. I had barely spoken to Trudeau for several years; his campaign team remained leery of Toronto Liberals. We met at the Prince Hotel, the Japanese-style hostelry that Trudeau favoured.

Pierre Trudeau had one uncanny knack. Dispassionately, he could separate himself from his persona and performance, and analyze his own strengths and weaknesses as if reading an X-ray.

After the usual family pleasantries, he asked, "How are we doing?"

"You, Prime Minister, are losing Toronto," I rejoined.

"Why so?" he asked softly.

"Because you, sir, have failed to engage Liberals. Besides, Liberals in Toronto are unhappy with your treatment of Mr. Pearson, and now he is dying." (By then, Mr. Pearson was suffering from cancer.) Trudeau fell silent and pondered, chin in hand, looking down.

Then he slowly raised his head, captured me with his penetrating look, and asked quietly and firmly, "Is there anything that can be done to change the situation?"

I knew that was why he had invited me. I immediately responded, "Yes, there is something that can be done."

"What would that be?"

"We would have to transfer the love and affection the Toronto Liberals have for Mr. Pearson to you."

His eyes narrowed and then lit up. "Is that possible now?" he asked, given that we were in the midst of the election campaign.

"Yes, I believe it is possible," I said.

"How?"

"You, sir, could throw an intimate surprise birthday party for Mr. Pearson. The Toronto Liberals know that Mr. Pearson is dying. Toronto Liberals are sitting on their hands. All we would need would be Mr. Pearson to attract them back."

"Would it work?" he asked.

"It can only help and it cannot hurt."

"Where would you propose to hold such an intimate surprise birthday party?"

"At Maple Leaf Gardens of course."

Trudeau broke up. "Where?" he laughed.

"At Maple Leaf Gardens."

"Why do you think we could fill Maple Leaf Gardens when our campaign crowds have been so sparse?"

"Because, Sir, every Liberal in Toronto would want to come and have a last chance to pay their respect to Mr. Pearson."

"Would you help organize it?"

"Yes, on three conditions."

"What are they?"

"First, your campaign team agrees not to interfere. Second, we must convince Mr. and Mrs. Pearson to attend, which I believe is possible with the help of Keith Davey, Jim Coutts, and others. Finally, you have to agree yourself to work that whole day in Toronto until midnight."

Pierre Trudeau was most curious about the third condition. "Why is that important?"

"Because, Sir, Liberals work hard in Toronto. Meanwhile, your campaign has been working half time and has been meandering."

Trudeau agreed and immediately instructed his national campaign chairman, Bob Andras, to support the event. We quickly set out to put the restless Toronto Liberal machine not only in motion but in high gear.

Keith Davey, Jim Coutts, Royce Frith, Dick O'Hagan, and I attended on Mr. and Mrs. Pearson's corner suite at the Park Plaza Hotel, which Mr. Pearson always preferred. Despite Mrs. Pearson's initial reluctance, Mr. Pearson overcame her irate vocal objections and agreed to be the "surprise" guest at "a surprise birthday party in his honour." He was amused by the idea and anxious to help the party.

Dorothy Petrie (later Davey), a superb Liberal organizer, agreed to be co-chair. One call to Leaf owner Harold Ballard, who revered Mr. Pearson, gave us the Gardens. Dorothy and I set out to call every Liberal candidate and riding president in the greater Toronto area to get their commitment to bring five hundred or more from their riding to the rally.

Elvio Del Zotto (then in the baking business) agreed to provide a six-foot-tall birthday cake, billed as "the biggest birthday cake in Canadian history." Popular Canadian musicians were enlisted to volunteer their talents. A snappy downtown Toronto media blitz was quickly deployed. Liberals came alive in Toronto. We decided to calibrate the seating capacity of the Gardens at eighteen thousand, confident of an overflow crowd. We prepared a wagon top outside on College Street, from which Pierre Trudeau could address the disappointed throngs unable to enter the Gardens.

The city buzzed with excitement. Mr. Pearson's appearance was not announced to the media. The event was billed as a Liberal rally to rejuvenate the Liberal team. The local media woke up. Liberal organizers were quietly informed about the "surprise guest" and outdid themselves to bring as many Liberals supporters from their ridings as possible by bus, car, and transit. A curious public appeared in droves.

At the rally, over twenty-eight thousand people showed up, effortlessly filling the Gardens and overflowing onto all the streets around. Trudeau spoke to those jostling outside just before the event. Loudspeakers were made available so outsiders could listen to the program inside.

Royce Frith, then a broadcaster, was MC for the event. All the Toronto Liberal candidates were on the stage to bask in the glow of their two inspired party leaders. Mr. Pearson was introduced as "the surprise guest." The giant birthday cake was wheeled in, candles ablaze, and Prime Minister Trudeau, Mr. Pearson, and all the candidates clustered around the cake and joined to blow out the candles, followed by a rousing chorus of "Happy Birthday." That was the image that would be pictured in the papers and TV.

Mr. Pearson spoke briefly and beautifully. There was not a dry eye in the jammed arena. Then Mr. Trudeau spoke. A stirring national anthem followed as the audience roared with one voice and the evening came to a tearful and emotional end. The volunteers streamed out of the building, energized with a new sense of purpose.

It was only 9 p.m. Mr. Trudeau came backstage to thank the organizers and take his leave. I asked him where he was going. He seemed surprised. He thought his job was done. I reminded him of his promise to work until midnight. He laughed and asked, "What is left to do?" I motioned him into a small room backstage, where there were a thousand or more small, white, cardboard cake boxes lining the walls. I then invited him to autograph every single white box.

Eyeing the huge stacks of cardboard warily, he asked, "Why?" I told him when he finished his final task, I would tell him. I smiled and said, "For Toronto Liberals, our work is never done," or – as Keith Davey would put it with apologies to Yogi Berra – "it's never over until it's over."

He began to autograph each box with his scrawled signature – Best Regards, Pierre, Best Wishes, Pierre, Thank You, Pierre, All the Best, Pierre. Shortly before midnight Mr. Trudeau completed his task. I then told him that each small cake box would now be hand-delivered to each newsman, radio reporter and commentator, TV anchor, TV reporter, and (for that matter) disk jockey in Toronto, and to each member of the national media covering the campaign. The national TV news coverage was upbeat that night, with sympathetic shots of the audience.

The next morning on CFRB radio, an ever-caustic Trudeau critic with the largest listenership in Ontario reported on the rally at length. The lines went something like this: "Even that arrogant Trudeau cannot be that bad. Look how he treated Mr. Pearson." That refrain was repeated endlessly in television, radio, and print. The media warmed to Mr. Trudeau, as did the Toronto public. The Tory momentum slowed. The polls in Toronto started moving up. Don Macdonald held his seat in Rosedale. The Liberal government held on as a minority government.

Throughout the many political challenges ahead, Toronto formed the bedrock of Trudeau's support that enabled him and Liberals to achieve such historic milestones as the Charter of Rights.

Two years later, in 1974, Trudeau, now fully supported by and engaged with Pearson Liberals, won a surprising victory and recaptured a strong majority government.

Trudeau never forgot the lesson. The Land was indeed Strong. So was Pierre Trudeau. So were Liberals.

❱ KEITH MITCHELL
Vancouver lawyer and Trudeau political campaigner

My knowledge of Pierre Trudeau was only through politics. In 1968, I served, along with my friend John Rae, as one of his two "advancemen" in his national election campaign. I would subsequently campaign with Trudeau in every national election he undertook. I shared with him the full range of the working parts of political campaigning, from the ludicrous, to the moving, to the downright exhausting. He persevered and mostly triumphed.

He came into politics in a tumultuous way, serving as the charismatic beacon of a new era. The 1968 election was a lot more than a political campaign; it was a national celebration. As campaign organizers, we learned to ask new questions of the police authorities every morning, generally along the lines of "How can we keep the crowds down?" In major Canadian cities, tens of thousands showed up; in towns and villages merely thousands; and in Toronto two hundred thousand. Part of Pierre Trudeau was obviously stimulated by the crowds, but part of him was overwhelmed, as people grabbed at him, reached out to him, and flung themselves at him by the thousands.

He was essentially a shy man. Not a modest man, but a shy and courteous man.

He had his limits and was committed to erecting a fence around his psyche to defend it against the public onslaught. This fence was fortified when he became a husband and father. He rigorously defended his time with his family and their privacy against governmental and political demands.

A memory: in the 1974 general election, Trudeau was making electoral breakthroughs in British Columbia. I wanted him to go to Powell River, a town up the coast north of Vancouver, which the Liberals didn't traditionally win, but were close to taking.

His schedule was full. There was absolutely no time for Powell River. But he did have private time planned during a campaign stop in Vancouver, to spend time with his wife – who was campaigning brilliantly for him in her home province – and the boys, who were the centre of his life. I called in a marker from his staff and gained agreement that his private time would be shortened, and I would fly with him by floatplane to Powell River. Then I received word that he was not amused.

At the appointed hour, I (along with the RCMP security detail) was at the floatplane. A driving rainstorm was pounding the dock. Trudeau emerged through the mist, carrying his two boys in yellow rain slickers. In case I hadn't got it, he most elaborately said goodbye to his protesting children and turned to me with a glacial expression. He clearly knew I stood guilty of violating his personal time.

We entered the small Otter floatplane and took the two adjoining rear seats. The moistness from the rain that turned the plane into a cold steam room did nothing to lubricate the silent atmosphere. We took off. The RCMP officer then passed me two damp cardboard-boxed lunches. I dutifully passed one of these delights to the prime minister. He peeled

Young Sacha and Justin study the platform carpet while Papa gives another campaign speech.

© Rod MacIvor

back the wet cardboard to reveal probably the world's soggiest tuna-fish sandwich. He picked up the offending sandwich, took one look at it, and somehow his disintegrating sandwich ended up on me. The expression on his face was such I knew he wished he had mushed it in my face. Just in case I ever wanted to breach his family time again.

Fast-forward to election night. I received a gracious call from Trudeau and Margaret, thanking me for helping her campaign in British Columbia, and acknowledging the Liberal-riding victory in Powell River. I told him it was due to his strong performance that day, which began as the floatplane touched down and the sun cleared, and he once again energized – as I had heard him so often before – another town of Canadians. All thoughts of a disintegrating tuna-fish sandwich were put in perspective.

▶ IONA CAMPAGNOLO
Worked with Trudeau as MP, minister, and latterly,
as president of the Liberal Party of Canada, 1974–84

*T*he 1976 Trudeau visit to Haida Gwaii (the Queen Charlotte Islands) took place on a number of levels. Long-horned cattle ("hippy cows" as the Islanders called them), sauntered along the roads as the prime ministerial cavalcade made its way through the island. There was none of that negative passion of the mainland, as happy spectators waved warmly, and fences and gates were hung with posters that said, "Bienvenue la famille Trudeau," and "You are Welcome here."

Pierre, Margaret, and the boys drove to a temporary cottage at T'lell, where wonderful island quilts had been specially sewn to honour them. Following the dedication of the Skidegate Museum, Pierre was given an honoured Haida name, which, with great hilarity, he was told allowed him to have four wives! He quickly reassured Margaret he would not be taking advantage of this offer. She and the boys were ceremoniously welcomed into the Raven clan.

There were many other events that day, but the one I remember most vividly now was Pierre – perched high up on a rocky outcropping

near Langara – looking out to the untamed Pacific. His love of the landscape was palpable. He was being earnestly briefed on the disappearance
of the sea otter, and he listened courteously.

The otter had been hunted to the brink of extinction in the last
century, and Pierre was presented with a proposal for the federal government to take a lead in restocking the sea otter here, where they had
once lived for thousands of years. (This idea was the *secret* agenda for his
visit.) He was noncommittal.

"Is it doable?" I finally asked him as he prepared to head back to the
mainland.

"That's up to all of you, isn't it?" he said, in his usual challenging
style.

Today, I am told, there are indeed transplanted otters thriving in their
ancestral waters around Haida Gwaii. The essence of Pierre Trudeau, I
believe, was his ability to teach us all how to take hold of the system and
make it work for society, rather than the other way round!

▶ GEORGE WILSON
Former executive assistant to principal secretary Jim Coutts,
and campaign advanceman, 1979–84

*T*his is fondly known as the "add-on story." Add-ons were last-minute
changes and additions to the PM's daily schedule, which, being planned
down to the minute far in advance, rarely allowed add-ons to happen.
During the 1980 election campaign, Allan Lutfy was the executive assistant, and he introduced the system of absolutely *no add-ons.*

This particular afternoon I met the PM's plane in Kamloops, where
he was scheduled to make a speech and then leave the next day. After the
advance trip for this campaign stop, however, I had learned from local
organizers that there was an elderly Indian gentleman, named Alfred
Trudeau, who was pretty insistent on meeting his long-lost relative.

I ran this by Lutfy.

"Whoa, George," he said. "It isn't going to happen. Remember, we
don't do this . . . we don't *do* add-ons."

I relayed this to the organizers when we got to the hall where the PM was about to speak, and then I moved to the back, as usual, to listen to the speech. When the speech was finished, I saw an organizer leading an old Native up to the stage. I was helpless. Lutfy looked at me and shook his head, *way* more than a bit annoyed.

A guy grabbed the mike and introduced the PM to his long-lost relative. Alfred Trudeau took one look at the other Mr. Trudeau, and collapsed on stage. Someone quickly called an ambulance and we got the PM out of there and into the car.

Lutfy said, "The PM doesn't know what to do now. Should we wait or leave?"

I told them to go to the hotel and call it a night.

The following morning, we got the news that Alfred Trudeau had died. We relayed this to Mr. Trudeau, who was genuinely shocked. A few minutes later, he said, "Well, that will teach you not to do add-ons."

Chapter Four

Just Watching Me

▌ EDITH IGLAUER
Journalist and author

*P*ierre Trudeau was the most difficult person I have interviewed in more than sixty years as a journalist. He simply talked a great deal faster than I could take notes. Sometimes I managed to write down only every other sentence, and then I retrieved missing sections from memory immediately afterwards in the nearest ladies' room or by racing home.

It took me the better part of a year – from summer 1968 into the spring of 1969 – to report and write my profile of Pierre Trudeau, entitled "Prime Minister/Premier Ministre," for the *New Yorker* magazine. It was published in the July 5, 1969, issue.

I have often been asked if I used a tape recorder, and if not, why not. Some years later I did try one with another profile subject, architect Arthur Erickson, and found it interfered with my mental sorting process and doubled the work. I am certain that Trudeau would never have spoken so freely if I had been taping; the introduction of a machine would have made him instinctively distance himself.

Early in 1968 I had proposed to William Shawn, the then-legendary editor of the *New Yorker*, that I write a piece about Trudeau. Mr. Shawn said I could go ahead if Trudeau became prime minister. When that happened, I called the Prime Minister's Office. Roméo LeBlanc, who had left the CBC to become Trudeau's press secretary, was my first contact, and wonderful to work with.

"Will the prime minister cooperate and grant me interviews?" I asked. LeBlanc replied that Trudeau was going on a six-thousand-mile trip across the Canadian North, a first for a prime minister, and could not reply until he returned; and in any event, he would have little time, if any, to see me. I asked where the prime minister was going, because I had travelled extensively in the North and was just curious. Roméo said that only three people, a combined press delegation, were permitted on the trip. And, he added, "You can't possibly go."

I had never thought of asking to go, but immediately called Mr. Shawn and said, "I have the funniest feeling they will take me along if I say you think it's essential." That evening, my first book, *Inuit Journey*, published two years before, went off in the diplomatic pouch from New York to Ottawa at Trudeau's request. At his regular meeting with four aides the next morning, he asked if anyone knew me. Gordon Robertson, then Clerk of the Privy Council, who had been deputy minister of Northern Affairs when I was writing about the North, is reported to have replied, "Take her with you. You won't be sorry."

So I went. We were ten: six in Trudeau's personal party, including his younger brother Charles, who replaced an ailing Michael Pitfield at the last minute; plus one member each from the CBC and the Canadian Press, Canadian Press photographer Peter Bregg, and me. I made a bargain with Roméo. In return for being able to observe Trudeau for eight days, I agreed not to interview him on the trip, to ask for only a single one-to-one interview in Ottawa, and to accede to Trudeau's stipulation that I would not interview his immediate family.

On our return, and after my one interview with Trudeau at lunch at 24 Sussex, his official Ottawa residence, I put down my objective for the profile in my letter thanking him. I wrote, "When people examine your achievements as Prime Minister . . . I would like them to be able to turn to my piece to find out what kind of a man you are."

Some nerve! I am amazed now by my temerity, but I believe I kept to that intention, judging by the long life this profile has had and the number of times it has been quoted over so many years. All the time I

Canadian Press, Peter Bregg

A prime minister going in circles.

was writing it, I had the feeling that I was actually painting a portrait. It seems to me I interviewed almost everyone who ever knew Trudeau well or worked with him – both friends and enemies.

I approached a member of his family only once. On the Arctic trip, at Cassiar Asbestos Mine, at Clinton Creek in northern British Columbia, I was standing next to Charles while we watched the prime minister ride a motorcycle in circles. I don't remember why Pierre was doing that, except that he always accepted dares and enjoyed showing off his expertise. I turned to Charles and said, "I am a younger sister. When you were growing up, what was it like to be his younger brother?"

He laughed. "Pierre always had to have the last word," he said, and I knew right then I had the beginning of my piece.

Trudeau was every inch the prime minister when we arrived at each destination, hastily combing over the bald spot on his head as our plane landed, then performing his formal duties with courtesy, charm, and enthusiasm, interested and inquisitive about everything he saw. The rest of the time, when he wasn't buried in state papers, he was a lot of fun, displaying the well-known acerbic Trudeau wit.

What surprised me was the amount of rest and sleep he needed. Leaders whom I admired – Presidents Franklin D. Roosevelt and Harry

Canadian Press, Peter Bregg

*Catching some sleep
on the Arctic trip.*

Truman in the United States, and Prime Minister Winston Churchill in Great Britain – needed less sleep and kept longer working hours than the average person. Somehow I had assumed that this was a prerequisite for the job. I observed that Trudeau, although he insisted he could go on four or five hours' sleep when necessary and make it up later, was somewhat frail and absolutely had to have eight hours of sleep, preferably nine or ten, while we were travelling. He often referred to himself as a "clocked person," and compensated for time lost sleeping with a prodigious capacity for hard work, discipline, and focused intelligence.

My one-hour lunch with Trudeau took place in the middle of his working day. He arrived half an hour late and was due at two-thirty in Parliament for Question Period, which didn't give us much time. I began by nervously disappearing under the table to pick up my notebook, pen, and then my fork, which had dropped in rapid succession; but I'd done my homework, and Trudeau made it a fascinating interview.

I used that lunch and the food we were served as the device around which I wrote the whole profile, divided into the subjects we covered. His quotes were in italics and were followed by extended indirect narrative. When I first discussed this concept with Mr. Shawn he said, "That's a device that will never work, but try it and we'll see."

The day after I turned in my manuscript, Mr. Shawn called me. "It's really marvellous," he said, and I wrote down his words so I could be sure I hadn't dreamed them. "It is a form that I don't ordinarily like, so you were working against a prejudice of mine, but this is right. It's wonderful not only at catching the personality and facts, but at writing about politics at a high level, which is very difficult." Then he added, "Trudeau needed special treatment, and the writing is worthy of the subject."

What was Trudeau's reaction to the profile? He never said and it didn't matter. I was writing for myself and my editor, and no one else. Years later, we met unexpectedly on a street in New York. His face lit up. He stopped and gave me a great hug.

▶ GEORGE BRIMMELL
Wrote about Trudeau from the Parliamentary Press Gallery, 1964–84

*I*t is Easter weekend, April 1968. In Ottawa, Pierre Trudeau – whom I have never met – has just been elected leader of the Liberal Party, which makes him prime minister-designate, soon to be sworn in with his own government. I am the Washington correspondent for Southam News Services (SNS), and though Trudeau has let it be leaked he was heading for an Easter weekend in Quebec's Laurentians, our Ottawa bureau knew better. He was, in fact, heading for the oceanside Beach Club Hotel, in Fort Lauderdale, Florida. Accompanying him were Treasury Board president Edgar Benson and Mrs. Benson.

As the whole of the United States was my beat then, I was assigned to fly from Washington, D.C., down to Florida and to shadow Trudeau in his hush-hush Easter holiday, without intruding on his privacy. "Observe what he is doing," Charlie Lynch, the SNS Ottawa bureau chief, suggested, "but don't let him know he's being covered, thereby spoiling his fun."

My dispatches back to Canada were in a terse, notebook form. They began on Good Friday. They went something like this:

FRIDAY: Check into Beach Club Hotel. No sign of Trudeau. No Trudeau registered. Contemplate disguises – dark glasses or false nose? Decide to play it cool and just look like ordinary, fat tourist.

My wife reports in: "He's at the front desk, hurry." Rush downstairs. There is Trudeau in blue jersey with white horizontal stripes, denim pants, and the famous House of Commons sandals. Benson still in dark blue suit and tie.

Conference with my wife: we've got to be extremely careful Trudeau doesn't get suspicious. Decide to use code name when referring to him. Why not initials like the Americans do: JFK–LBJ fashion. We'll call him PET. (Note: this assignment *was* early on in the PET era.) Also important not to let eleven-year-old son know who PET is. He's bound to yak and give game away. Not accomplished snooper like parents.

SATURDAY: PET emerges from second-floor hotel room #234, dressed in blue shorts, same blue jersey, sandals. Ambles to coffee shop. Time: 10:45 a.m. Wife volunteers to sneak by coffee shop to adjacent gift shop, for closer observation. I agree. Wife buys beach coat first trip. Buys beach hat second trip. Buys sandals third trip. Question: Can SNS afford overhead for sleuthing?

PET sauntering around, then back to room, emerging in blue and white vertically striped swim trunks, hip-hugger variety. PET settles into chaise longue thirty feet from where I am hiding behind Arthur Hailey novel. Appears to snooze. Fine spot for surveillance. Open-air bar handy if need arises.

12:30 p.m.: PET gets up, heads for pool. Tests springboard. Does fancy dive, touching hands to toes. Then does ten-minute series of spectacular dives from high and low diving boards. Jackknives, swans, half-gainers, half-nelsons. The works. Easy to see how he's a brown belt in judo.

1:00 p.m.: PET heads for beach. He has little blue gob hat, to protect bald spot from sunburn. Very trim in swimming trunks. PET talks to no one. Shows no interest in bikini-clad coeds. Must be contemplating affairs of state.

Observation: he really seems a lonely figure. Wonder how he gets reputation as playboy. PET is circumspect in the extreme.

More superb dives from high board, witnessed by my son and his pal. Son doesn't know diver is subject of Dad's cloak-and-dagger assignment. Son reports later: "He's cool."

SATURDAY AFTERNOON: New arrival in lobby from Ottawa. Manpower Minister Jean Marchand, pipe clenched in teeth, carrying bulging briefcase.

SUNDAY: PET activities much like yesterday. Lots of pool performances.

MONDAY: No sign of PET. He has checked out earlier this morning. Discover he was registered as Benson's son. Wonder how this will go over with Mrs. Benson, who is far too young to be mother of PET.

Discover my sleuthing story has broken in the Vancouver *Province* around midnight last night. Canadian Press picks up story. PET gets phone calls from Ottawa, telling him jig is up. He flees. I get call from our Glorious Leader, Ottawa bureau chief Charlie Lynch. "Turn in your Mickey Spillane badge," he says.

Six years later: I am now running Southam News Services from the Ottawa headquarters and am well acquainted with Prime Minister Trudeau. Following a Parliamentary Press Gallery dinner, I receive a note from him, thanking me for souvenir photos I had sent of the evening. He signs the note Pierre (Benson) Trudeau.

▶ JOHN FRASER
Former St. John's Evening Telegram *reporter; journalist, author, editor; Master of Massey College, University of Toronto*

*T*he smile was devastating. It warmed your soul and made you think the times were ripe for change. That's not nostalgia. I remember the first time I saw the smile. It was directed straight at me, and the combination of sheer exuberance and mischievousness was the most infectious thing I had ever seen. Surely I wasn't the only man to be vamped by that smile. In fact, I know I wasn't. Rossie Barbour was, too.

Barbour was one of Joey Smallwood's most venal backbenchers in Newfoundland's House of Assembly of the late 1960s. This was a time when Smallwood's Liberal Party controlled thirty-nine of the forty-two seats in the provincial legislature. Pierre Trudeau was justice minister in the minority federal administration of Lester Pearson, and he had been dispatched across the country – *a mare usque ad mare* – to explain the startling contents of the proposed Criminal Code amendments – the ones that were going to keep the state out of the bedrooms of the nation.

In 1968, the contrast between Late Smallwood Liberalism (LSL) and New Trudeau Liberalism (NTL) was astonishing: LSL meant sleaze, bribery, corruption, sexual constipation, nepotism, governmental stagnation, fear, and loathing. NTL meant youth, idealism, hedonism, legislative emancipation, courage, and admiration.

Later, after Trudeau became party leader, and there was an election campaign under way, I was part of the Newfoundland "People and Pierre Movement" with Rex Murphy. Our aim was to disassociate LSL from NTL and we had many tricks up our sleeves. We would need them, because Smallwood controlled the federal wing of the party in the province. There was an old hack of a candidate named Mr. Tucker in the federal riding of Trinity, for example, and we fashioned a campaign sign that read: "Tolerate Tucker in Trinity for Trudeau." It didn't work. Tucker went down, as did most of the Liberals. Hatred for LSL turned out to be stronger than love of NTL.

But this was later. On the first occasion that I saw Trudeau in person, he had just addressed the legislature from the bar of the House and had sat down in one of the guest seats just the other side of the floor. Above, in the press gallery, we all stared intently at him. I say "we" laughingly. There was me, representing the *Evening Telegram*, the *St. John's Daily News* reporter, and a Canadian Press reporter. Trudeau was looking all around the legislature, when suddenly he looked up. I smiled and he let out a huge grin. Oh, I melted, just melted. He was my leader then and there. It dawned on me later that I had seen elected parliamentarians laugh raucously and loudly and cynically in Ottawa, in Ontario's Queen's Park, and in St. John's, but I had never seen anyone *smile*. That was interesting, right from the start.

All my subsequent encounters with Pierre Trudeau stem from that smile. I can name and remember every one of them, partly because there weren't that many, and partly because they were always special. We met once at a private rendezvous at the Wakefield, Quebec, farm of Hon. C.M. Drury. Margaret was pregnant with Justin at the time, and the Drury boys had a small field of mature hemp growing nearby. We met in China when he was out of office and I was posted there.

We met in his Centre Block office when I interviewed him formally for the *Globe and Mail* and he told me (astoundingly) that part of the reason he wanted a proper constitution for the country was to control people like himself during moments of national emergency. We met in London, England, and went for a wonderful two-hour walk (complete with a rest in one of the Wren churches in The Strand), mostly along the Thames Embankment. And finally, my best luck, we met quite a few times when he stayed at Massey College, where I am the Master; he liked the relaxed, intellectual atmosphere when he came to Toronto to see his young daughter, Sarah.

But that first smile never seemed to change. Old Rossie Barbour, the Smallwood hack who hardly ever said a sensible thing that I overheard, came up to the press room half an hour after Trudeau left the Confederation Building that first day I ever saw him.

"I saw ye smiling at Purr Trudoo," Barbour said.

"Yeah, I was smiling," I said, somewhat condescendingly. Rossie was a butt of humour in the press gallery. "I'd smile at you too, Mr. Barbour, if you ever looked my way."

"Do ye know him den?" insisted Rossie. He was *very* serious. I'd never seen him so serious.

"No, not at all. It's the first time I've laid eyes on him in the flesh. What's your problem, anyway?"

"No problem, me son, no problem. He's something wonderful, that's all, and I wanted to know more about him. Go back to yer work if dat's what ye call it."

That's what I called it, and that's how I remember the first time I saw Trudeau.

▶ ARNIE PATTERSON
Press secretary, 1978–79

Before joining the PMO press office in 1978, I was a radio broadcaster and had also run twice for the Liberals in my hometown of Dartmouth, in 1968 and 1974, so I knew the PM from, shall we say, several angles. When my long-time friend Dick O'Hagan left the PMO for a job at the Bank of Montreal, I was a candidate to succeed him. After meeting in Ottawa with Senator Keith Davey, Jim Coutts, and Dick, I agreed to take on the task for one year.

Following our discussion, Dick and I went up to the Hill to meet the PM. He gave us a warm reception, but near the close of our conversation, I said to him, "Prime Minister, the only concern I have is that you don't like reporters."

"Arnie, Arnie, that is not so," he said. "I like you very much." That settled it. I took the job.

However, I was to find that his assurance, though sincere, was not quite accurate. While he was exceptional in so many ways, Pierre Trudeau was never totally comfortable with journalists. On the other hand, while he was not loved by the media (not even liked by some) he was, nevertheless, much respected. I asked him once why he was sometimes hostile to them.

"Perhaps it is because, as a professor, I was used to people being polite and respectful."

When the 1979 campaign got under way, the travel was unrelenting but there were moments of great fun. One Saturday morning in Vancouver, we had a press conference and, with the sun shining and a light work schedule for that day, both the PM and the media were in a happy mood.

As we walked back to the elevator following the conference, Mr. Trudeau said to me, "Your colleagues were in a good mood today."

"I think the sessions are helping out," I responded.

"What sessions?"

I hastily explained that at night I gave etiquette lessons that focused on how the media ought to treat the prime minister.

"My God!" he said. "Does anyone show up?" I told him that twelve journalists had shown up just the night before. When we got on the elevator, Bruce Garvey of the *Toronto Star* and the CBC's Don McNeill were also en route to their rooms. I had been out late the night before with the two of them, and I could see they were slightly hungover.

"Say 'Good morning, Prime Minister,'" I said to them. Almost automatically, these two wily veterans politely chanted the greeting. When we got off the elevator the PM was incredulous.

"I am flabbergasted," he said. "I can't believe what I just saw."

Pierre Trudeau was probably the smartest guy in any room he entered – but maybe not elevators. I never did tell him I was just kidding.

▌ PATRICK NAGLE
Reporter, who covered most aspects of Trudeau's life in
Montreal, Ottawa, and Vancouver

*D*espite finding love in British Columbia, Pierre Trudeau was never able to find happiness there. For some reason, Trudeau inspired the province – and some of its citizens – to an almost incendiary level of provocative behaviour. As prime minister, he travelled to British Columbia on official business with some reluctance, and his staff always wondered what could possibly happen next during visits that became less and less frequent as his prime ministry grew longer.

The first big event after the 1968 Trudeaumania election was probably definitive. Trudeau slugged a British Columbian.

The location was the Seaforth Armoury on Burrard Street, where the new prime minister was to address a Liberal fundraising supper. As has been obligatory ever since, a protest demonstration manifested itself outside the armoury on that warm August night in 1969.

In those days, Trudeau did not travel with much security and, along with a couple of Mounties and Vic Chapman (at that time, the staff "baggage-smasher"), Trudeau chose to walk through the crowd into the armoury. He was wearing a pale tropical summer suit that showed up clearly against the surrounding sea of hair and denim. Just before he got

Canadian Press, Peter Bregg

Pierre and Margaret
in happier times.

to the armoury door, he paused briefly. The white-clad arm shot out. The crowd parted, and Trudeau disappeared inside.

As a PMO staffer, Chapman was also a very good bodyguard. A former B.C. Lions football player, he still had good stature and a physical robustness that added presence alongside Victor Irving, the superintending RCMP officer in attendance. Had Trudeau been in serious trouble that night, Chapman and Irving would have been in the middle of it. (Years later, Chapman chuckled admiringly when remembering the incident. "It all happened so fast," he said. "The guy never knew what hit him.")

On that night outside the armoury, Richard Bruce Jesmer was crying that the prime minister had clouted him, and he had witnesses to prove it. When asked later what might have provoked the country's leader to inflict an act of violence on a voter, Jesmer said he had called Trudeau a "creep." He also said he used a modifying phrase implying maternal incest. Jesmer swore a citizen's prosecution at Vancouver police headquarters later that night, before a justice of the peace. It was a charge of common assault against the prime minister of Canada. But the matter would be quashed, as an abuse of process, by the end of August.

In later years, the prime minister's marriage to Margaret, a British Columbian, and the birth of their children did nothing to soften the heated combativeness between the citizens of the province and their federal leader. Protesters once staked out a Kamloops railway siding to challenge Trudeau, even though he was on vacation with his children. The man did not disappoint. The international proctology salute was delivered from the window of his private railway car.

The enmity pursued him right to the end of his public life. During his last major visit to the province, Trudeau tried to reason with his listeners. He pointed out – quite pleasantly – that he thought the mountain ranges separating the province from the rest of Canada restricted the vision of British Columbians as to their position in a federal state.

Needless to say, it didn't go over well.

▶ PETER BREGG
Canadian Press photographer on Parliament Hill, who covered Trudeau through most of his years as PM

*I*n October 1967, at the tender age of nineteen, I was promoted from copy boy to photographer at the Canadian Press in Ottawa. I wasn't even old enough to vote or drink at the time. Six months later, Pierre Trudeau was elected leader of the Liberal Party to become prime minister of Canada, and a few months after that, in July 1968, I was assigned to travel to the Arctic with Trudeau on a week-long trip. That assignment as the only still photographer travelling in a small party provided my introduction to the most fascinating subject of my career.

It was my first trip to the Arctic. We were travelling in a small executive jet and the seating configuration had us all facing each other. Once we were in the air, the steward started to serve dinner. The main course was Chinese food, and he presented me with chopsticks. I leaned over to the steward and asked for a fork. Trudeau overheard this remark, and asked me if I knew how to use chopsticks. I had lived a very short and sheltered life. He then held up his chopsticks and showed me

Canadian Press, Peter Bregg

PM celebrating Peter's birthday in the back of the plane during the 1972 campaign.

how to use them. With a little work, I managed to eat dinner and have been able to use them ever since.

From that point on, Trudeau was always kind to the young shooter who was constantly in his face with a camera – and who managed to earn a few news-photo awards along the way with pictures of him.

It was, I think, 1972, when I decided to enter in a Miles for Millions walk for Oxfam. I was working on Parliament Hill by then, and so I started gathering pledges. One day, I was outside External Affairs Minister Mitchell Sharp's office, having just managed to extract a pledge of 25 cents per mile. Most people had pledged 10 cents. It was just after Question Period, and I saw Trudeau approaching his Centre Block office with his legislative aide, Joyce Fairbairn, so I approached him for a sponsorship, and he offered 25 cents. Boldly, I told him that I just got 25 cents from Mitchell Sharp and, as prime minister, maybe he could go for 50 cents per mile.

With a quick huff and an about-face Trudeau walked off, saying, "Forget it. I'm not going to bargain with you."

I was so angry with myself. I had just embarrassed the prime minster and myself. About twenty minutes later, I was back at my office when I got a call from Joyce Fairbairn. She told me she had convinced the PM that it was for a good cause and that he should reconsider. He did, and boosted his offer from 25 cents to 50 cents per mile. I walked thirty-two of the thirty-five miles, before I dropped out with a bad knee. Trudeau paid up, and I made a photograph of the cheque before mailing it to Oxfam.

His quick reaction and combativeness when he decided he didn't "want to bargain," were played out many times over the years. I always enjoyed covering him and listening to his quick comebacks, especially to young people.

For example, during a question-and-answer session at one high school in northern Ontario, he was asked about legalizing pot. His reply was that he was puzzled by the fact that many of the students were complaining about air pollution and now wanted to inhale more smoke. A round of applause followed as he quickly diffused a touchy question.

In another confrontation, he was heckled by some long-haired youths on the steps of the Winnipeg legislature as he was leaving. Without stopping to look, he just walked over to them to discuss their complaints. One shirtless man, in his late teens, had his hands in the pockets of his jeans and was forcing them down low on his hips. Trudeau was just three feet away, face to face. I don't remember exactly what they were discussing, other than the Vietnam War, but I was surprised at the boldness of the young man, whose ever-lowering pants waist was now close to exposing his pubic hair. Without looking down, Trudeau asked him, "So do you expect to solve the world's problems by pulling down your pants?" The question period ended with a sheepish protester having been put in place by the prime minister.

On another occasion, Trudeau looked out over a crowd of protesting farmers in Saskatoon and responded to some of their chants. But he complained angrily about some of the signs they were holding, which he felt were more personal insults than legitimate complaints. He spoke from a wagon that had been equipped with a microphone. At one point, he leaned over to a little boy of about twelve, who had been pitching kernels of wheat at him as he spoke. Under his breath, Trudeau warned the boy he would "kick his ass" if he didn't stop. Trudeau did not realize many people heard this remark. But that was pure PET.

▶ JANE FAULKNER
Family friend

The first time I met Pierre Trudeau was in 1971, while I was working on my book *House on the Hill*. I was in Ottawa for a few days to gather material for the chapter on Trudeau, and I needed to draw his office. As a member of the Press Gallery, I had many opportunities to draw the prime minister himself, but I was informed that a written request was required to get permission to draw his office.

Of course, I had no time to wait around for the permission process, but, as luck would have it, Trudeau came out of the chamber after Question Period without the usual crowd around him. With little or no thought I seized the moment.

"Would it be possible for me to draw your office?" I asked him directly. Well, I was young and he not yet married, and he visibly perked up.

"You want to draw *me* in my office?"

"No," I said, "not *you*. It's your office I want to draw."

His mood changed instantly. He caught the eye of a staff member, coolly asking them to arrange it. Then he turned on his heel and was gone and, with him, the opportunity to do a close-up portrait.

▶ PETER CALAMAI
Former correspondent and editor, who spent thirty years with the Southam newspapers

It might have been Ivan Head, then executive assistant to Pierre Trudeau, or it could have been the RCMP officer in charge of the PM's security detail, but one of them took me aside one January day in 1974 to whisper, "Stick around tomorrow morning."

"Sticking around" the next day wasn't all that simple for a Canadian reporter in St. Moritz, Switzerland. Trudeau had stopped off there for a few days skiing en route to a gathering of elite thinkers in Salzburg, Austria, which had been convened by the Club of Rome. He had the prime-ministerial jet, of course, but the tiny gang of trailing Canadian hacks were flying commercial, and that meant leaving first thing next morning in order to reach Salzburg in time to send back the requisite bulletins when Trudeau arrived there. The concierge at the five-star Hotel Kulm, however, came up with a solution involving a charter flight to Zurich (those were the days when Southam News spent money). So, the next morning, when the prime minister headed out to the ski slopes, I was the lone reporter standing in front of the hotel. And I got a lift with Head and Trudeau. Except that they weren't going skiing.

Instead, they veered off to the Cresta Run, a diabolically dangerous bobsled ice run that descends more than five hundred feet along a three-quarter-mile corkscrew path down a gully at the edge of town. The run was originally created in late Victorian times to fight off boredom among the idle British rich who had flocked to St. Moritz.

The British made it as dangerous as they could, with walls much lower than standard bobsled runs, ten testing corners, and flimsy toboggan sleds on which the rider lies prone while shooting downhill head-first at speeds that can reach eighty miles per hour. Broken bones are common in the daily morning runs, which start just before Christmas and continue until the end of February. There's even a special tie worn only by men who fail to negotiate Shuttlecock, the most famous and tricky corner of the run. (Since 1929, only men have been allowed to ride, a rule made by the private club that builds the Cresta every year.)

Head and Trudeau had obviously schemed in advance to test themselves on the Cresta Run. They had brought along tight-fitting red and white bobsledding suits, festooned with maple leaves. Each also sported pads on elbows and knees, a black crash helmet, boots with metal "rakes" on the toes (the only way to brake), and yellow goggles. As well, they had a cheering section of three Canadian visitors in St. Moritz, who were wearing maple-leaf getups as well and, from the banter, it seemed obvious that they had been expecting the prime minister to show up.

As beginners, Trudeau and Head launched their sleds from a spot called the Junction, which is one-third of the way down from the top of the run. From there a time of between sixty-five and seventy-five seconds was considered respectable. The PM's first descent took somewhat longer, so he was given pointers by Christian Fishbacher, a sixty-two-year-old Swiss Cresta expert. Fishbacher showed Trudeau that, by pressing down on the nose of his Morgan Special 2 sled, he could increase the speed. (I was scribbling feverishly in a notebook at this point.)

When the PM announced he was eager to hazard a second run, the RCMP officer with the party visibly blanched. Trudeau swooshed through Shuttlecock corner with ice chips spraying from his boots and reached the finish in sixty-nine seconds.

"*Bonne sensation*," he said, posing for a photograph with Head and the three vacationing Canadians.

While Head's times for both his runs were a few seconds better than his boss, someone from the Cresta Club said that Trudeau's time was a record for a national leader. It doubtlessly still is.

▶ GEOFFREY STEVENS
Author; former Ottawa columnist and managing editor of the Globe and Mail, *1965–81*

*E*very journalist who spent any length of time covering Pierre Elliott Trudeau came away from the experience with a collection of vivid memories. I have many, but two of them stand out.

One was the day in January 1976 when Trudeau, who was touring Latin America, arrived in Cienfuegos on the south coast of Cuba. It was a steamy day and the huge crowd – somewhere between thirty thousand and fifty thousand – had been waiting for six hours under the broiling sun. After Fidel Castro had lavished praise on Canada's continued support for the Cuban people, Trudeau took over. Speaking in fluent Spanish, he held the crowd enthralled as he talked about, of all things, the need for a more stable and balanced world economic system. The crowd cheered lustily and happily.

My second indelible memory is of Washington in February 1977, when he became the first Canadian prime minister to address Congress. Although Trudeau was no favourite with many people in the U.S. capital, especially Republicans, you could have heard a pin drop as he talked – clearly, logically, and with quiet passion – about the cause of national unity in Canada. It was a great speech. No one demurred when

Senator Edmund Muskie of Maine called it the best speech he had ever heard by a foreign leader.

In Washington as in Cuba, I felt a small thrill of national pride – the sort of thrill that cynical journalists are supposed to be immune to. Trudeau was brilliant. He was compelling. And he was Canadian.

As a reporter and columnist, I had the privilege – and I counted it as privilege – of covering Trudeau for fifteen years – in Parliament, in every corner of Canada, and around the world. I watched him when he arrived on Parliament Hill in 1965, when he was elected as the Liberal leader in 1968, when Trudeaumania carried him to a majority government later that spring, and when he faced down the FLQ terrorists in the October Crisis of 1970.

When he secretly married Margaret Sinclair in Vancouver in 1971, it fell to me to track down the wedding photographer and negotiate the purchase of the spectacular colour picture that appeared a few days later on the cover of *Time* magazine, my employer at the time. And I travelled with him to, among many other places, Mexico City and Caracas, New Delhi and Singapore, Moscow and Norilsk in the Siberian tundra. (Not to mention Halifax, Trois Rivières, Hamilton, Brandon, Lethbridge, Victoria, and most points in between.)

On the trip to Russia in 1971, Trudeau was intrigued by Norilsk, a mining town of about thirty thousand that was seldom, if ever, visited by Western dignitaries. At one point he turned to his hosts and told them how impressed he was with the Soviet ingenuity and enterprise that had carved a modern community out of the frozen Siberian permafrost – either not realizing, or having forgotten, that Norilsk was built by slave labour during the regime of Josef Stalin. His gaffe made headlines at home, naturally.

On our first evening in Norilsk, after Pierre and Margaret had retired to a government guest house – it was their first official trip after their marriage – the members of the press pool and Canadian diplomatic officials gathered in the press room at the hotel to drink and talk. Before we knew it, we had run out of booze, but then discovered that a case of liquor that had been on the Trudeau plane had not been delivered to our hotel. Ed Ritchie, who was then the deputy minister in External Affairs, went off to track it down. He came back laughing. "The box was taken to the guest house," he reported. "Somebody put it under the prime minister's bed. Pierre and Margaret have gone to bed and no one on his staff has the guts to go in and retrieve our booze." So much for our party!

Covering Trudeau may have been a privilege, but it was not always a pleasure. Trudeau could be charming and engaging, but he could also be remote, irascible, and occasionally obnoxious. He displayed both sides of his complex character in the years I covered him. Historians will remember him for the patriation of the Constitution and the entrenchment therein of the Canadian Charter of Rights and Freedoms. I will remember him for something else – the impact he had on young people.

When he died, I wrote an appreciation in *Maclean's*. "He did what no politician before or since has done: he touched the dreams of an entire generation of Canadians," I wrote. "He made them excited about politics and public affairs. He caused them to believe they could actually change the country and even the world. He inspired them to get personally involved in the life of their nation and community. . . . [H]e changed their lives. He set them off along paths they might not otherwise have taken. He made them, and the country, better."

I believe that still.

▶ JERRY YANOVER
Parliamentary affairs adviser, 1969–84

One day in the late spring of 1973, a minister telephoned me to say that he had a nephew who had just returned from studies abroad and who, having missed Canadian politics for more than five years, was having difficulty understanding Mr. Trudeau's great appeal to young Canadians. The minister thought that, being in the same age group, I might be able to explain matters, perhaps over a meal, with greater success than he had been having.

I agreed, and took my new friend, John, to a recently opened Lebanese restaurant in Ottawa that I had heard about. Fortunately, there were no other patrons in the place to hear my not very successful explanations of how different it was to have a political leader who actually seemed interested in the ideas and experiences of young people.

I was just about to give up when I saw, outside the restaurant's front window, two men wearing earpieces. I had barely enough time to tell my dinner companion that he should try not to look surprised, when in walked the Trudeau family, with the toddler Justin in the arms of his father.

The prime minister and Margaret came over to our table and, when I told them that John had just returned from foreign studies, Mr. Trudeau engaged the increasingly shell-shocked young man in a discussion of the universities he had attended, the subjects that he had studied, and his professors, several of whom the prime minister knew, either personally or through their work.

After several minutes, the Trudeaus went to their table, while, to the prime minister's chagrin, the restaurant owner let Justin play with the shiny new cash register.

For a few moments, my friend was silent. Finally, he smiled and said, "I think I understand now."

▶ RALPH COLEMAN
Assistant press secretary and chief advanceman, 1974–79;
press secretary, 1980–84

*T*he prevailing image of Pierre Elliott Trudeau's relations with the news media is an adversarial one. Although they would never admit it, most journalists were intellectually intimidated by him. He, in turn, liked to tell them that he did not like them, and did not bother to read or watch what they said about him. My experience as a press officer, however, was that he was always remarkably aware of what the media were saying, and not just from the news summaries and analyses that we prepared for him. Nevertheless, he could never resist a chance to tease them.

I found this out on the very first trip that I did with the prime minister. It was May 1974, on the eve of a general election. I had just joined the Prime Minister's Office and he was doing a day trip down to Duke

University in North Carolina to receive an honorary degree, give a speech, and return immediately to Ottawa. My job was to look after the news media on the trip.

In those days, the only aircraft that could carry the prime minister, some staff, and a small number of media was an old, slow, propeller-driven Air Force Cosmopolitan. As a young army officer, my only flying exposure had been my parachutist course, when I had trained to jump out of aircraft, not ride in them for long periods of time, and I was extremely sensitive to motion sickness. The trip would last several hours. As bad luck would have it, on the trip down to Duke University, we ran into a storm just after everyone – including me – had consumed a seafood lunch. The old Cosmopolitan could not fly above or around the storm; we had to go through it, and there was considerable turbulence.

After a few minutes, my stomach reacted in the expected fashion. Many of the news media could see me, and those who couldn't soon got word that the prime minister's new press assistant was airsick. They loved it and teased me relentlessly for the rest of the trip. Fortunately, the prime minister was well forward in the aircraft and not aware. I managed to survive the rest of the day and an uneventful return flight to Ottawa.

After exiting the aircraft in Ottawa and while waiting on the tarmac for the motorcade to come, the prime minister asked the news media waiting with us how his new press assistant did on the trip.

Mike Duffy, then with CHUM Radio, and a journalist with a great sense of humour, piped up with a smile on his face saying that the new assistant did not do very well because, on his first day with the news media, he was sick to his stomach. Without missing a beat and with a twinkle in his eye, the prime minister replied, "Coleman is going to do very well in my office then, because he shares my opinion of the press!"

▶ JIM FERRABEE
First met Trudeau in 1962, and covered him as a journalist until 1976

Pierre Trudeau did not like journalists, something he made clear to all of us in the pack very early on in his political career. He did not like the media emphasis on the negative, its lack of perspective, and its tendency to get things wrong. Mostly, though, it was because we did not agree with his view of Canada or the world.

He was not alone among prime ministers in despising the media, a view prime ministers usually come to at one point in their careers. The difference with Trudeau was that he had been contemptuous of the media before he came to office and remained contemptuous of them until he died. One consequence of this view was that he had few favourites in the media and fewer friends, although he had many admirers among editors and editorial writers.

Like him or not, however, everyone recognized his draw as a story on TV, on radio, or in newspapers. He played to our daily need to feed the hungry animal that is the insatiable appetite of viewers, listeners, and readers. So, while he may not have liked us, he knew how to use the media to his advantage.

He was the first visual prime minister we had. TV cameramen and newspaper photographers were under orders always to have Trudeau in their sights. They never knew when they might miss one of his double tucks off the high board in a hotel pool, or a slide down a banister in the parliament buildings, or his flirting with a Hollywood star. This was all front-page material for newspapers and guaranteed first-item coverage

Montreal Gazette, Richard Arless, Jr.

Using the media . . .

. . . and feeding the
hungry animal?

Canadian Press, Peter Bregg

on the nightly TV news. The photographers and TV camera crews knew
it, and so did he.

Though other prime ministers understood how important visuals
were in election campaigns, they were not as deft at using them. Louis
St. Laurent, for instance, was an avid golfer, and one of the memorable
pictures of him is on a golf cart with U.S. president Dwight D. "Ike"
Eisenhower, who never missed an opportunity to play golf. Lester
Pearson was a baseball fan and from time to time his handlers would lure
him to a baseball game and put a cap on his head and a bat in his hand
for a photo opportunity. John Diefenbaker used his right index finger
when photographers were nearby, grabbing attention by waving it at
someone. Brian Mulroney was occasionally seen doing a soft-shoe dance
and singing Irish songs. But none could match Trudeau as an athlete, as
well as a shameless and successful performer before the cameras.

On the other hand, Pierre Trudeau tried to avoid the media as much
as he could when he wasn't using them. His staff knew this, and when the
media were travelling on the prime-ministerial plane on a foreign or
domestic trip, he rarely moved from his up-front cabin to the back-end
media section for a chat, even though it was the custom of most other

prime ministers and party leaders to do so. There were many reasons why he did not like mingling with the media. He was shy, he was uncomfortable with small talk, and he had very little sense of humour about himself or anything else.

The lack of humour showed most noticeably at the annual Parliamentary Press Gallery dinners in the 1960s and 1970s. This was when the Governor-General of the day, the Opposition leaders, and the prime minister were invited to be humorous about the issues of the day and about themselves. In the Trudeau years, the Press Gallery dinner was one of the most sought-after tickets in Ottawa – not because of Trudeau, but because then-Conservative Opposition Leader Robert Stanfield was the best stand-up comedian in the town. Stanfield's speeches left everyone weak with laughter except for Trudeau, who invariably looked uncomfortable and embarrassed.

Visitors to the country who met both Trudeau and Stanfield must have wondered how Canada could have produced such contrasting characters. Stanfield looked like a stuffy, humourless figure from a British comedy of manners, more at home in the dusty drawing room of an English manor house than in the House of Commons. He was none of that. In fact, he was one of the most engaging and intelligent figures in Canadian politics through the 1960s and 1970s, and he came close to scuttling Trudeau as a one-term prime minister in the 1972 election, the outcome of which was not decided until the day after the vote.

After that near-defeat, Trudeau paid more attention to political strategy and won back his majority in the 1974 election. In 1976, he embarked on one of the strangest state visits a Canadian prime minister has ever made – to Cuba and Mexico. It was the Cuba visit to President Fidel Castro that caused much anguish and confusion both at home and in the United States. Trudeau seemed to relish the controversy. Castro, of course, was delighted. But if there had been a list of twenty-five countries Trudeau could have visited at the time to increase Canada's influence or beef up its trade and sell its products, Cuba would have been the twenty-fifth. Pierre Trudeau obviously had reasons for making the trip, even if they were never convincingly explained to Canadians, Americans, or anyone else. Maybe it was just the maverick in him.

Fidel Castro, one of the most fascinating leaders on the world scene, is still admired and feared by many Cubans. Outsiders could admire Fidel, and many do, without supporting his political ideas or applauding what he has done to the Cuban people and its economy. No doubt, Trudeau was a "Fideliste."

The trip itself was bizarre, if only because it seemed heavily weighted in Castro's favour. It was, in short, an unequalled chance for Castro to legitimize himself in the eyes of the world. The benefits to Canada – or Pierre Trudeau – were not so evident. Castro took Trudeau to schools; the Canadian delegation stayed in guest houses; and the climax of the trip was a two-hour plane ride for the media and the Canadian delegation to a sugar factory. There, Castro and Trudeau spoke to about five thousand sugar workers for more than two hours. Not far in the background was Margaret Trudeau, sitting on the platform wearing a Liberal Party T-shirt.

That was only the beginning of Margaret Trudeau's involvement in the diplomatic and political aspects of the visit to Cuba and Mexico. By the last night in Mexico City, when she stood up at the formal diplomatic dinner Canada gave for its Mexican hosts with her guitar to sing a song, she had taken over the print headlines and the top of the radio and TV newscasts. The Prime Minister's Office, while trying to be protective, was worried and humiliated by the last incident.

Back in Canada, to which the official delegation and the media returned the day after her singing episode, opinion was fiercely divided on Margaret Trudeau's behaviour, even among editors. A few of the Southam papers I wrote for published my story, which featured Margaret's performance rather than Pierre's.

The reaction was almost instant on my home phone. The story, most callers said, was mean, unfair, biased, anti-feminist, and worse. That strong reaction reflected the sharp division in Ottawa about Margaret's role – and her lifestyle – that dominated cocktail conversation in that period. The debate coursed through the country for the next week. Only weeks later did it peter out. But by then, journalists had seen a different side of both Pierre and Margaret Trudeau that highlighted the challenges they faced in their marriage.

That moment occurred in the National Press Club on the Friday night after the Cuba–Mexico visit. Members who visited the club that night for booze and chatter before the weekend saw Margaret standing at one end of the long bar with her Mountie escort. She was defiantly smoking what smelled like a banned substance and blowing it around the room. Clearly, she was challenging someone. When word got back to the PMO, the prime minister arrived and managed to persuade her to leave.

Given the place where the incident happened, and that it happened in front of journalists, it took immense courage for the prime minister to walk into the National Press Club that night and confront demons that had never been exposed publicly. The relationship between the two of them understandably deteriorated after that, but during the sad denouement of their marriage, most people in the media came to see Pierre Trudeau more sympathetically. Much to his credit, he handled his private trials with stoicism and grace.

▶ PATRICK WATSON
First met Trudeau in Ottawa in 1962, at the Liberal Party convention they were both covering

I have written elsewhere how I met Pierre Elliott Trudeau early in the *Inqui'ry* days, which ran from 1960 to 1964, and worked enough with him to want him to replace Davidson Dunton as host of that series. When we started *This Hour Has Seven Days* in 1964, both co-producer Douglas Leiterman and I were convinced that Trudeau would be a superb host. He turned us down, but agreed to do some interviews, the most notorious being a Hot Seat encounter in which Trudeau and Larry Zolf – an unlikely but effective partnership – grilled René Lévesque.

As I recounted in my autobiography, *This Hour Has Seven Decades*, in the chapter on Jacques Cousteau, Jacques never forgave me for abandoning a second voyage with him on the *Calypso* in order to go back to Ottawa for the leadership convention. Well before Lester Pearson had announced his retirement, Roy Faibish, Ottawa editor of *This Hour*, and I had each called Pierre Trudeau, independently, when he was Minister of Justice, urging him to try for the leadership, and I found it unthinkable that I should miss that contest. I reported from the floor of the

Ottawa Coliseum during that very dramatic three days, and Roy Faibish arranged for me to do an interview with Trudeau in the CJOH studios on the eve of the vote.

While that interview was broadcast only locally, it is not surprising that excerpts were picked up by many news services, especially by CTV, a member station. It was the first time the country had seen him, *in extenso*, in an informal, self-searching mood. When he talked passionately about how it was time to leave behind the "old guys with old ideas and go after the new guys with new ideas," banal and unoriginal as the phrase was, there was a passion and a believability that struck hard.

In the following years, our friendship remained intact, but we agreed that, once I began my regular interview program out of Ottawa, it would be best to keep some distance. My second interview with him in that period, on *The Watson Report*, was during the Watergate scandal, when the impeachment of U.S. president Richard Nixon seemed a real possibility. Douglas Leiterman phoned me proposing, inspiredly, that I ask the prime minister whether his own experience being at the top allowed him – during these days of tribulation for Nixon – to think of the U.S. president with a certain amount of sympathy. When I asked him about it during the live interview, Trudeau said with a thoughtful half-smile, "Yes. As a matter of fact, I phoned him today to tell him so."

My second-last *Watson Report* encounter with Trudeau may well have been the worst. It was the eve of his imposing wage-and-price controls. Uncertain of my grasp of the economic issues, I had broken a long-standing rule and taken notes into the studio. My concern for those notes attenuated my focus on how he was, and indeed on what he was saying; he knew I wasn't listening to him, but instead was pressing my own agenda. He closed up. It was just horrible and we could scarcely look at each other on the way out.

Dick O'Hagan, his press secretary, without admitting the blackout, never let him come on the program again, and when O'Hagan left and the new man called me to propose an interview, Pierre greeted me, saying, "I've just read the transcript of our last one. That was two years ago. We were both awful."

Our relationship had that kind of candour, and that was characteristic of the man.

When I began to work intensely on *The Struggle for Democracy* in
1985, it was clear to me that a major contribution from the recently retired
Canadian head of government, on what he had learned about democracy
after his turbulent decade as a politician, would be of enormous value.
But, having stepped down, Pierre Trudeau had also stepped out of the
spotlight. When I called to ask him to give me a number of interviews
over the two or three years that I expected to take in making the series, he
refused, cordially enough, saying that he had turned everyone down, and
that if he did it for me, then that would open the floodgates. My arguments about the special nature of a twelve-part, internationally funded
series on a major world issue did not, at first, move him.

We had a few meetings in Montreal, over lunch or in his office, in
which he fully and generously answered my questions about what he
had learned and what he felt about the nature of democracy. He guided
me in the development of the program, and a few days after one of these
meetings – which had been very rich, we both felt – I called again and
did my best to persuade him that this project was unique. My British
partners who had the offshore distribution rights (international except
for the United States and Canada), were saying confidently that it would
be seen in at least thirty countries; I had full PBS distribution through
my Pittsburgh partner WQED, and it would be an opportunity for him
and for the world. This time he did not say no straight out.

"When do you have to know?" he asked. I said that in just less than
two months I would have to lock up the final shape of the program, so
let's say six weeks.

"I'll call you within six weeks and give you a definite answer," he said.
He was travelling, would think about it while he was abroad, would be
back in a month, and would call soon afterwards.

At around the five-week mark, I woke up one morning at seven
o'clock and told my wife, Caroline, that I had just had a vivid dream in
which Pierre had phoned and accepted. She scratched my head affection-
ately and chuckled something about wishful thinking. At ten o'clock that
morning the phone on my desk rang. "Mr. Trudeau is calling," a secretary
said, and on he came to say that, yes, I was right, he had an obligation to
do this. He was reluctant, but he knew he must. Would I call in two weeks
after he'd settled down from his trip, and we would set a time?

And then when I made that call, two weeks later, he had changed his mind once more. He was very sorry, he said, but it was the floodgates thing. He couldn't bear having to tell all the other journalists, with whom he had long-standing cordial relationships, that he would not do something with them when he had done so with me, and, please, I must not ask him again.

So I buried it.

Three years later, in December 1988, and a couple of weeks before the first broadcast of the *Democracy* series, Tom Axworthy gave an elaborate party at the Mount Royal Club in Montreal for his wife, Roberta's, fortieth birthday. I arrived about twenty minutes after the announced start time, and there was already a big crowd in the main reception bar area on the ground floor, a smaller number of us having been invited to stay for dinner after the drinks and welcome for a hundred or so.

I was standing in that crowd with a drink, about twenty feet from the door, when Pierre Trudeau came bouncing through it. All eyes turned in his direction. He paused at the threshold and surveyed the crowded room. Then his eyes lit on me. He called across in a loud voice, "Well! Patrick Watson! I hear that you are about to launch a big international television series on democracy. Why the hell didn't you ask me to take part in it?"

Every eye in the place turned on the idiot producer who had made such an egregious omission, such a goof, such an idiotic goof. He glided by me, on his way to shake hands with Tom Axworthy, and winked conspiratorially as he went by.

I admired that; I remember it with affection.

Chapter Five

Just Watching Me Too

▶ VICTOR IRVING
RCMP officer in charge of PM's security detail, 1969–71

*P*ierre Trudeau and I got off to a strange start when he learned that I was related to the Irving family of Saint John, New Brunswick. However, after several interesting incidents with him in British Columbia, I was able to gain the PM's confidence, and he certainly had my respect.

In July 1969, I was appointed officer-in-charge of the PM's security detail (a ten-man detective squad) in British Columbia. I was responsible for his physical and personal protection. On the day of my appointment, my immediate superior explained my new duties and added that, although he didn't know too much about the prime minister, there were "a lot of rumours about his personal lifestyle and left-wing politics." Over the course of the next several years, I learned my superintendent's suspicions were unfounded.

I have many recollections of working with the PM, some too personal, but others I am willing to share since they were featured on the front pages of most newspapers.

INCIDENT ONE: August 1969.
A Liberal fundraising rally was held at the Seaforth Armoury at the south end of the Burrard Street bridge in Vancouver. A large group of protesters had gathered in front of the Burrard Street entrance, because

of some local labour unrest, so my security detail was being assisted by the Vancouver City police. When the PM, his press secretary, Roméo LeBlanc, and I tried to enter the armoury, the crowd closed in around us. With Inspector Bud Errington of the Vancouver police leading the PM, and with me pushing from behind, we tried to make our way to the entrance.

A young man, wearing an NDP ski cap, came up on Trudeau's right side and yelled at him.

"You're a mother-fucking creep."

I saw the guy's head snap back, and then we were inside the armoury.

The next day Pierre Trudeau was charged with assault.

I received an urgent telex from RCMP headquarters in Ottawa, requesting an explanation as to how we *allowed* this incident to happen. I replied (with my fingers crossed) that there was nothing to it, that the case would be dismissed forthwith.

It was "an alleged summary conviction assault offence," so the court arranged to hold a hearing before a justice of the peace to determine the validity of the charge, prior to proceeding further. I was called as the first defence witness.

My evidence was the following: I was the closest person to the PM when the complainant was hit. I did not see the PM throw the punch. As I was pushing people out of the way, I may have accidentally been the culprit myself. If the PM had actually *hit* the guy, I should have seen him do it.

What I didn't tell them was that I believed Trudeau did punch the guy in the nose, but I was never asked what I *believed*. The guy got what he deserved, I thought. The case was dismissed.

INCIDENT TWO: March 1970.
Pierre Trudeau and Gordon Gibson, his executive assistant, arrived in Vancouver from Ottawa, for a ski trip. We drove them up to a motel in Whistler. Three days later, on Saturday, Margaret Sinclair was due to arrive at the Sinclair's Whistler condo, and Pierre was going to move in with her, as planned. It was arranged that Gordon would receive all important government phone calls on his motel-room phone, which were routed through the Squamish telephone exchange to Whistler. I, on

the other hand, had a direct (and secure) line to RCMP headquarters in Vancouver. All fine so far.

At 1:30 a.m. Saturday morning, Gordon woke me up.

"There is a problem," he said. "I've just had a call from Barbra Streisand, who's in Vancouver. She wants to come up here and ski with Pierre."

"Oh," I said, trying to gather my thoughts.

"The last thing Pierre needs is two girlfriends up here at the same time."

"This is not a *police* problem," I said.

"You have to help me."

Gordon then said he had no return phone number for Ms. Streisand, but thought she was staying at the Bayshore Hotel. I offered to trace the call, and then either he – or Pierre – could contact her later in the morning and make some other arrangements. I contacted the RCMP in Vancouver (on my secure line) requesting information.

Gordon and I then put on some coffee and waited for the return call. At 5:30 a.m., we finally heard back from two RCMP detectives, who were then standing in the matron's office at the nurse's residence of the Royal Columbia Hospital in New Westminster.

Three student nurses, the detectives reported, had gone to a Streisand movie on Friday night and afterwards had picked up a bottle of wine and some fish and chips. The newspaper the fish and chips were wrapped in was the front page of the *Vancouver Sun* that showed a photograph of the PM skiing at Whistler. The story mentioned the motel he was staying at.

After several glasses of wine, the detectives continued, the nurses decided they should go skiing with their prime minister. One of them – who could sing like Streisand – had made the 1:30 a.m. call. The scene in the Matron's office was not pretty. The matron was very angry, the nurses more than distraught. I told the detectives to wait in the matron's office, and that I would call back as to what further action was required.

Pierre was always up by 6 a.m., as we usually went jogging before breakfast. At 6:05 a.m. Gordon and I relayed the whole "Streisand" story to him. I told Pierre he had several options, including the nurses being charged with public mischief. "Sir," I said, "it's up to you."

"Oh," he coolly replied, "just tell them not to do it again."

"Yes, sir," I replied.

I passed on the information to the detectives, and that was the end of that. Margaret arrived on Saturday and Pierre disappeared, as planned.

The next day I went skiing and happened to be sitting on the lift with a young woman and we began talking. I had no idea who she was and nor she me.

"Isn't it wonderful that Pierre Trudeau is skiing on the hill today," she said, "and that Barbra Streisand is coming up to join him."

"How do you know that?" I asked.

"Oh," she replied, "my sister is the long-distance telephone operator at Squamish."

INCIDENT THREE: March 1971.

The Trudeau–Sinclair wedding was a "top secret" affair, and I was taking my instructions directly from the PMO and RCMP headquarters in Ottawa. Even my RCMP superiors in British Columbia were unaware of the event. I couldn't even tell my wife, Louise, who was a huge Trudeau fan. The thinking was that the fewer people who knew, the better. It was decided, for example, that a sergeant from the Squamish detachment would obtain the marriage licence for a "P.E. Trudeau and M. Sinclair, of Whistler, B.C." (Later, the secrecy bothered this guy so much he had to take a leave of absence.)

Pierre, accompanied by his brother, Tip, and sister-in-law, Andrée, arrived in Vancouver by government jet about ninety minutes before the wedding was scheduled. The raincoat he wore shrouded his formal wedding attire. We left Vancouver airport in two unmarked police cars, followed, as usual, by a car containing the press, who knew something was up but not what. They were able to monitor the radio frequency of our normal car but, unknown to them, I had a new special radio channel in my car, which was carrying the Trudeau party.

I knew if we kept going in this three-car lineup, we would lead the press right to the front steps of St. Stephen's Church in North Vancouver. So I called in a third police car, to tail the press vehicle, and we then proceeded (slight detour) to Chinatown and into a narrow alley, where car number two and car number three stopped, thereby boxing in the

Victor Irving (on right) guarding the honeymoon couple.

reporters. Our car then proceeded to the church on time with a bemused prime minister sitting in the back.

Their wedding went off without incident – even the uniformed RCMP personnel we had outside the church were unaware of the history occurring inside. After the wedding, we drove the Trudeaus to their wedding reception at Capilano Golf and Country Club, where Gordon Gibson released a statement that finally let the country in on the secret wedding.

At 11:30 p.m. (2:30 a.m. Ottawa time) we drove the Trudeaus to the Sinclair condo at Whistler. Another officer, a corporal originally from Saskatchewan, was assigned to drive, while I sat in the passenger front seat. From my ten years as a detective, and driving with Pierre, I was able to observe what went on in the back seat of a car. (By this point I also knew Pierre's body language well.) From the rear-view mirror I observed that he seemed perturbed by our slow and cautious speed, even though there was some snow on the highway.

When we reached Squamish I asked the driver to stop. I took over the driving, hitting fifty to sixty miles an hour. I could see a smile on Pierre's face. We reached Whistler in short order.

The next morning I received a request from them for ice cream and all the Vancouver papers. I delivered these, leaving the happy couple kneeling on the living-room floor reading the papers.

(Pierre still owes me $5.75.)

▶ BARRY MOSS
Retired RCMP chief superintendent, responsible for the security of the PM, 1971–76

I accompanied Mr. Trudeau and Margaret on many foreign trips, both official and private, and through two election campaigns in 1972 and 1974. We travelled to, among other places, Jamaica, Barbados, Antigua, China, Japan, Mexico, Cuba, Venezuela, England, Finland, Denmark, and Washington, D.C. In those days he had only one accompanying bodyguard, amazing as that sounds now, except when Margaret accompanied him, and a second RCMP inspector travelled with the group. He was an easy man to work with, and was always concerned about your life.

I remember one trip early on when he was travelling without Margaret and phoned her frequently. I used to place the call to the PMO switchboard for him, and then they would connect the call.

"You call home to Edith [my wife] on these foreign trips, don't you, Barry?" he asked. I said that I didn't.

"Well," he said, "you'd better start." So, from then on, when I placed a call to his office for him, the operator called (my wife) and held her on the line until Mr. Trudeau was finished, and then I would talk to her.

I kept a card in my wallet that listed his height, weight, shoe size, shirt size, and blood type, just so I'd have them handy in case I needed the information in any emergency. Fortunately, on my watch, there was never a big emergency.

He rarely got mad, but you knew when he was annoyed, because he'd just give that stare without saying anything and you knew you had to fix whatever it was that bothered him. In Jamaica one night, he and I were both reading in the living room of the residence where we were staying. He was sitting on the sofa beside a rather dim lamp. I was across the room in a chair with a brighter light, smoking my pipe.

Barry Moss (top) arrives in Mexico with Margaret, baby Michel, and the PM.

Moss Collection

"Don't you want a better light to read by, sir?" I asked him.

"I would, but your darn pipe smoke bothers me." I didn't smoke it in front of him after that!

On a private vacation trip to the Caribbean (when I first started to travel with Mr. Trudeau), Dr. Joe MacInnis, the PM, and their wives went scuba diving. We went out to a large raft in the ocean and the four of them went diving while I remained onboard the raft. When they resurfaced, Mr. Trudeau asked me if I wasn't concerned about him being so long underwater, and didn't I worry about what might happen to him?

"No, sir," I said. "My job is to protect you from others, not yourself."

▶ R.H. "HAP" MACDONALD
Retired RCMP Inspector, responsible for the security of the PM, 1976 until the early 1980s

My first trip with Prime Minister Trudeau was over the New Year in 1976–77, when I accompanied him, Mrs. Trudeau, the three boys, and their nanny to St. Lucia. We stayed in a private residence about five miles from Castries. The first thing that impressed me about the PM was his care for his children, and the time he spent with them.

We all went swimming every day. In the afternoons, after the boys had their rests, we would go all over the island to see various historical sites, from the Old City Market to various banana plantations. I remember the boys being really impressed at seeing bananas growing.

"Look, Dad," young Justin said to his father. "Bananas grow upside down!" The PM got a real chuckle out of that, and he allowed them to take some bananas home to Ottawa.

A few days after we returned, I went back to my regular work, and when I got home one evening, my wife, Merlene, told me that Sacha and Miche and their nanny had baked banana bread, and the boys wanted to give some to "Hap." Justin was back at school, so the other boys came by and dropped it off.

On another trip, just after Christmas 1977, I accompanied the PM and three boys to Jamaica. We flew on Air Canada to Montego Bay, and then stayed at a private beach house in Ocho Rios. It was a quiet, restful holiday and the PM spent all his time with the boys, until Justin developed a high fever.

The PM gave him two baby Aspirins and put him to bed, and soon he was fast asleep. But when Justin awoke the next morning, he was covered in chicken pox! (This was a day before we were due to leave, and the PM was concerned we couldn't fly back on Air Canada, for obvious reasons.) So I contacted the airline, whose policy was not to fly anyone with a contagious disease.

"What will we do now?" the PM asked. "How will we get home?"

I informed him there was only one alternative, and that was to have a government Jet Star come down and pick us up. The PM didn't say anything, but I knew what he was thinking. Then he wondered aloud about what "people would think" if it became public that he'd used a government aircraft to return from a Christmas vacation.

I pointed out that, given the circumstances of Justin's condition, those people would have egg on their face.

"Leave it with me for a while," he said, and wandered off to think it through.

About an hour later, he returned and asked me to contact Bob Murdoch, his executive assistant in Ottawa, to make the arrangements. We returned home without incident and nothing was said in the House, or in the press, about using the government aircraft. The PM was needlessly worried.

▶ ROBERT H. SIMMONDS
RCMP commissioner, 1977–87

During my years as commissioner, the Right Honourable P.E. Trudeau was twice the prime minister of Canada.

Occasionally we had one-on-one luncheons at 24 Sussex, where we discussed a wide range of Canadian and world issues. Throughout these encounters I was always impressed by his seemingly genuine interest in my views on current (and at times historical) events.

Prime Minister Trudeau had a great talent in getting you to bare your soul and disclose your inner thoughts. He would muse about an issue, set a probable scene, and then just let it hang in the air while he looked you in the eye, thus inviting a response. Before long, you were expounding your views, and (as he continued his silence) you would keep adding to them as justification until all was said.

After my first private luncheon with him at 24 Sussex, I recall that, as I drove back to headquarters, it occurred to me that either the prime minister was suitably impressed with my reasoning and interpretation of events or, alternately, he considered me a complete fool. I shall never know which it was.

To me Mr. Trudeau was much more a scholar and statesman than he was a politician. In fact, I sometimes thought that he probably found the requirements of party politics to be somewhat distasteful to his instincts, and to his much broader interests in history and the evolution of humankind. I don't suppose that I am really qualified to make such an assessment, but I *am* quite competent to say that he would have been a very successful detective.

One Sunday afternoon I was skiing at Camp Fortune, just moseying along and minding my own business, when suddenly a voice at my shoulder rang out: "Commissioner, you should appoint some better skiers to the Security Detail, these fellows have trouble keeping up." I looked to my right and there was the prime minister with a big smile on his face, but before I could respond, he shot away down the slope, seemingly without a care in the world. Upon enquiring, I learned that the prime minister and his sons were skiing at the resort for a couple of hours. I also realized that, although I was the commissioner of the force, I would not qualify for the Security Detail if the criteria that he suggested were a prerequisite.

My last discussion with Prime Minister Trudeau was on the street in Montreal after he had retired from government. He greeted me like an old friend and we sat and chatted for a few moments. I was once again impressed with his great courtesy and the genuine interest that he reflected in all that was ongoing. At that time, he had some concerns regarding his personal security, and the security of his Montreal home, and we talked about that. He thought that, perhaps, it would be wise for him to carry a pistol (!).

I (naturally) advised against such an approach and suggested that he leave all that to the force, which retains responsibility for the security of a retired prime minister as long as there is an actual or perceived threat. I believe that he accepted my assessment of the situation. And I promised that I would follow it up with the commanding officer in Montreal. However, his suggested approach served as one more example of his strong streak of independence and desire to take care of himself, no matter the circumstances.

Chapter Six

Creative Canada

▶ GORDON PINSENT
Actor, director, writer

I first felt the major impact of Pierre Trudeau's arrival on the political scene in the mid-sixties, when we were filming *Quentin Durgens, MP* on Parliament Hill. The series ran successfully for three years. We filmed in black and white, and were doing quite well. Then Mr. Trudeau arrived on the Hill in living colour. Helped by his everlasting red rose, his style, and his incredible charisma, he lit up television, lit up the country, and lit up our imaginations in a way that our fiction never did. Our government-by-television seemed to fade very quickly after that. My character had two suits, two ties, and a sad-looking turtleneck. Trudeau had a wardrobe to die for, and wore it better than me as well. While my character was falling on his face, Trudeau made backflips off diving boards and twirls for royal visitors. So it could be said that the man had some impact on the demise of our series.

In 1972, Pierre and Margaret came to a premiere of my film *The Rowdyman* in Ottawa. I was sitting next to him in the theatre. I remember this distinctly, because the film started upside down. While this was being dealt with, Pierre – sensing my discomfort – leaned over to me and said, "Never mind, we have popcorn." There was a lot of bloat by the time the show started, but they gave us no reason to think we'd never be allowed in Ottawa again. At the end of the film, he kissed my leading lady

Nancy Southam Collection

*Who is Quentin
Durgens, MP, anyway?*

– Linda Goranson – and Margaret said: "If he can, so can I!" and she kissed me. Not bad. I recall thinking at that precise moment: I hope I can hold onto her until the cameras get it. And one photographer did. Unfortunately, I'm facing the lens, and from the back the girl could have been anyone.

When U.S. president Ronald Reagan visited Ottawa in 1981, I was the English host for the gala at the National Arts Centre. The following morning, I was packing up to return to Toronto, and I got a phone call from the Prime Minister's Office. This nice woman asked me when my flight was. I told her, and she told me the prime minister was wondering if I wanted to hear Reagan's address in the House of Commons that afternoon. Terrific. What a way to cap the trip. Trouble was I didn't have a tie. Brought a tux for the event, but that was it. Never mind, she said, we will get you one, don't worry.

So I headed over to the Hill and was ushered to the Speaker's Gallery corridor, where Trudeau's other guests had been waiting. Among them were the Trudeau children; their nurse; Robert Charlebois – the great Montreal singer; Trudeau's sister, Suzette Rouleau, and her husband; and a young woman of indeterminate age and identification. I couldn't get the entire business out of my mind: the extent of Trudeau's generosity in including me in this small special group. Then, a lady I took to be in charge of guests welcomes me. I tell her I don't have a tie! She says that's okay, she'll get me one, and adds, "He'd like to see you in his office." I wasn't sure which "he" she'd meant for a moment. Turns out, she had been referring to the PM.

Now, I'm in his office. Again, terrific. My God, he's *finally* going to apologize to me for the drastic reduction in my television numbers since his arrival on the Hill. What a man. About time! The PM was doing up the top buttons of his shirt, straightening his tie, and putting his jacket on, and I'm thinking, God, I bet Reagan's been all suited up, had breakfast, and been to the boys' room three times already.

"I don't have a tie!" I said to Prime Minister Pierre Trudeau.

"Oh," he said in flawless English. "Get Gordon my emergency tie!"

This he said to the woman poised half-in and half-out of his doorway. The tie arrived. (Made me wonder what else I could have asked for.) Anyway, it was green. The tie. Plain green. And kind of Irish in colour, which I hadn't related to him somehow. I remember thinking, that's what happens when you have other people shop for you. Plus, the green tie had spots on it. None that could not be hidden by a done-up jacket, but spots nonetheless. Strange, I thought, for such an immaculate gentleman. His "emergency tie," I kept thinking, where has it been? I was suddenly feeling a lot like an authentic MP. It had a hook at the top. Yes, a hook. And this hook was not small. You did the shirt up to the top, and then jammed this hook business down between collar and neck, and it looked for all the world like an . . . emergency tie! The tie of someone in a hurry a lot of the time. He tells me how to apply it. And then he says he wants it back.

"You don't wear this, surely," I said. "This has got a Windsor knot in it!"

"What's wrong with that?" he said.

"I didn't think it was you," I said, realizing as soon as I said it that it was stupid. The man could look good in prison clothes.

"I'll try and return it to you," I say, fumbling with it.

"No, no, Gordon, I *really* want it back." He sounded serious. And then my prime minister says, "Oh, by the way, would you like to come for lunch today after Reagan's speech?" To Sussex Drive this was.

Of course, I accepted his kind invitation now that I'd be suitably dressed – in a huge unlikely green tie and the lot. The luncheon guests at Sussex Drive were Charlebois, Mr. and Mrs. Rouleau, the mystery girl whose name I can't remember, the PM, and me. During the course of the meal, I mentioned something about Reagan doing very well in his remarks.

"Yes," Trudeau says, "but I think I'm a better actor." I had a feeling he'd said this before, but it was good enough to be original, because to me he would never be accused of redoing or copying anything, even himself. I'm sure that those who knew him better would know better.

I remember the lunch being a bit awkward because Charlebois kept directing all his remarks to Trudeau, in French of course, and I felt a little lost, but to his credit, Trudeau directed everything back to me. As I said beforehand, I did not expect such generosity. I was very touched by the grace of the moment. And for a second, I saw us as buddies. Me and him. Him and me. Over a small, round table of draft ales in some pub. I, at least, would like him to have known how appreciative I was of his gesture.

After lunch, Trudeau had to go back to the Hill, but he kindly offered a lift in his limousine to the mysterious girl and me. She, it turned out, was returning to the same hotel and was on the same Toronto flight as me. All three of us sat in the back, the woman between us. I recall looking out the window and pretending I wasn't there for the entire six-minute drive, while they had a very private conversation that I did not want to hear. The girl – I had never been a beard before – and I were dropped at the hotel, and the prime minister went on to Question Period. Arriving at the hotel, I asked if she was going to catch the same flight.

She said to me in the smallest voice since Lillian Gish in *Perils of Pauline* – "I don't know what I'm going to be doing now. I may stay a while."

There was another gala at the National Arts Centre, the following year, when the Queen was in Ottawa to sign the Constitution. A whole bunch of us were lined up to meet the Queen and Prince Philip in this vast room before the gala performance. We had all been reminded not to stick our hands out when meeting the Queen, and were standing waiting to be introduced. Knowlton Nash was there, plus Karen Kain, perhaps, Oscar Peterson, Anne Murray . . . not sure. Anyway, they arrived at my wife, Charmion, and me. Of the whole line of us, guess whose hand was stuck out toward Her Majesty? Quentin Durgens, MP.

Pierre says to Her Majesty, "This is Gordon Pinsent, one of our better-known actors, directors, and writers."

And the Queen says: "Well, that's a bit greedy, isn't it?" and moves on. And so did Pierre – move on – wearing just a hint of a fun-smile, or so I thought.

A few months later Trudeau was at a Genie Film Awards evening in Toronto. He happened to see me above the heads of his many admirers and shouted, "Where's my tie?"

That was the last time I saw him. I did return his tie, though. I sent back his "emergency tie" after he brought back the Constitution, saying in a brief note: "It's the least I could do, for bringing it home!"

▶ MICHAEL SNOW
Visual artist, filmmaker, and musician, who met Trudeau in 1968 during the event described below

When Pierre Trudeau first ran for election as prime minister, my wife at the time, Joyce Wieland, an artist like myself, and I were living in New York. From afar, as it were, Joyce became very interested in Trudeau and wanted to support him. She decided to organize "Canadians in New York for Trudeau." Getting in touch with other Canadians led to the happy desire to host Trudeau in New York, and to personally and publicly show our support for his candidacy.

Working with Mary Mitchell, a playwright, and me, Joyce conveyed her invitation to Trudeau's Ottawa office. We were pleasantly surprised to receive a prompt reply, and subsequently we were (more surprises!) visited by Marc Lalonde, who came to investigate our offer of support. Joyce proposed to Lalonde that we would organize a party of sympathetic Canadians – and sympathetic Americans – in Trudeau's honour at our (very humble) loft on Chambers Street in lower Manhattan. Despite Lalonde and his team checking our (definitely crude) loft, there was another surprise: they agreed, and a date was set.

Joyce and Mary got to work issuing invitations. Joyce suggested that I arrange for some music to be played at the party. That wasn't a good idea, because I was deeply involved in an area of music that I felt was a powerful new movement within the jazz tradition. This kind of music was, at that time, decidedly "underground." It was called free jazz and was generally feared and disliked even by jazz fans.

Since I was very supportive of this music, I naturally chose such a group to play for the Trudeau party. It wasn't dance music and it was kind of fierce but it was very avant-garde; these guys were doing something new, so I thought being really daring would be good for a really daring Pierre Trudeau.

The evening of the party, Trudeau and his entourage arrived, *running* up the three flights of stairs to our loft. I had been asked to introduce people to Trudeau, to describe who they were, what they did, and to try to keep moving with him. There were many talented and celebrated people there, and I was continually astonished by Trudeau's tact and charm, but especially by his knowledge of the various art scenes in New York.

He knew that there was experimental film, that there was Off-Broadway theatre, and that there was an avant-garde dance scene. (In this respect, the rest of my story will register only with a reader who knows something about jazz, but what the hell.)

We had scheduled the music as "a concert"; the group, a trio of two saxophonists and drummer Milford Graves, would play for half an hour in the first half of the party. I was wise enough to know that they would ruin the party if they played longer. I was very impressed with Milford Graves's playing, and before the group began its set, I introduced Milford to Trudeau.

"Mr. Trudeau, I'd like you to meet a man I consider to be the greatest drummer in jazz today, Milford Graves."

Pierre Trudeau shook Milford's hand, saying, "Oh! Well, what about Max Roach?"

Incredible, I thought. Roach was/is a great drummer, who defined the New Jazz (or bebop) when he played with the great innovators of this style: Charlie Parker, Dizzy Gillespie, Miles Davis, and Bud Powell.

Milford was very taken by Trudeau's knowledge of jazz.

Trudeau then sat down, unfortunately kind of close to where the trio had set up. At the first note, his bodyguards jumped to their feet protectively. Trudeau flinched, but otherwise paid attention (I think) to the music, which someone new to it could, I suppose, take for excessive screaming and pounding.

The musicians were amazing, Trudeau was amazing, and the party survived.

▶ JIM HARRISON
Writer and poet

*I*t was in the late 1960s, certainly in another century, while I was teaching at Stony Brook University on Long Island, that I was invited to an international poetry conference in Montreal, part of their world's fair celebration. I felt distinctively out of place among a hundred poets from all over the world whose names I recognized, knowing that only a few of our group of Americans had any idea who I was, with only a single volume of verse to my credit.

There was a great deal of camaraderie and free-form carousing, but the singular event that embedded itself strongly in my memory was a formal luncheon given us by Pierre Trudeau. There were waiters in white gloves, three different wines, and an array of silver, china, and stemware that confused most of us. Above all there was the great man himself, who, in a speech of welcome, quoted from memory lengthy passages of Valéry and Rilke in French and German. We were all simply stunned. I wondered if I could possibly belong to a greater world, one that did not include the ignorance of our own president to the living vitality of poetry. The world leapt into something larger.

Of the dozens of politicians I've met in my life, no one came close to making the impression that Trudeau did on me – though I was struck positively once by the company of England's Harold Wilson at a dinner at Edna O'Brien's, and was startled by the intelligence of our own Senator Bill Bradley.

Many years later at my cabin in Michigan's Upper Peninsula I listened to the Trudeau funeral on CBC and wept.

▶ TIM PORTEOUS
Friend since 1957; speechwriter in PMO, 1968–70;
executive assistant, 1970–73

*T*here is a theory among political organizers that, if a politician is photographed in the company of a popular celebrity, some of that popularity may rub off on the politician and result in additional votes in future elections. A good example would be Pierre's meeting with John Lennon and Yoko Ono on December 21, 1969.

In 1969, the Cold War had divided the world into two nuclear-armed camps competing for global dominance. In this volatile situation, John Lennon, who had recently abandoned the Beatles, apparently decided that the celebrity he had earned as a songwriter and performer would make him an effective advocate for peace. In the spirit of the decade, peace was to be achieved by the relaxation of tensions between individuals, leaders, and states. John and Yoko would set an example by lying in bed in a Montreal hotel.

For the prime minister's staff, the principal objective of the PM meeting John and Yoko was not the discussion of how to achieve world peace. The proposal was for fifteen minutes of conversation and – more importantly – fifteen minutes of photography. The meeting would be arranged during Christmas week, a time when the prime minister's schedule is less crowded than usual, and the news media are looking for stories.

Since Pierre's childhood, music and the other arts had been part of his life and he enjoyed the company of performers. Among his friends were Leonard Cohen, Barbra Streisand, Jean-Pierre Rampal, and Guy Béart. He was happy to accept the staff's suggestion.

As far as I know, I was the only songwriter in the Prime Minister's Office (although there was at least one poet in the correspondence section), and that may have been why Pierre invited me to join him for the occasion. As I remember it, the meeting started almost on time, but it lasted well beyond the scheduled fifteen minutes. Pierre, who could have ended the encounter whenever he wanted, was enjoying himself.

In an interview later, Yoko claimed that John was nervous, but to me he seemed quite at home, and he easily dominated the conversation. He

Getting the youth vote out.

was utterly charming, highly articulate, an amusing raconteur, and, as you would expect, very entertaining. He spoke with a delightful "scouse" (Liverpool) accent that you could have cut with a knife. Pierre, unusual for a politician in such a situation, didn't say much. He did not attempt to take over the conversation, content with occasional interventions.

Much of the talk dealt with the Cold War. They both agreed that, since neither side could achieve victory without suffering unacceptable damage to its own population and territory, the conflict was irrational. Somehow a climate of mutual trust had to be created in which disarmament and peaceful diplomatic relations could begin. Each of them, in very different ways, would work toward this goal.

"If all politicians were like Mr. Trudeau, there would be peace," John said. Pierre said, "'Give Peace a Chance' has always seemed to me to be sensible advice."

Did the photo op win any votes? In the next election in 1972, Pierre came within two seats of losing to Robert Stanfield, a politician who had never been photographed with John Lennon or Yoko Ono. Perhaps some would argue that there were enough voting John Lennon fans in two of the seats to make the difference. Who knows?

▌ ARTHUR ERICKSON
Friend, travelling companion to Tibet, and architect of Trudeau's country retreat in the Laurentians

I first met Pierre Trudeau when, freshly chosen as our prime minister, he gave a dinner for a selection of arts leaders from across the country. A dinner for about twenty-four: composers, painters, poets, authors, actors, performers, and a sole architect. He was intent on hearing our views on the support of the arts as an important aspect of Canadian identity. The dinner went on around the long table until the early hours. I can't remember what was resolved, except that we were all flattered by the attention.

The next occasion was shortly after his marriage to Margaret, on their honeymoon on the West Coast. Margaret had mentioned that they would like to meet Gordon and Marion Smith, to see the Smith House and Gordon's paintings. I arranged it with Marion and volunteered my caterer, so that she would be free of any worries regarding the prime minister's visit.

Pierre and Margaret arrived from the Black Tusk meadows, laden with alpine flowers, which Margaret had made into a crown. They were both so radiant, joyous really, in their mutual adoration.

The only sad note to an otherwise informal and amusing lunch, was provided by the caterer, who fainted when she saw Pierre. Once she recovered, she had an attack of nerves, and when I went out to the kitchen to correct something, she burst into tears and left! Marion, however, had a backup supply of her usual West Coast fare – fresh shrimp and crab – and we ate that instead.

In 1976, there was a wonderful gathering at my little home in Vancouver during the Habitat conference. Vancouver was host to an international group of visitors, yet no one had volunteered to entertain them, so I sent out a blanket invitation to all of them to visit my garden. I was surprised and delighted when Pierre and Margaret arrived, bringing the governor of Caracas, Diego Arria, and his stunning wife, Ticqui. They were two beautiful couples who clearly outshone the likes of Margaret Mead and Buckminster Fuller, also in attendance, in casting their charismatic spell over the guests. Pierre, forever the statesman indifferent to the vulgarities of politics, moved with grace and ease amongst the assembled delegates, showing rapt concern over the issues raised.

There was also an intimate dinner in Montreal at my partner Francisco's Le Cartier apartment, for the Trudeaus and Paul and Eileen Lin. Paul was the head of Chinese studies at McGill and later U.B.C. As a veteran of the Chinese revolution, he had arranged Trudeau's trip to China, as well as the Kissinger and Nixon visits, which led to the complete reconciliation between East and West. It was also a dinner where I strained my culinary skills to make a large brioche to be filled with chicken, pineapple, and ginger, but this required throwing the dough violently against the plastic cupboard doors, to force the requisite layering of the dough for brioche. It was the last time I would do it.

A subsequent encounter in Canada was at their private lake north of Montreal. It was a perfect retreat for the hot summer days, isolated in the Laurentian forest. Pierre asked me if I would design a home for him. It had to be burglar proof, he said, and capable of being entirely closed-in for long periods of time. It had to be, basically, indestructible – with no exposed glass, or wood, for that matter.

I suggested we finish it in a traditional metal of corrugated aluminum. Pierre agreed. He also wanted an attic space for the boys to play in, and for their bedrooms. The main floor would contain a living-dining space, a kitchen, and an office, with the master bedroom next to it.

After our discussion, I already had ideas. Then we stripped and went for a swim *au natural*. After the swim, Margaret made a picnic, and we sat on the rocks by the silent lake.

▶ JUNE CALLWOOD
Journalist and social activist

I knew Pierre Trudeau slightly, because I was writing a magazine piece on Margaret for *Maclean's* in the early seventies, and I travelled across the country with them during an election campaign. I remember one time he and I were side by side on the ferry, sailing from Toronto Island to the mainland, and he asked me what Margaret had been telling him.

"Everything," I said.

"Thank God you don't publish until after the election," he said, very glumly.

"That's insulting," I shot back. "You've just offended me and your wife." And I wheeled away.

Later that day, as we were collecting our luggage at the Ottawa airport, he found me in the melee, and astonished me with a contrite apology.

My favourite story, though, was when I was national spokesperson for the Canadian Council of Christians and Jews. Somehow I had an appointment with Pierre in his PM's office. I had some doubts about our meeting, because I knew he was hot – I was told – about my opposition to the War Measures Act.

We sat uncomfortably in armchairs opposite one another, and he spoke first.

"So, just what is it you do as chair of this Brotherhood Week?" he asked.

"First, I get to meet you," I replied. "And second, I am not to be bigoted for a week."

Without a pause, he said, "Well, the latter will be easier for you than the former."

▶ TONI ONLEY
Painter

*D*espite the things we had in common, Pierre was always an enigma to me. He was like a solitary Arctic landscape, and I felt that no one could ever really *know* him. We shared a Catholic education of the kind that prepares one for the worst in life. It taught survival, mind over matter – when stung by the cane, you never complain. In me, he saw some of those qualities that he himself enjoyed: the pleasures of absolute withdrawal, and frugality, but at the same time, generosity toward one's friends.

On one cloudy day, we simply carried on skipping stones on the St. Croix River. We then headed into the New Brunswick woods, where he explained to me that one can always light a fire by using the bark from a birch tree.

"It will light even when wet," he said, peeling off a piece of bark. As a pipe smoker, I had a lighter, and I fired it up as he held out the piece of bark, a demonstration of wood lore that greatly alarmed his two RCMP security men.

Pierre was a good listener, and despite his reserve, we had some revealing conversations. But when I questioned him occasionally about such matters as taxation rules for artists (which I found unfair, and later won a battle over), or the use of bilingualism in air-traffic control in Quebec (which as a pilot I found dangerous), he would flare angrily, refusing debate.

But his gift for friendship always rose above any momentary irritation with my questions.

At our first meeting, in 1972, Pierre told me that my large minimal abstract collage of the early 1960s, which he owned, reminded him of the Arctic. Like me, he gravitated to lonely places and appreciated remote landscapes. We both enjoyed travelling alone in the vastness of the Canadian North, in what Glenn Gould called our "miles and miles of miles and miles."

Some time after our first meeting, I wrote to him that I wanted to go to the high Arctic to paint. In 1974, he arranged to have me travel there on an icebreaker, the CCGS *Louis St. Laurent*, so that I could depict the land's magnificent solitude. My very first paintings of icebergs were made possible by Pierre, a thought that humbles me. After I returned to Vancouver in October, I sent him a copy of the diary I kept during the voyage, and he wrote me back in November to tell me how much he enjoyed reading it. The diary gave the location of an ancient Thule site that I had found on Cornwallis Island, and he later visited this site on one of his solitary trips into the far North.

After 1974, I sometimes found myself on the guest list for dinners for visiting heads of state. I remember a state dinner in Ottawa for German chancellor Helmut Schmidt. Yukiko, my wife at that time, accompanied me, dressed in her finest kimono. The chancellor and Pierre were obviously the best of friends, because the formal dinner soon turned into quite an informal party, and several cabinet ministers got rather tanked. Another invitation came when the Queen and Prince Philip visited Vancouver after the ceremonies in Ottawa that brought home the Constitution. Pierre invited us to the dinner party the Queen held aboard the royal yacht *Britannia*. Those were heady days.

A couple of decades later, I arranged for Pierre to join me on a July rafting expedition down the Firth River to the Beaufort Sea. Just before we were to meet in the northern Yukon, I received a letter from Pierre apologizing that he could not make it. He had been invited to give an important lecture at Cambridge University in England and had decided to spend the rest of the summer in Europe. He suggested that I go ahead, but keep a diary and send him a copy, which I did.

When he wrote back, he did not comment, sadly, on this one passage: "Another long, wet day on the river. We unexpectedly entered Surprise Rapids and then plunged straight into the rollercoaster of Big Bend Rapids. During our daylong transit of a succession of rapids, we pulled off into an eddy behind a huge rock jutting into the river, a rock that looked like a giant fist with a raised finger. This landmark was known among rafters as 'Trudeau's Finger.' There we had lunch, wrung out our socks and shorts, and jogged to get warm."

I sit here, still wondering what he thought of the naming of that petulant bit of rock.

Trudeau was wildly unpopular in British Columbia, for the majority of British Columbians believed that he had won the 1980 election by ignoring the concerns of the West. On one of his last public visits to Vancouver, he was giving a dinner speech before a less-than-sympathetic crowd, when somebody heckled him. There was a group of people in the back of the room that were there to make a statement, and they took over the room for a few seconds. Where were the prime minister's staff and security? They ought to have expected interruptions like this, it being downtown Vancouver and all.

Pierre looked surprised, then said, "I don't know what you are complaining about. You live in the most beautiful land in Canada, and you have my friends Arthur Erickson and Toni Onley, one to create magnificent architecture to grace your city, and the other to interpret the magnificent landscape in which you are so fortunate to live." That didn't go over very well. I was sitting at a table in the front row, and I remember feeling pleased at the compliment, but embarrassed at the audience's reaction to his remark.

Since that fateful icebreaker trip in 1972, I have gone back to the Arctic three times to paint. I shall always be grateful to Pierre for having the insight to see that the Arctic was my kind of landscape. And also for that cloudy day in the New Brunswick forest for taking time out of his very public life to connect me with the land. I will always remember him as a generous friend.

▶ KAREN KAIN
Ballerina with the National Ballet of Canada, 1968–97

At the end of June 1973, Frank Augustyn and I were dancing at the Second International Ballet Competition in Moscow; we were just kids really – it was very early in our careers – but I won a silver medal in the women's category and together we won a prize for the best *pas de deux*, the Bluebird from *The Sleeping Beauty*. It was all thrilling, of course, but what really topped it off was receiving a congratulatory telegram from Prime Minister Trudeau. Thanks to the regular updates on our progress in the *Globe and Mail*, from then-dance critic John Fraser, the whole country had taken notice, including the prime minister!

After that competition, Frank and I were to fly back to Canada, with a connection in Montreal and then to Toronto. Well, we didn't get home to Toronto, because the attendant on the flight came over to us and said she'd received a message from the Prime Minister's Office, notifying us that we were going to Ottawa to have a dinner, in our honour, with the prime minister. We couldn't believe it.

We arrived in Ottawa, with no bags, just the clothes on our backs, because our luggage had gone on to Toronto. After a hasty shopping expedition, which yielded an oversized dress for me and a jacket for Frank, we safety-pinned ourselves together and headed off to 24 Sussex Drive. The combination of extreme jet lag and nervousness leaves me with few recollections about who was actually there that evening except, of course, Pierre Trudeau, who impressed us with his knowledge of music, ballet, poetry, and philosophy. From then on, every time we appeared in Ottawa with the National Ballet of Canada, Pierre would be in the audience, and we sometimes dined with him and Margaret.

He was such a generous man. I remember a very touching moment, when I received my Order of Canada, in 1977. Pierre invited me and my parents over to 24 Sussex after the ceremony at Rideau Hall. He gave us a tour of the house and swimming pool, showed us the paintings, and was very gracious to my parents. He was a single dad by that point, and the one time he excused himself for a few minutes was because he had to potty-train Michel.

What was so unique about Pierre, as a politician, was his deep appreciation for the culture and the arts of this country. In my experience, no one in our country's leadership has ever had that understanding. He was a Renaissance man, whether he was canoeing in the wild or quoting philosophy in German.

And he had such flair and grace, whether it was the way he spoke, the way he dressed, or the way he reacted so spontaneously and joyously to things around him. Remember that pirouette behind the Queen?

I never actually danced *with* Pierre, regrettably. In his last years I would see him at the annual Gala des Étoiles in Montreal, an evening of dance featuring stars from around the world. He would always alternate which son he brought, continuing to imbue in them not only a love for the outdoors, but also an appreciation for the fine arts.

▶ CATHERINE McKINNON
New Brunswick-born singer and actor

*I*n the late 1970s, I was asked to perform in Ottawa for the Liberal caucus Christmas party. I performed two selections, the most important song being "Christmas Child," from the musical/film *Irma La Douce*. I dedicated this number to Trudeau's two sons, Justin and Sacha, who were born on Christmas Day.

In those days (in the last century) the late-night news was "live" and, as the prime minister moved forward to thank me, the scrum of political reporters surrounded him. Later, when they were out of earshot, he leaned over and asked if I would like to "come back to Sussex Drive for a swim."

I was rather stunned by the request, but I responded with a very enthusiastic "Yes!" An offer like that, I realized, comes only once in a lifetime, even if I was terrified of swimming.

I was told to be in – of all places – Iona Campagnolo's office at midnight. Until the appointed hour, I passed the time talking to politicians and reporters. I must have appeared anxious, because, apparently, I kept checking my watch. One keen observer asked me if I "was going someplace," and I replied with an emphatic "No!" A second reporter asked if I "was meeting the PM," to which I replied, "Don't be ridiculous." I quickly said my goodbyes and headed to Campagnolo's office.

A guide led me through the dark halls and tunnels of the parliament buildings and, when I finally made it outside, I was met by two plainclothed RCMP officers. The female officer was the driver, and we quickly got into an old car and headed toward the PM's residence.

Once inside the prime minster's home, he asked if I would mind if he "went upstairs to check on my sons." Then he asked me to join him. Looking in on his youngest son, Mr. Trudeau mentioned that Michel was missing his mother, and then the prime minister picked him up and carried him to the bathroom. Returning to the bedroom, and tucking him back into bed, he then kissed each of his three sons goodnight.

We went downstairs and raided the kitchen. We enjoyed a wonderful terrine (made by the chef) and some white wine. We played a tape I had recorded, listened to music, and talked.

"How do you see your professional life? What is your purpose?" he asked me.

"My job is to make people feel." Then I added, "Do you want me to tell you the truth?" He did.

"Well, sometimes you, sir, make the problem, and I make them feel better."

"Oh, don't put yourself down."

"What I do is not rocket science. It is a joy for me. I am a diversion from the pressures of everyday life."

It was then the prime minister asked if I would like to go for a swim. Oh God, I thought, there's no turning back now. We went downstairs to the pool and the next thing I knew this very attractive man dove into the pool.

I changed into a bathing suit and slowly waded into the water.

"Don't be such a chicken," he cajoled.

I'm not a very good swimmer, and I was nervous in the water, but for the remainder of the evening/morning we moved from pool to sauna and back again. My hair, by the end of the evening, could best be described as "God's Brillo pad."

It was getting late . . . or, rather, early . . . so I changed back into my clothes, threw on my coat, and Mr. Trudeau arranged for a cab to whisk me back to the Château. My parting vision is of the prime minister standing at the front door of Sussex Drive with an RCMP officer saluting him.

▶ OSCAR PETERSON
Pianist

*T*hroughout most of my adult life, I have been a supporter of the Liberal Party. The primary origin of this allegiance and dedication was not only sparked by some of the party's early leaders, but was most definitely deepened by the years Pierre Elliott Trudeau was prime minister. I was in his presence only a few times, but on each of these occasions his vivacious candour and spirit served to deepen my belief in his leadership. I recall being on an extensive tour of Europe, during which I was queried by numerous Europeans as to whether I knew Trudeau personally, and if so, what was he like. I found countless Europeans had an unbridled admiration for him.

I vividly remember a fleeting vision of him in the 1970s dashing up the outside stairs to the concert hall in Ottawa, where I was performing that evening. He came backstage and chided me in a kidding way about my sounding not unlike Dave Brubeck on a certain tune (this has yet to happen).

On another occasion I attended a presentation to some young aspiring classical players. Following the presentation, there was a reception at which I had a chance to say hello to Mr. Trudeau. He had just returned from a trip abroad and teased me about having had to come all that distance, supposedly to hear if I could still play. I bade him welcome home and had barely finished my hellos, when he became distracted by one of the young female recipients. He quickly thanked me for my welcome and then informed me he was certain that I would excuse him so that he might properly congratulate this pretty young female award winner, which of course was part of his duty as prime minister. Then he immediately moved off in her direction.

Canadian Press, Fred Chartrand

The famous Mercedes-Benz,
packed with Trudeaus.

I have always had great admiration for Prime Minister Trudeau and his illustrious reign as the head of the Liberal Party. However, my real admiration was predicated on the fact that he had impeccable taste in his choice of automobiles. He drove the same make of sports car as I did at the time, which served to tell me that we were on the same track when it came to cars.

▶ JEAN-LOUIS ROUX

Actor, director, author, and theatre producer, who first met Trudeau in the mid-1930s

*I*t was at the end of a rather official luncheon in the University of Montreal's main lobby in 1994, and Pierre Trudeau was being honoured there for some reason I can't recall. As guests were about to return to their daily chores, I went over to offer him a friendly handshake. Knowing him to be a great fan of Claudel, I mentioned I'd soon be playing the King in *Tête d'Or* at the Éspace Go theatre, and told him I hoped he could take in a performance (which he in fact did later on). And without the least hesitation, he broke into the following verse:

> Here am I,
> Stupid, ignorant,
> A new man before the unknown . . .

I was staggered: those were precisely the first words spoken by the character Cébès at the very beginning of the play. Besides, I remember another occasion when, commenting on the unexpected misfortunes of politics, he'd said, with a half-smile (clearly intended for my benefit): "The worst isn't always certain!" We were likely the only two people among all those in attendance who knew that this was how the announcer had subtitled *Le Soulier de Satin*, before the curtain rose on the French playwright's huge masterpiece.

Pierre Trudeau displayed his knowledge of literature, as he did many things, with elegance, spontaneity, and often with a hint of amusement and mockery, somewhat like a little boy. It was as though he were saying, "You're likely amazed that a prime minister can devote himself to reading things besides newspapers and Machiavelli's *Prince*!"

His literary erudition was indeed extremely broad, ranging from T.S. Eliot, to William Butler Yeats, through Northrop Frye, Victor Hugo, Charles Péguy, Arthur Rimbaud, Edmond Rostand, Antoine de Saint-Exupéry, William Shakespeare, Robert Louis Stevenson, Henry David Thoreau, and Voltaire, to name only a few.

Examining some of the passages he quoted in his own books provides a glimpse of his "hidden garden," and a hint of his concerns at the time. For example, in *Against the Current*, we find the following words from T.S. Eliot:

> This is the way the world ends,
> Not with a bang but a whimper.

A "whimper" that Pierre Trudeau never let anyone hear, but whose echo perhaps resonated in the depths of his soul.

In *This Mess Deserves a Big No*, he quotes Péguy, not the practising believer, but the man of action and polemicist:

> Everything begins with mysticism
> And ends with politics.

Do we detect a certain disillusionment before the constraints of *realpolitik*?

In his *Memoirs*, he calls on Rimbaud:

> I was going along, fists in my torn pockets
> And even my topcoat was becoming ideal
> I walked beneath the sky, Muse! And was your vassal
> O, dear me! What sublime loves I dreamed of!

The symbolist poet's *Gypsy Life* is no doubt the one he wanted to live, had he not been so committed to public affairs.

Elsewhere, in *Approaches to Politics*, he lets Henry David Thoreau speak: "Under a government which imprisons any unjustly, the true place for a just man is also a prison . . . the only house in a slave state in which a free man can abide with honour." This is a profession of faith from the man of opposition, which Pierre Trudeau was, first and foremost, before becoming a man of government.

Moreover, Pierre Trudeau often referred to the "murdered Mozarts" whom Saint-Exupéry mentioned at the end of *Terre des hommes*, on seeing – in a third-class train car – a child who was a model of charm and grace, born of a couple marked by misery and back-breaking work, whose destiny was severely compromised as a result. Trudeau was very sensitive to this situation and waged a tireless battle seeking equal opportunities for all, right from the cradle. He wanted his just society to ensure that no Mozart was ever murdered.

But Pierre Trudeau's relations with the world of literature weren't limited to quotations. He sometimes turned up as a character in certain works, and the portrait wasn't always flattering. Is he recognizable in Jacques Ferron's *Le Ciel de Québec*? At other times, however, Pierre Trudeau is portrayed as an almost mythical hero. For example, in 1956, the year the Rassemblement was created, Pierre Trudeau had journeyed along the Mackenzie River with F.R. Scott and a few friends. This inspired the Montreal poet to write the following verse:

> Pierre, suddenly challenged,
> Stripped and walked into the rapids,
> Firming his feet against rock
> Standing white in white water,
> Leaning south up the current
> To stem the downward rush,
> A man testing his strength
> Against the strength of his country.

This picture of a young man in his prime, measuring himself against the forces of nature, was impossible to evoke without a twinge of sorrow when one saw the fragile old man he'd become toward the end of his life.

But the energy of the character remained. As had many believers from his generation, he'd read the works of the unorthodox Pierre Teilhard de Chardin with passion, and I wouldn't be surprised if he'd meditated on these inspired words:

> When the signs of age begin to mark my body (and still more when they touch my mind); when the illness that is to diminish me or carry me off strikes from without or is born within me; when the painful moment comes in which I suddenly realize that I am ill or growing old; and above all at that last moment when I feel I am losing hold of myself and am absolutely passive within the hands of the great unknown forces that have formed me; in all those dark moments, O God, grant that I may understand (provided my faith is strong enough) that it is You who are parting the fibres of my being to penetrate to the very marrow of my substance and bear me away within You.

▌ CHRISTOPHER PLUMMER
Actor

*T*hough I knew the inscrutable Monsieur Trudeau only a little, this wily old "pro," with all the tricks at his command, has somehow wormed his way, uninvited, into my Canadian consciousness and will, undoubtedly, remain there till hell freezes over. I have no objection to his being there. After all, it's extremely flattering – he was a most remarkable man. I merely object to the odd twinge of envy I feel for his charismatic sense of theatre, his mental agility, and, of course, his well-known prowess with women.

He materializes for me every now and then as in a dream, wearing either a ballet shirt, a cap and gown, those terrible beige corduroy suits of his, or in some instances completely stark naked, with only his customary red rose pinned to his left pap! Whatever he may be sporting, he always seems to be slicing through the turbulence with the sharpness and accuracy of a finely cut sabre.

Canadian Press, Chris Morris

*Cruising Montreal in
his favourite corduroy suit.*

Let me say that, as a Canadian, I thank my lucky stars I was raised in the province of Quebec. Back in those days, there was more life going on there than in any other part of the country. My apologies to Hugh MacLennan, but to me there was only *one* solitude: we Anglais. Scottish Rule had begun to collapse all around me by the time I was a schoolboy in Montreal. The indolent, spoiled sons of the Anglo rich – too lazy to work as their forefathers had done – were drinking themselves into early oblivion, while les Français – whom they had treated for the most part as second-class inhabitants – were rapidly gathering in strength and in spirit.

Snubbed and ignored by France (as we Anglais had been somewhat patronized by Britain), the French Canadians, unlike us, had long ago formed their own identity. We are *still* floundering for ours! Theirs was a personality different and unique. It was loud, brash, gregarious, and hilariously funny. Their very patois, mixed with half-breed woodnotes wild, had a music all its own. "Joual," as it was called, with its querulous amusing inflections, made life around it seem carefree, positive, and vital. Like a light in a tunnel, each sentence ended with a ring of hope. I began to feel as Canadien français as they. I clung to them at every opportunity. They were like a warming pan in a frigid bed. Besides being delightfully wacky, they seemed able to survive anything – the bitter north winds had taught them how. They had fought fiercely and valiantly in two great wars and waged several cold wars on home ground in order to keep a grip on what they were convinced was theirs. In many cases they had intermarried with the native Indian to secure that conviction. They cared for and cherished the land under their boots, and loved it with a pride and passion a hundredfold stronger than ours, and the land had no choice but to love them back.

Out of this emotional mélange came Pierre Elliott Trudeau – a most unlikely figure in that *galère*. Elegant, urbane, with sharply chiselled features, he had those piercing eyes, a mind as clear and cool as a diamond, and a mysterious smouldering sexuality, hard to describe but never far from the surface. Montreal was his beat. Because he was well-to-do and supremely well-educated in both tongues, he cleverly kept one foot in the Square Mile and one on the other side of the tracks – the downtown ghettos of the *vrai* Montreal.

I have an image of Pierre Elliott in the wee hours, discarding his pinstripes, whirling a dark cloak about him and disappearing into the bowels of the city to sip absinthe and listen to the plaintive sound of Gallic blues, the angry young *chanteurs* with their message for the future, the new wave of separatism on the march – the poets of the night. Pierre Elliott too was a poet, and this dual existence made him all the more intriguing – a Metternich by day and a Rimbaud by night.

I met Pierre Elliott for the first time in the late forties. He was already a successful young lawyer. He had also earned himself equal stature as one of Montreal's more sought-after boulevardiers. I was about seventeen at the time, and concentrating hard on cutting a dash for myself as an up-and-coming man-about-town. We met at the long-extinct Café Martin on rue de la Montagne, where he frequently lunched with a young reporter named René Lévesque. Other favourite hangouts in which we continued our nodding acquaintance were the Colony Club on Drummond Street, and the much-frequented – and much-missed – Maritime Bar at the Ritz-Carlton Hotel. When I reminded him of all this some years later, he said with typical Trudeau candour that he didn't remember me at all.

The next time I bumped into him he was prime minister. Years had flown by. I had spent a good portion of them in England and on the

Continent, and so had missed the stunning impact my homeland witnessed at his meteoric ascendancy. But word had spread fast that Canada
had a new boss, and pretty soon, uncharacteristically, the world sat up
and took notice. None of our leaders had ever been as radical, as unconventional, or as daring.

What Glenn Gould was to Bach, Trudeau was to Canada. He interpreted it with a freshness that was bold and utterly original. Few could
match him in intellect or sophistication. Few had the political savvy, or
the wisdom and timing, to use it sparingly and to great effect. Very few
came close to his knowledge and understanding of the two cultures, and
none possessed his mystique or his curious glamour. There was also
enough old-fashioned gossip hovering around him to add spice to any
cause he undertook. Suddenly, for the first time perhaps, Canada was in
fashion. And Pierre Elliott had firmly placed it on the map.

Return visits to my beloved Montreal brought us together occasionally over drinks – at the old Maritime Bar and in the company of a
mutual friend, Jimmy Domville. Trudeau always checked his eminence
at the door. The more the waiters genuflected, the more he dropped his
formal manner, and we all relaxed. He was exceptionally articulate on a
great variety of subjects. With his profound knowledge of literature and
his keen sense of the music of language, he had a wonderful way with
words. He could quote with astounding recall whole passages of Milton
or Keats and then move into Ronsard, Corneille, or Racine. Then he
would come down to earth and be one of the boys, and the conversation would revert to fishing and the fair sex.

What also made Pierre Elliott attractive was his ability to listen. He
was a great listener. When he spoke he was riveting. When he listened
he was magnetic. While we were thus conversing, women would come
over to the table (some he knew, some he did not) to pay their respects
and flirt outrageously. He would flirt back. While theirs seemed calculated, his was second nature.

Of course, his exalted position was the major attraction, but I think
his eyes had a lot to do with it. Abandoning the cold, professional stare that
could electrify a room full of senators, a look of shyness would come over
him, a hunted look that made him vulnerable, and which drew women
to him like a magnet. Add to that the danger and unpredictability, and

Margaret Trudeau Kemper

Canada's éminence grise.

he became irresistible. Could there be a smoking gun somewhere? I have a vision of Pierre Elliott making love and invoking the War Measures Act at one and the same time.

It's strange but, long after his retirement, his mystique and popularity never waned; it grew increasingly stronger. Everyone sought his advice, tapped into his wisdom. He became Canada's éminence grise and a cult figure to boot. At one of his rare public appearances in the early 1990s, I was MC and had to introduce him. The country at the time was in poor straits, and totally disenchanted with its current government, and I couldn't resist saying, "Ladies and gentlemen, a man we need now more than ever – Monsieur Trudeau." Well, the room went wild! He got one of the longest standing ovations *I've* ever seen. I thought it would never end. (I made a mental note at once to put the line into my act. What better way was there to get an audience on their feet?)

With the exception of a few brief encounters, I saw little of him after that. He had gone into private exile, living out his legend with his writing, his books, and a few close friends. What was going on in his head those last years, I wonder? Had he thrown up his hands in despair at the dichotomy that was Canada? Had he wearied of the insipid conventionalism his beloved country insisted on breeding? Whatever, we certainly could use him now. Why, he might even negotiate our country back into being a major player. At least he would bring vision and guts to the table.

When he died, there was that extraordinary funeral attended by the most controversial list of mourners imaginable. From all over the globe they came, world leaders and vagabonds. Even his enemies had come to pay tribute to a man they couldn't help but admire. It was as if Pierre had been feasting with panthers.

The last time I saw Trudeau in the flesh was in the late 1990s at a tennis match in Montreal. André Agassi was defeating Michael Chang, and I was seated in the box with Trudeau. Rumour had it he was fading fast, and that his memory had gone. There was no evidence of it that day! We spoke of the early times in Montreal, and his eyes lit up and a flood of anecdotes poured forth from him like a fresh stream. He asked me what I was doing with myself. I told him I was trying to write a memoir and – as a running gag – I had him and René Lévesque in their youth as the Bobbsey Twins, turning up everywhere unexpectedly – huddled in a corner of the Café Martin bar; watching eighty-three-year-old Mistinguette dance the Apache at the Club Montmartre; sipping drinks at 3 a.m. at Rockhead's Paradise; or popping up behind potted palms in the old Windsor Hotel lobby; always together – plotting the future and carving up the country between them.

I asked him if he would forgive my impertinence and give me permission to use the gag. Two satanic eyes burned holes in my forehead for the longest time. And then he burst out laughing. To this day, I'm still out in left field. Was this just another of his old tricks? Oh, to hell with it – I'll print it anyway.

Chapter Seven

24 *Sussex and Harrington Lake*

▶ ALISON GORDON
Author

*P*ierre Trudeau, the man who had become prime minister of Canada just weeks before, came out of the summer residence at Harrington Lake. A number of people who had been involved in his leadership campaign and subsequent election were there for the weekend, but most were off walking in the woods or in canoes on the lake.

He had been inside, with the "PM's Eyes Only" boxes delivered by the RCMP the night before, running the country, I guess. I don't think he noticed me where I sat on the lawn that terraced down to the lake, reading a book. He wandered down to the shore and stood for a moment, stretching and bending. He picked up a rock or a piece of wood and spun around, throwing it far into the lake like a discus, then did a somewhat astounding series of flips and cartwheels along the lake's edge.

He seemed to be completely free in that moment, comfortable in his body in solitude, as he never seemed to be, in all the years I knew him, in company. It was as if the coiled spring he seemed to carry with him had been released and let him go. It was just a small bit of time – three, four minutes, maybe – but it is something I remember clearly thirty-six years later. I envied him that.

The Harrington Lake residence.

▶ JOYCE MASON
Along with her husband, Bill, introduced Trudeau to wolves in 1970,
and shared informal broomball games, meals, and canoeing adventures.

We'd all just gotten back from local backcountry in the Gatineau Hills and were sipping hot chocolate, sprawled around our blazing fire, thawing out our toes. Paul, our son, heard a knock, and both he and Becky, our daughter, raced to the door. Much to the surprise of my husband, Bill, and me, Paul whispered around the corner to us that the prime minister (our neighbour) was at the door, with a young woman. This was shortly before Pierre married Margaret (though we had no idea).

We invited them to our fire and they told us they had been out walking and decided to pop in to see what was up. We enjoyed visiting with them and telling them all about our pack of thirteen wolves, and Bill's National Film Board wolf-film project. I think our friendship started then, sitting around our hearth, trading outrageous stories.

One spring a few years later, Margaret, Pierre, and baby Justin joined us to make maple syrup at our backyard sugar bush. During the conversation, the topic of winter broomball games on our rink was mentioned. A group of friends gathered at our rink every Saturday evening to play broomball. We had a large rink, so this allowed us to have eight to ten players on each team, plus goalies.

Soon Margaret and Pierre joined us as often as possible in our regular broomball games. The games were hilarious and noisy as we slid on the ice while trying to pass to a teammate or score on the goalies. During her first game, Margaret got whammed in the face with the ball while playing goalie. Fortunately the ball was very soft so she didn't get a shiner. Pierre was just one of the players and right in the thick of things like everyone else.

At every game, the RCMP officers diligently stood in the snowbank at the side of the rink watching the on-ice mayhem. It must have been a bit disconcerting for them as they were supposed to be "guarding" the PM. Perhaps that is why they started waiting in their car! After the game we would gather in our house for tea and goodies and laugh over our crazy shoot-and-score stories.

At the end of our broomball "season" in 1974, Margaret and Pierre sent out invitations for a "Broomball Awards" dinner at 24 Sussex. Most of us showed up on time. Bill had made individual cartoon awards for each player and they were presented after a tasty dinner.

David Selwyn, one of the regular players, had made a fake broom for Bill, as Bill was notorious for breaking his broom. This broom was made from a piece of hose and it bent in half as it was presented to him. We all roared with laughter. It was so typical of our after-game gatherings. But the wobbly "broom" did not stop Bill from stickhandling around both sides of the elegant dinner table at 24 Sussex Drive. The kitchen staff peered through the glass in the door, wondering what kind of rowdies had been invited. It was definitely our most memorable Broomball awards dinner.

I was going through some files recently and came across a newspaper clipping from the *Ottawa Citizen* that referred (indirectly) to our rowdy evening with the Trudeaus. The press rarely got stuff right about Pierre's private time, and here's a great example.

"Guests in formal attire were being received at Government House for the state reception for Ontario Lieutenant-Governor designate Pauline McGibbon. Prime Minister Trudeau was not among the guests. Apparently the Trudeaus had made plans for a dinner party of their own before the state reception was announced, and couldn't change their plans....

"Hanging back from the receiving line at Government House were a man and a woman, dressed well, but not formally. They seemed nervous. An aide approached them, listened to their problems, and pointed out the party they were looking for was down the lane [sic] and across the street, at 24 Sussex."

They were late, but they made it!

▶ LESLIE KIMBERLEY-KEMPER
Nanny, 1977–78

As all caregivers of young children know, days spent looking after young ones are long and full of challenges. You are tired at the end of the day and sometimes feel that you need a pat on the back. As much as you love "your" children, a word of thanks is always appreciated.

When I was working as nanny to Justin, Sacha, and Michel, Mr. Trudeau was not one to hand out compliments or words of thanks gratuitously. He was a disciplined man, who had high expectations of himself as well as those around him. Compliments and words of thanks from him were rare, and therefore all the more treasured.

While Mr. Trudeau was *my* "boss," he was also, as a young Justin once referred to him, "the boss of Canada." I was acutely aware that running the country was a full-time job and that thanking nannies was not high on the to-do list. Words of appreciation typically came indirectly – usually via the household coordinator, Maryalice Mullally, not directly from Mr. Trudeau.

The family often spent weekends at the cottage at Harrington Lake. There, the atmosphere was more casual, there were fewer staff, and the schedule was more relaxed. Although Mr. Trudeau worked every day, he timed his breaks to be with the children for swimming, canoeing, or nature hikes. Sometimes he had his dinner with the children and me; at other times he would dine after the children were in bed.

Yannick, the chef at 24 Sussex Drive, usually made the weekend meals ahead of time, sending them to the lake to be reheated and served

Nannies Monica Mallon and Leslie Kimberley-Kemper
presiding over snack time with Michel, Sacha, and Justin.

by one of the maids, either Hildegard or Tara. Hildegard or Tara usually travelled up from Ottawa to Harrington Lake on Saturday afternoon in the Mounties' car at shift change, returning to the city at the end of the shift (midnight). It was a long time to take just to serve one meal.

One particular weekend, Monica Mallon and I were sharing the care of the children. We decided that we could easily reheat and serve Mr. Trudeau his dinner, saving the maid the trip. Fine. All was arranged.

It was dinnertime. We had tucked the children into bed and we were in the kitchen heating up Mr. Trudeau's dinner. Monica and I were teasing each other about how we felt like "exhausted suburban housewives"; after a full day with the children we were *still* working in the kitchen slaving over a hot stove. We joked that "no one ever thanks us for all the extra things we do for our family."

The meal was by now sufficiently warm and we took it into the dining room, placing it in front of Mr. Trudeau. As we did, we were surprised to hear Mr. Trudeau thanking us. "*Merci, les filles,*" he said.

We could barely contain ourselves as we walked back to the kitchen. Perhaps Mr. Trudeau had heard us in the kitchen. Monica, forever the tease, said kiddingly to me under her breath and in a droll voice, "In

English please." We arrived back in the kitchen in virtual hysterics. We didn't really *mean* it! We *knew* we were appreciated. Had he *actually* overheard us?

Monica and I stayed in the kitchen, tidying up between our giggling fits, and trying to compose ourselves. Suddenly, Mr. Trudeau walked in. He placed his dirty dishes beside the sink and said, "Thank you, girls." Monica and I exchange horrified glances! Had he heard us yet again? We never asked; we'll never know; but we'll certainly never forget that night!

Being part of, and living with, another family has its benefits; you grow close to the family, but sometimes it can be too close!

Evenings at 24 Sussex Drive often followed a predictable routine. The children would eat with the household staff at approximately 5 p.m. Mr. Trudeau would arrive home as we were finishing dinner, and the children would run out to greet him. After dinner, I would take the boys upstairs to help them put on their robes, so they would be ready for a swim with Daddy. Mr. Trudeau would go down to the pool ahead of the children to swim his laps. Every day, Mr. Trudeau scheduled time to be with the boys. The plan was for the nanny to arrive precisely as Mr. Trudeau finished his last lap.

When Mr. Trudeau was with the boys, he gave the impression of having all the time in the world. This was great for children who knew nothing of the constant daily pressures that their father faced. The nannies, however, knew otherwise. There were many demands on Mr. Trudeau's time and, to accommodate them all, that time was tightly scheduled. Therefore, in order for Mr. Trudeau to maximize his time with his children, it was important that the nanny and the children arrive at the pool at the designated time. Mr. Trudeau was a very precise man. You didn't want to arrive one minute late and be asked, "Was there a *problem* getting the children down here on time?"

"A *problem*?" one might say to oneself. "Three preschoolers finishing dinner, upstairs into robes, and downstairs at a precise time! Why would there be a *problem*?"

After the swim, it was "jammies and bed" for the children. Mr. Trudeau, who often had a guest or guests for dinner, would get dressed and head to the dining room. I would get the children ready for bed, brush their teeth, read them a story, and bring them down to meet the guest(s). The children were sometimes allowed to stay for bread and butter. If Mr. Trudeau was alone, he would often take them up to bed between courses. Otherwise, I would wait for the boys to return upstairs and tuck them in. After dinner, the guest(s) would leave, and Mr. Trudeau would retire to the Freedom Room (the family's personal living room) to work.

I recall one particular evening, after Mr. Trudeau had put the children to bed, I heard the pitter-patter of tiny feet. I waited for the loud roar and the squeal of little boys' voices, telling me that Mr. Trudeau was playing "Monster" with them. In this familiar family game, Mr. Trudeau would hide and the boys would try to find him. When the boys approached his hiding spot, Mr. Trudeau would jump out with a loud roar and chase them, squealing, back to bed. But this particular evening there were no roars or squeals. I guess they aren't playing "Monster" tonight, I figured.

I headed down the hall to the boys' bedrooms. "Those little monkeys," I thought to myself. "They're out of bed." I looked in Michel's bedroom – he was sound asleep in his crib. I looked in Justin and Sacha's bedroom. Sure enough, they were out of bed.

I began searching the bedroom level for them. I headed toward Mr. Trudeau's bedroom, but as I passed the stairs leading down to the first floor, I just about died of fright. Who was standing there, poised with his hands stretched out, ready to pounce, but Mr. Trudeau. He didn't roar, but I'm sure *I* screamed.

When Justin and Sacha were finally "caught" and put back to bed, Mr. Trudeau said, almost apologetically, that they kept coming to the Freedom Room to visit him. He said he just couldn't be serious with them when he, himself, was having as much fun as *they* were.

▶ VICKI KIMBERLEY-NAISH
Nanny, 1978–79

My first public appearance with Mr. Trudeau, Justin, Sacha, and Michel was so traumatic it is permanently etched in my brain. I was going to accompany Mr. Trudeau and the boys to the Remembrance Day service at Confederation Square in 1978. I had been thinking about what the boys should wear, for a number of days. The weather office said that it would be a sunny but cold day.

The boys had beautiful wool duffel coats that I thought would be fine. I planned that Sacha and Michel, who had red coats, would wear freshly pressed red corduroy pants. Justin, whose coat was navy blue, would wear navy-blue corduroy pants. They were ready to go. They had been to the bathroom. They had brushed their teeth, washed their faces, and combed their hair. I, too, was ready to go, as I had given a lot of thought about what I should wear, for I was in the delicate position of needing to be present and smartly dressed, but not in such a way as to draw attention to myself.

While waiting in the front hall, I heard Mr. Trudeau coming down the side staircase and just about died when he appeared around the corner. He was in a top hat and tails. My heart sank; the children were woefully underdressed. There was no time to wish that I had been instructed of the function's dress code before he spoke: "Vicki, I thought you might have dressed the boys better."

I summoned up my nerve and, instead of telling him I had not been informed that this was a formal function, I said boldly, "Give me five minutes, just five minutes!" I grabbed the boys and raced upstairs with them. I threw open their closets and got out their grey flannel pants and white turtlenecks. Sacha (who always wore red at that time) didn't let out a peep of protest as I yanked off his favourite clothes and threw on the dressier ones.

We reappeared in next to no time, and Mr. Trudeau and the boys got into the limousine. I went in the RCMP backup car, which drove directly behind the limousine and provided security for the PM. Smiling goodbye to the boys, I had noted with dismay that their hair needed re-combing. Would Mr. Trudeau notice?

Sure enough, as soon as the limousine was rolling, I could see in the back window Mr. Trudeau frantically combing the children's hair. There was so much activity going on, I wondered in what state the boys would arrive. And yet when the limousine pulled up to the edge of the red carpet and the door opened, out stepped a very composed Mr. Trudeau and his neatly turned-out sons.

Sacha and Justin holding hands with best dressed guy in the crowd.

I was introduced to an official who instructed me where to stand with the boys. Later, when the service was over, we joined Mr. Trudeau at the edge of Wellington Street to watch the parade move from Parliament Hill down Wellington Street, to pass in front of Confederation Square. Things were progressing quite well, until the parade ended and the crowds, which, up to that point, had been calmly lining the roadway, suddenly started to surge into the street, thereby blocking the limousines of the Governor General and the PM.

Before I knew it, the crowds were around us. The people wanted to talk to Mr. Trudeau and shake his hand. People also tried to touch the children, and I suddenly realized that I was so compressed by the crowd that I could no longer see any of the PM's police. I encircled the boys with my arms and pushed out against the crowd to try to give them more space. They were small, and I was terrified they would get trampled, or that someone might try to harm one of them – or the PM.

Mr. Trudeau joked that, if the limousine didn't come soon, they might have to walk home. (Although I wasn't aware of it at the time, the RCMP who were in the crowd near the PM, heard his remark and apparently were concerned about being able to provide adequate security should he decide to walk.)

Finally, a black limousine inched its way down Wellington Street. The street was still packed with people. Without warning, a local police officer grabbed Michel from my grasp and attempted to put him into the limousine. He did not realize that the black limousine was the Governor General's car and that the PM's limousine was silver. I wrestled Michel from him and told him that I was the nanny, and that he was putting Michel into the wrong car. When I returned, Mr. Trudeau said to me, "Let's make sure we get in the right car!"

I didn't know whether to laugh or cry. Ever so slowly, the silver limousine pulled up to where we were waiting. The children got in with Mr. Trudeau, and I went toward the backup car. While inching my way toward it, however, I saw the PM's police get into it. As I mentioned, the RCMP are there to protect the PM, not to drive the nannies. Whenever the PM's chauffeur drives away, the police backup driver instantly follows. And that is exactly what he did.

Unfortunately, I had just opened the rear door, when the driver started to pull away. I let out a cry, and they stopped, allowing me time to get in. It wasn't until I was in the car that I started to tremble. By the time I got back to 24 Sussex, I was more composed, but still shaken. It had been quite an initiation.

▎ ROBERT H. SIMMONDS
RCMP commissioner, 1977–87

During the Christmas season I received a telephone call advising me that the prime minister was hosting a reception at his residence the following evening to express his gratitude to the members of the force that took care of his personal security, and I was invited to attend. When I arrived at 24 Sussex Drive, I found that not only were the off-duty members of the Security Detail present, but also their spouses and children. The children, along with the prime minister's three young sons, were all playing and romping around on the floor. It was bedlam.

In the midst of it all was the prime minister, seemingly having as much fun as the children. As I looked upon the scene, I just wished that all Canadians could see what I was seeing. Because whether or not they agreed with the policies of his government, they would certainly relate to the humanity of the man who was at its head.

▶ HEIDI BENNET
Household coordinator, 1978–83

My predecessor, Maryalice Mullally, had told me she would usually stand by the front door when the PM left in the morning just in case there were some last-minute instructions or changes in the daily schedule that had been discussed over breakfast. So here I was, my first day of work at 24 Sussex, in October 1978, standing by the door waiting for the PM to come down the stairs. I was more than a bit nervous, and rather doubtful whether accepting this job had been such a good idea after all. All I knew about Pierre Elliott Trudeau was what I read in the newspapers, and that was not encouraging to say the least! I wondered whether I could work on a close personal basis with someone who had a reputation for being arrogant, impatient, petulant – in short, *difficult*.

Suddenly, Mr. Trudeau came bounding down the stairs, one little boy tucked under each arm. He grinned at me. "Welcome on board. Where's Michel?"

I had no idea where Michel was, but supposed he was with his Nanny, Monica. The PM gave Justin and Sacha a goodbye hug and kiss, told them he would be back home for lunch, and headed into the kitchen in search of Michel. A few minutes later he was back, rather put out he'd not found his youngest son.

"I like to say goodbye to the boys before I go to work," he told me. I took a mental note to have all three boys lined up in the front hall every

Heidi Bennet with the Trudeaus at 24 Sussex Drive; Christmas 1983.

Bennet Collection

morning from now on. Mr. Trudeau looked at his watch, hesitated, and then reluctantly went out to the waiting car. The door had shut, the car had begun to move, when out of the front door shot a toddler, diapers around his ankles, yelling "Dad! Dad! Dad!!"

The car stopped. A smiling dad got out, caught Michel up in his arms, gave him a hug and a kiss, and brought him back inside. Then the prime minister of Canada finally went to work.

I went downstairs to my office, thinking that a man who so obviously loved his children couldn't be all that bad. I felt we might get along just fine. And we did. Over the years, I grew to love Pierre as a friend. He was one of the kindest people I have ever known.

Everyone who worked at 24 Sussex – from the chef to the laundress – considered the Official Residence of the Prime Minister of Canada to be first and *foremost* the home of a very busy dad and his three little sons. This was their home and he wanted his boys to have as normal a life as possible. We all felt that, in some small way, we were a part of the family. In the course of the five years I was at 24 Sussex, I came to realize that Pierre too felt we were "family," and he often showed it.

I remember one morning I found the cleaning maid quietly weeping as she pushed the vacuum cleaner. She told me her son was dying of cancer. Naturally I told the PM about this. His reaction was spontaneous.

"Oh no, poor Gertie," he said. "Where is she? Could I talk to her?" Before I could answer, he was already heading downstairs in search of her.

Of course there were times when "home" turned into the prime minister's residence again. Pierre did not enjoy those official dinners, but he put up with them because they were part of the job. But no matter how tired he was, he always, without fail, came into the kitchen after an official dinner to thank the staff and the waiters who had been hired for the occasion.

The PM usually preferred small lunches and dinners, often with long-time friends. One summer day, he and his old friend Jacques Hébert were enjoying an aperitif in the garden before lunch. I was just going out to announce that lunch was served when I saw the PM leap up and sideways like an acrobat! At the same time, a cascade of water descended on M. Hébert, whose reflexes were clearly not as fast as his host's. They both came inside, Hebert drenched and laughing, the PM not at all amused. It turned out that, unbeknownst to anyone, the gardener had chosen this moment to test the automatic sprinkler system that had recently been installed.

When I came downstairs during the lunch, Zeph, the gardener, was already standing in my office, terribly upset, and asked me to apologize to Mr. Trudeau on his behalf. I did, adding a compliment about his lightning reflexes. He was still not amused. But later in the day, I saw the PM and Zeph walking through the garden, laughing and talking as Zeph showed him the location of every single sprinkler in the lawn. The PM didn't like surprises, and he wasn't going to be surprised again – at least not by the sprinkler system.

Mr. Trudeau had a reputation for being very careful with money, and that was true from what I could see. He was of a generation that believed that socks with holes in them should be mended, not thrown away, that one ought to take good care of one's belongings so they last a long time. He was proud of the fact his favourite hiking boots had belonged to his father. He cleaned and oiled them himself.

He was equally careful with the taxpayers' money and never spent a cent on the Official Residences that was not – in his view – absolutely necessary. For example, when Her Majesty the Queen came to Ottawa for the repatriation of the Constitution, the PM was to host an official luncheon for her at 24 Sussex. Buckingham Palace had informed us that Her Majesty would require a private room with bathroom for the occasion. At 24 Sussex, the upstairs library had its own bathroom, so this was where the Queen would powder her nose.

The bathroom had a particularly ugly wallpaper in a green, black, and silver octagonal pattern, which I had always thought was an eyesore in an otherwise beautiful house. Here was my chance to get rid of it, or so I thought. I selected three different wallpaper samples that were elegant, discreet, and – above all – not too expensive. After going over all the plans for the luncheon with the PM, I brought out the samples and made my case. He listened attentively.

"So," he said, after I finished, "you think the wallpaper is ugly?"

"It's hideous," I confirmed. "I don't know why it wasn't changed when the rest of the house was redecorated."

He looked at the samples. "You think one of these would be more suitable for the Queen?"

"Yes, I do," I said emphatically.

"Well," he said, handing me back the samples, "I don't know about the Queen, but *I* like the bathroom the way it is."

After I left 24 Sussex, Pierre and I kept in touch as friends. He had always taken a genuine interest in my daughters, Nancy and Jennifer, and continued to do so, even though we did not see him very often after he and the boys moved to Montreal. But I remember one memorable day we spent with him at his new country house in the Laurentians.

We arrived well before lunch, so Pierre suggested "a little hike" to the Upper Lake. We had never seen the Upper Lake and were keen to go. Pierre warned us the walk might be a little difficult in places, because there had been a tornado the previous summer, which had uprooted a few trees. We assured him this wouldn't be a problem, that we had brought our hiking boots, and were ready for anything, and so we set off.

Well, it was the Hike From Hell! We crawled under fallen trees, clambered over fallen trees, and detoured around fallen trees by scrambling up big boulders and sliding down the other side. Pierre was very solicitous, asking every now and then if we wanted to turn back. Of course we didn't, we told him. Where would he get *that* idea?

Heidi Bennet

Bennet Collection

*Nancy Bennet looking
hot and tired with a
fit and cool hiker, midway
through the Hike From Hell.*

*What Hike From Hell?
Heidi and Jennifer Bennet
with the tennis-shoe-
wearing leader.*

We *finally* made it to the Upper Lake, where we had a refreshing swim, and then did the whole trip in reverse! After four hours, we were back at the house, scratched, dirty, sweaty, hot, our hair and clothes sticky with pinesap, but we felt very proud of ourselves. Still, it was a little galling that Pierre had done the entire hike clad only in shorts and a pair of flimsy tennis shoes.

▶ CLAIRE MOWAT

Author who, along with her husband, Farley, was a friend and weekend guest of the Trudeaus

*F*arley and I were invited to spend the weekend at Harrington Lake with Pierre and Margaret and Justin in May 1972. On Sunday evening, after five-month-old Justin had been put to bed, we four gathered for a Japanese meal prepared and served entirely by Margaret. Neither Farley nor I were familiar with Japanese cuisine, but we were adventurous eaters and were ready to try anything they put in front of us. However, the one thing they hadn't put in front of us was a knife, or a fork, or a spoon. There were only chopsticks.

Pierre, who had turned up for dinner dressed in an authentic Japanese kimono, seemed surprised we didn't know how to eat with chopsticks. He assumed we were as worldly as he was, and that we would have acquired this skill somewhere along the way. We had, indeed, travelled to – and eaten in – exotic places. We had dined on horse ribs in Siberia, whale blubber on the shore of Hudson's Bay, boiled squid in Italy, turtle soup in Mexico, and shark's liver in Iceland. Yet none of these meals required they be eaten with chopsticks.

Margaret's meal consisted of a large tureen brimming with soy-flavoured sauce, in which small pieces of chicken were floating about. A separate dish contained boiled rice. How were we supposed to get any of this on our plates? I was too proud to ask for a spoon, but neither could I rudely dip my fingers into the sea of broth to retrieve a chunk of chicken. I had absolutely no idea how anyone could possibly pick up rice with chopsticks.

Pierre must have seen the look on my face.

"Here," he said. "It's simple. I'll show you."

He placed the chopsticks just *so* between my thumb and fingers. It did turn out to be fairly simple and, after a few tries, I got the hang of it. Very slowly, I picked up a few bits of chicken and then small clusters of rice, and put them on my plate and then into my mouth. I ate far less food that evening than if I had had a fork. It occurred to me that one way to lose weight would be to limit yourself to using only chopsticks at meals.

Lounging on the Magdalen Islands (without chopsticks) in 1971,
Farley Mowat, Margaret, Pierre, Justin, and unidentifiable security officer.

Farley wasn't nearly as compliant as I was. He simply asked Margaret for a fork and spoon, and he ate his dinner with his accustomed tools and gusto.

"Just think," I said to Farley when we were in the privacy of the guest room, getting ready for bed, "someday I might appear on one of those television quiz shows . . . you know . . . the kind where a guest has a fascinating secret and the panel has to guess what it is."

"And what's your big secret?"

"The prime minister of Canada taught me how to eat with chopsticks. I bet you not too many other people could make that claim."

"It could be you're the only one in the world," he laughed.

▌ JANE FAULKNER
Family friend

After the 1979 election defeat and the loss of thirteen ministers, Pierre gave two goodbye dinners, as he could not get twenty-six ministers and wives around the Sussex Drive dinner table. We were invited to the first of the wakes, and I was sitting in the middle of the table opposite Pierre. At one point in the dinner, he leaned across the table toward me and, in a soft voice, announced to me that he was going to tell a joke! This was something I was unaware he had a reputation for.

He told me I was to say a few lines in order to set up his punch line. However, I have no gift for memory and, anyway, I was certainly enjoying the good wine of Sussex Drive for the last time. (The joke went something like this: I ask Pierre if he is the funniest man in the world. He answers "Yes." I then ask him what the secret to his success is, but before I get the sentence out, Pierre is supposed to yell out "TIMING!")

Pierre tapped his glass, and the whole table fell silent. He announced that he was going to "tell a joke," and that *really* had everyone's attention, and off he went. When I was to say my first line, I drew a complete blank. He gave me an uncomprehending and pleading look. I whispered I couldn't remember, and he whispered a clue, but by then the moment was lost.

He was most forgiving, even though he wouldn't have understood short-term memory loss. I always wondered if he tried to tell a joke on his second dinner.

▶ ALASTAIR W. GILLESPIE
Cabinet minister, 1971–79

Most of us know what it's like to tidy up in preparation for a meal at home with friends. In the case of the prime minister, even with all his efficient staff, there were occasionally last-minute details to tend to. One particular evening, the family living room was the scene of a few quick touch-ups.

Pierre Trudeau was not known as an animal lover. There were no cats or dogs in the household – at least not until Farley and Claire Mowat gave the Trudeaus a black lab puppy. Labrador was important to him. The Trudeaus named the dog Farley, and he soon became a much-loved member of the family. He was *accepted* perhaps more than loved by the prime minister.

One of the younger Trudeau children displayed a very creative talent early on. He noted that almost always at dinner parties, there was a saucer or two of assorted nuts on the dining-room table. He also noted there were almost always a lot of nuts left over. So, after the grownups had left the table, he would move in and surreptitiously hide them behind sofa cushions and, occasionally, *under* the sofas – a little like a squirrel before winter sets in.

When heads of state were entertained at 24 Sussex, it was the living room that had the pride of place. On this occasion Prime Minister Ali Bhutto, the Pakistani leader, was to be the guest of honour. Very careful preparations were always made. Pierre Trudeau was fastidious about his parties. On this evening that planning was seriously challenged.

Pierre asked me to come early, because he wanted to be briefed on an animated discussion I had had with the Pakistani foreign minister regarding nuclear non-proliferation, and Pakistan's plans for a repro- cessing facility. The PM met me just inside the front door and, as we entered the living room, it was apparent that Farley had left a big deposit – a large mound of dog "moonies" – in the centre of the carpet. Pierre rushed away and returned himself with a dustpan, which he insisted on personally using to clear up the mess.

No sooner was this done than he spotted a large photograph of Indira Gandhi on a nearby table. He rushed over and removed it from view, shovelling it into a nearby drawer. At that point the peanuts and cashews showed up.

I can't remember whether they were under the sofa and he trod on them, or if they spread themselves all over when he was puffing up a cushion. In any event, I couldn't help by being impressed by the little- known domestic skills of our prime minister.

Chapter Eight

Notwithstanding Everything and All of Us

▶ HUGH FAULKNER
Cabinet colleague, 1965–79

*F*ollowing my election to the House of Commons in November 1965, I became focused on the Quebec and Confederation issue. The initiatives of Prime Minister Pearson had already taken hold as the best promise of getting at the political and constitutional issues raised by the "Quiet Revolution." So I talked to key spokesmen for the NDP and Conservative parties on constitutional questions.

We all agreed we had to open up the BNA Act for basic amendments, but also agreed we should consult Trudeau and Pelletier. I convened a lunch in the parliamentary restaurant.

Trudeau listened to us patiently, but in the end his comment was, "To open the Constitution is to open a can of worms, and I would be strongly opposed."

Pelletier agreed.

The rest is history.

▶ MARC LALONDE
Cabinet minister, 1972–84

When they talk about Trudeau's relationship with Robert Bourassa, the Quebec media have tended to concentrate on the remark made by Trudeau after a meeting with the provincial premier, in the middle seventies, after a luncheon they had together on top of the premier's office building in Quebec City (commonly called "The Bunker"). It was reported that Trudeau, on the way out, had told the media that Bourassa was a "*mangeur de hot-dogs*" (a hot-dog eater). In fact, Trudeau had spoken less disparagingly and said, when asked by the press how the luncheon had gone (he did not want to talk about the substance of their discussion), that the premier "seemed to prefer hot dogs." This was a well-known fact. Bourassa used to like to have a barbecue lunch every summer day on the roof of his building. The misquote nonetheless became part of the political folklore about Trudeau's scorn for everything having to do with Quebec, including its premier!

However, the press was right in perceiving that Trudeau did not have great trust in Bourassa, but I do not recall any journalist trying to

Canadian Press, Peter Bregg

So why do *you prefer hot dogs?*

identify the source of that falling out. In my view, this lack of trust all came out of the Victoria Charter fiasco in 1970.

When Bourassa became premier in 1970, Trudeau was well-disposed toward him and was looking forward to a positive relationship with him. This was specially so, after the continuous conflicts he had had with the Union Nationale of Daniel Johnson, although the situation had improved significantly under Johnson's successor, Jean-Jacques Bertrand. Unfortunately, Bertrand was only premier for a few months before he was defeated by Bourassa.

In spite of the subsequent public perception, Trudeau was never a great fan of constitutional reform. As he had stated frequently before he became prime minister, he saw it as a hornet's nest and as an easy escape route for Quebec politicians hoping to avoid addressing the real economic and social problems faced by the province. However, the issue had been opened by John Robarts, premier of Ontario, when he subsequently called the provincial premiers' Confederation for Tomorrow Conference in Toronto, in 1967. Prime Minister Pearson followed up with a federal-provincial conference in Ottawa in February 1968.

With the election of Bourassa, Trudeau's colleagues and advisers felt that there was an opportunity to make significant progress on the Constitution, if not to settle the issue. Trudeau maintained his reservations on the subject but, after months of internal pressure, he agreed to approve preliminary discussions – but with a major proviso: no constitutional conference would be called unless there was, beforehand, a firm agreement with Quebec about the amendments to be put forward at such a conference.

Contact was established with Bourassa, and an agreement was reached on the process. Bourassa designated himself and Julien Chouinard, an experienced public servant, who had been deputy minister of justice in Quebec before becoming secretary of the cabinet, to be the Quebec representatives. Trudeau appointed Gordon Robertson, Clerk of the Privy Council, and me to speak for the federal government. At our first meeting in Quebec City, Bourassa made it quite clear that our conversations were to remain completely confidential, and that we should not talk to any provincial civil servant or politician about the matter. He emphasized that he would take charge of the matter when the time was ripe, and told us not to worry; he would make sure that his cabinet would support what we had agreed upon.

Then started a series of meetings in Quebec City among the four of us (or sometimes we met with Chouinard alone), during the winter and spring of 1971, which led to a firm agreement between Bourassa and Trudeau. Bourassa personally initialled the proposed amendments to the Constitution. These amendments, if adopted, represented a major achievement for Quebec, which was obtaining the recognition of at least some of its "historical" demands: right of veto for Quebec on any future amendment; recognition of official language rights not only at the federal level but also in Ontario, Quebec, New Brunswick, and Newfoundland; in addition, a very innovative formula was to be introduced into the Constitution, whereby provincial attorneys general would, for the first time, be formally involved in the appointment of judges to the Supreme Court of Canada.

With such assurance from Bourassa, Trudeau agreed to call a federal-provincial conference for June 1971, and, in the meantime, bilateral discussions were initiated with the various provinces to try to obtain their support for the proposed package of amendments. After considerable arm-twisting, most provinces agreed to our proposal, Alberta and British Columbia being the only ones that refused to budge.

A couple of weeks before the conference, we suddenly got reports from Quebec that Bourassa was facing difficulty with his colleagues, and that further amendments, dealing in particular with social affairs, might be required. There is little doubt in my mind that some key Quebec officials dealing with federal-provincial matters were miffed at having been kept in the dark, and they were determined to throw their weight against the proposal. They convinced the new Minister of Social Affairs, Claude Castonguay, that he should oppose the project unless Quebec was to be given a major extension of its constitutional powers in social matters, a subject that had not been raised by Bourassa in our discussions. And, in the minutes of the Quebec cabinet meetings at that time, which were released to the public recently, Minister Jean-Paul L'Allier (now mayor of Quebec City) is reported as objecting that, if that proposal was accepted, there would be no way Quebec could later achieve independence!

Rather than pressing ahead, Bourassa started hesitating and twisting. Meanwhile, the press and the ultra-nationalists were informed of the developments. Claude Ryan, as editor of *Le Devoir*, wrote editorials opposing the project, and the ultras launched public gatherings to the same effect.

Needless to say, Trudeau was outraged by Bourassa's lack of backbone, but it was too late to cancel the conference. He hoped that, at the conference itself, it would be possible to assuage the two Western premiers and that, in the face of otherwise unanimous support from the other premiers, Bourassa would realize that he had a unique opportunity offered to him.

The conference took place; Bourassa arrived with his delegation, including Claude Castonguay, Julien Chouinard, and Claude Morin (deputy minister of Federal-Provincial Affairs). The conference was not an easy one but, in the end, the premiers of Alberta and British Columbia relented. The package was, word for word, what had been agreed upon with Bourassa. The latter, however, said that, while he was not opposed to the proposal, he would need additional time to discuss the matter with his cabinet.

I remember coming back on the plane and making bets on the chances of the deal being approved by Quebec. I, for one, was confident that Bourassa would take the bull by the horns and get his cabinet's support for what was an unprecedented victory for Quebec (one, in fact, that proved unachievable since, and, I dare say, could not be repeated in the future). Trudeau was of the contrary view and as usual, in the end, he proved to be right.

From that day on, Trudeau knew that he could not trust Bourassa, and he never did. I saw this clearly, a few months later, at the time of the October Crisis, when Bourassa pressed Trudeau for weeks to send the armed forces to Montreal and, then, to use the War Measures Act. Trudeau resisted and resisted, until it appeared clear that the federal government definitely needed to intervene. But Trudeau refused to do so until he had in hand an unequivocal document signed by Bourassa (or by his attorney general) that specifically requested such an intervention. I remember Trudeau telling me that he did not want to find himself in a situation where, when the soup would get hot, Bourassa would disappear in a cupboard or distance himself from any action taken by the federal government. Who could blame him for his circumspection?

More importantly, the failure of Quebec to endorse the Victoria Charter was a tragedy for Quebec and for Canada. I am convinced that, had it been enacted, the following thirty years would have been very different from, and much better than, those we have known.

▶ ALLAN BLAKENEY
Saskatchewan premier, 1971–82, who had many meetings
and conflicts with Trudeau over oil prices and the Constitution

I remember vividly my first dinner at 24 Sussex as premier of Saskatchewan, in the fall of 1971. Both Peter Lougheed and I were newly minted premiers. While we were the greenest, others were still in their first terms of office, including Richard Hatfield of New Brunswick, Bill Davis of Ontario, Ed Schreyer of Manitoba, Gerald Regan of Nova Scotia, Robert Bourassa of Quebec, and, of course, Mr. Trudeau.

During the course of the evening, talk turned to constitutional change and the fact that consensus for change – the Victoria Charter – agreed to the previous June, had shortly thereafter been shattered by the withdrawal of Quebec. At the dinner, Mr. Trudeau berated Mr. Bourassa with phrases like "If you had any guts we wouldn't have this problem" and (worse) words to that effect.

When the evening was over, Peter Lougheed and I left together. I don't remember exactly who said what, but clearly we were thinking the same way. It went something like this:

"Well, what did you think of that?"

"I was flabbergasted."

"I know if Trudeau had spoken to me like that, I would have said 'Thank you, Mr. Prime Minister. Thank you for your hospitality. I don't think I can be of any further use in our constitutional discussions. So I

Circled by premiers, at 24 Sussex Drive.

bid you, and everybody else, goodnight.' And I would have been out of there." On this, we both agreed.

Sometime after 1976, a similar event took place at a dinner for premiers at 24 Sussex. Mr. Trudeau taunted Mr. Lévesque. Only this time, Mr. Lévesque replied in kind. They began insulting each other in ever-more-rapid French. And then they looked about the table and realized the rest of us were not able to fully appreciate their verbal sallies. So they kindly switched to English, thereby allowing us to more fully comprehend the barbs being tossed.

We learned a lot about each other at those dinners, not the least of which was that leaders from Quebec – when addressing each other – are often long on invective and short on civility.

▶ EDWARD R. SCHREYER
Manitoba premier, 1969–77, and Governor General, 1979–84

I recall well one of the many occasions when all ten premiers were invited to the prime minister's residence. After dinner had been served, discussion was well under way regarding oil production and pricing issues. There was, at the end, a brief lull.

As we began to chat casually, a young boy of about five entered the room. He looked about tentatively at this small room full of new and strange faces. However, his uncertainty vanished quickly when he recognized one person, and he ran over to him and sat on his knee. It was René Lévesque that young Justin ran to, whom Canadians knew as premier of Quebec, the separatist and rival to Prime Minister Trudeau on most constitutional issues of that decade.

The symbolism of it all was truly left to our individual imaginations.

▶ ROY McMURTRY
Ontario attorney general, 1975–85; High Commissioner to the Court of St. James, 1985–88

My association with Pierre Elliott Trudeau during my ten years in the cabinet of Ontario premier Bill Davis was largely related to the patriation of the Constitution process. Conversations with the prime minister ranging from, say, federal budgets or the constitutionality of the anti-inflation initiatives of 1976, seldom seemed to strike a meaningful chord with Pierre Trudeau. I recall that one of his very rare visits to Queen's Park took place shortly after the delivery of a federal budget. When I made a comment on the budget, I was met with one of Pierre's famous shrugs and the unenthusiastic observation that "budgets come and budgets go, life goes on."

Pierre Trudeau's return to office in 1980, after the brief Joe Clark premiership and a few months before the Quebec sovereignty-association referendum of June 1980, clearly re-energized him in relation to constitutional reform after the last-minute failure of the First Ministers to reach an agreement in 1971. He had promised Quebec meaningful constitutional reform after the successful No campaign in 1980, and he became strongly committed to the project.

As a participant in many of the meetings, I became fascinated by the dynamic of the rivalry between Pierre and René Lévesque. Trudeau took many opportunities to remind Lévesque of his defeat in the 1980 referendum, while René could be quite adept at needling the prime minister in return. Often, in a loud whisper, Lévesque would refer to Trudeau as "The Princeling." But both René and Pierre were determined never to appear provoked by the other, and an exchange of verbal barbs would usually end in a frosty silence.

Curiously, it was the mutual enthusiasm of Trudeau and Lévesque for the referendum process – and the competition that another referendum would provide for the two aging warriors – that broke the constitutional impasse. However, the seven premiers who had bonded with Lévesque in their opposition to the patriation proposals were opposed to any federal referendum that might be conducted in their provinces in relation to constitutional reform. For them, a national federal referendum would enable the federal government to ignore the views of the provincial governments. René Lévesque's embrace of the referendum process for constitutional reform ultimately resulted in his isolation when the historical accord was reached in November 1981.

It is, of course, well known that Pierre Trudeau could be both quite aggressive and a little condescending when there were differences of opinion. While Pierre enjoyed a good argument, it could sometimes be quite counterproductive, particularly when a high degree of diplomacy was required in relation to the patriation issues. As we approached the First Ministers' Conference of November 1981, my conversations with my provincial colleagues across the country indicated that there was a real possibility of a breakthrough in relation to the Constitution logjam that had persisted, even though the "gang of eight" premiers who opposed the Trudeau proposals were publicly still united in their opposition.

Several days before the First Ministers' Conference in November, I arranged a lunch with Jean Chrétien in Ottawa to review possible strategies. I advised Jean of my cautious optimism, but expressed my concerns with respect to the prime minister's argumentative style at this highly sensitive time in federal-provincial relations. I urged Jean to convince Pierre of the importance of avoiding verbal confrontations during the meeting, even when faced with the provocative styles of some of the premiers.

I well recall Chrétien conceding that "the Boss sure like to argue [pause] and he win a lot of arguments," but after a few moments of reflection he stated, "but the Boss can lose the war."

In fact, Pierre Trudeau was a model chair during the critical meetings that took place during the week of November 3, 1981. He generally ignored the barbs of some of the premiers and the only indications of his impatience occurred when he would speak of adjourning a session, simply so that he could have his daily swim. Later in the week, though, he did reveal his growing impatience and frustration when he threatened to end the First Ministers' meeting and hold national referendums on both a proposed constitutional amending formula and the entrenchment of a charter of rights. (It was Lévesque's embrace of the referendum proposal that led to his break with the other members of the "gang of eight.") As a result, an agreement was reached between the federal government and nine provinces in the early hours of November 6, 1981.

However, it was with considerable reluctance that Trudeau agreed to a "notwithstanding clause" in the Constitution that would allow legislatures to override a decision of the courts with respect to the entrenched Charter. The important and (in my view, principled) compromise that led to the insertion of the "notwithstanding clause" in the Charter was essential to the obtaining of the agreement between the federal government and nine provinces.

Nevertheless, this compromise was a major irritation for the prime minister and he did not conceal his disappointment. In fact, for a few moments before the signing of the historic agreement, I thought that Pierre Trudeau's irritation might scuttle the accord at the last moment. In tabling the document outlining the agreement for signature by Canada's premiers, he expressed his personal displeasure with the notwithstanding clause and his disappointment that "we could not do better."

Fortunately, the document was signed by all of the First Ministers with the exception of Lévesque. After the signatures, both Trudeau and Lévesque stomped out of the room, their individual displeasure obviously fuelled by very different reasons.

▶ PETER LOUGHEED
Alberta premier, who, like Trudeau, remained in
his position for a substantial period (1971–83)

I have pondered for some time the request that I provide an anecdote relating to my relationship with Pierre Trudeau. Unfortunately, most of my memories of my dealings with Mr. Trudeau are of a very serious nature, because we looked upon our country in two very different ways.

I saw Canada then – and see it now – as a federal system responding to the regions through its provincial governments, with all coming together on a unified basis – for the benefit of all Canadians. Mr. Trudeau saw Canada much differently. He visualized it as more of a centralized nation, less fractious, and presenting a more unified approach. Both of these views of Canada have validity, and I respected Mr. Trudeau's intellect and leadership very much.

The only incident I can recall that might fit was when he and I were consulting on serious energy issues, and I visited him at Harrington Lake in the summer of 1980. Mr. Trudeau suggested the two of us go out onto the lake in a rather dilapidated rowboat.

My aide, Jim Seymour, inquired as to what should be done if we did not return. Mr. Trudeau immediately responded that, if we were lost, "all of Canada would cheer."

▶ ALLAN BLAKENEY
Saskatchewan premier, 1971–82, who had many meetings
and conflicts with Trudeau over oil prices and the Constitution

*P*ierre Trudeau could be testy when challenges to his ideas could be regarded as challenges to the office of prime minister. I recall the dinner that preceded the Federal-Provincial Conference of September 1980. The dinner was held at the Lester B. Pearson Building on Sussex Drive and was presided over by Governor General Ed Schreyer.

The date was September 7, my fifty-fifth birthday. A birthday cake was produced, and good wishes were expressed all around. Those were about the only terms of endearment expressed during the evening.

Sterling Lyon, premier of Manitoba, was chair of the Council of Premiers. He was putting forward the idea that the conference, which was to begin the next morning, should have two chairmen: the prime minister and himself, representing the premiers. He was putting the idea forward vigorously, as was his wont, but some of us doubted whether it was tactically sound to launch a conference with the federal government by an approach that could be seen as a baiting of our likely adversary – with whom we hoped to reach some kind of compromise. Mr. Trudeau was getting more and more irritated at what he clearly regarded as a discourteous affront to his position as prime minister, and indeed, an idea a little short of *lèse-majesté.*

Finally, before dessert was finished and before the governor general had left, Mr. Trudeau stood up and strode out of the room. The prime minister had reacted to Premier Lyon's perceived discourtesy by allowing himself to appear disrespectful of the position of Governor General.

Subtlety and deftness of touch were not Premier Lyon's outstanding attributes, and on this occasion neither were they Mr. Trudeau's.

▶ MICHAEL KIRBY
*Assistant principal secretary, 1974–76; secretary to the cabinet
for federal-provincial relations, 1980–81; and deputy clerk of
the Privy Council, 1981–82*

*T*he date: January 30, 1981. The time: 4 p.m. The location: the Prime Minister's Office on the third floor in the southwest corner of the Centre Block. The issue for discussion at the meeting: Should the rights of aboriginal Canadians be entrenched in the Constitution, through the Charter of Rights and Freedoms?

The participants in the meeting: the prime minister; the minister of justice, Jean Chrétien; the secretary to the cabinet, Michael Pitfield; the deputy minister of justice, Roger Tassé; and myself, secretary to the cabinet for federal-provincial relations.

The context: In January 1981, there was limited political support for the patriation of the Constitution and the inclusion of the Charter of Rights and Freedoms. Only the federal government, the federal Liberal caucus, and the Progressive Conservative governments of Bill Davis in Ontario and Richard Hatfield in New Brunswick were on side. Negotiations with the other eight provinces had broken off, and they had turned to the courts to block unilateral federal action.

At the same time, the federal government had been seeking to ensure the support of the British government, led by Margaret Thatcher, for a resolution of the Parliament of Canada to patriate the Constitution with a charter of rights, even if it was backed only by the federal government of Canada, and by New Brunswick and Ontario.

Mrs. Thatcher was personally committed to do whatever the Parliament of Canada requested. However, she was concerned that a significant number of British MPs would be likely to vote against the resolution, because they believed that it lacked support in Western Canada. This was because the federal Liberal caucus contained only two western members of Parliament. Mrs. Thatcher was not concerned about opposition from the Province of Quebec, because the federal Liberal caucus contained seventy-four of the seventy-five MPs from Quebec, which could be taken as an indication of political support for the resolution from the people of that province.

As a result of Mrs. Thatcher's concern, in the late fall of 1980, I was asked by the prime minister to see if it would be possible to get the support of the federal NDP caucus. There were thirty-four NDP MPs: seven from Ontario, seven from Manitoba, seven from Saskatchewan, twelve from British Columbia, and one from the Northwest Territories. If the NDP caucus could be persuaded to support the resolution, it would bring on side twenty-seven western and northern MPs.

After protracted negotiations with the NDP leader, Ed Broadbent, and several members of his caucus, notably Ian Waddell and Nelson Riis, it was agreed that all but the Saskatchewan NDP MPs would support the resolution if – and only if – it included a clause entrenching Aboriginal rights in the Constitution. The Saskatchewan MPs would not back it in any case because of continued opposition from the premier of the province, Allan Blakeney.

The purpose of the meeting in the prime minister's office was to decide if the federal government would agree to the negotiated deal. The prime minister began by asking for the opinions of those in the room. Roger Tassé forcefully argued that, since the courts had never determined the scope of the existing rights of Aboriginal Canadians, he could not support an entrenchment of rights whose details remained unspecified.

On the other hand, I argued that the Aboriginal-rights clause was essential to gain NDP support and hence ensure passage through the British Parliament. Moreover, since only existing Aboriginal rights, whatever they were, were to be entrenched, and no new rights created, it was difficult for me to understand why the proposed agreement with the NDP created such a problem for the Justice Department.

As was his style, the prime minister encouraged a vigorous exchange among the other participants in the meeting. After allowing the debate to continue for a while, the prime minister, who had said nothing to that point, concluded the discussion. He looked at the four people on the other side of his desk and began by observing that there was considerable validity to both sides of the debate.

Then, showing his concern over the problems faced by Aboriginal Canadians, the prime minister reflected at length on how poorly Aboriginal Canadians had been served by politicians of all parties since 1867. Finally, he concluded with these words: "How could judges possibly do worse?"

The meeting ended, and Jean Chrétien went directly to appear before the Joint House–Senate Committee on the Constitution. He began his testimony by saying: "I am pleased on behalf of the government to say that the Aboriginal rights of the Aboriginal people of Canada will be entrenched in the Constitution." Thus, section 35 of the Charter of Rights and Freedoms – the so-called Aboriginal-rights clause – was born.

▶ JUDY EROLA
Cabinet minister, 1980–84

The mood around the cabinet table was festive. After a long, tortuous process, the patriation of the Constitution was finally a reality. The cabinet meeting was to be a scene of celebration, following the agreement (earlier that morning) with nine of the ten premiers on an amending formula, as well as on the Charter of Rights and Freedoms. True, Quebec was still an issue as a result of the evening before, "The Night of the Long Knives." But no one had paid much, if any, attention to something else that had been excised by the knives: Section 28 of the Charter.

The section reads simply: "Notwithstanding anything in this Charter, the rights and freedoms referred to in it are guaranteed equally to male and female persons."

As the minister responsible for the status of women, the excision had not escaped my attention. I was in shock. This had been one of the most studied and deliberated sections of the Charter, fought for hard by women across the country. Years of briefs, hearings, public meetings, and intensive lobbying had produced Section 28, which was included in a draft passed unanimously by both Houses.

The new accord contained a rider giving the provinces the power to override certain rights set out in the Charter. The effect of the rider could have been to render Section 28 inoperative.

So, I rained on the cabinet parade.

In a cold anger, I protested the override. It was unacceptable, I said, and the women of Canada would protest. We had broken faith with 52 per cent of the population of the country. The cabinet room became quiet, with only the voice of the prime minister saying, "But we did not insist on the override; it was the provinces."

The room remained quiet, as The Boss and I engaged in a heated debate. The other ministers watched and listened. They knew they were mere bystanders who loved a good fight at the cabinet table, and they had front-row seats. It was always that way in cabinet when Mr. Trudeau challenged a minister.

Anger sustained me, but logic carried the day. I informed the prime minister that I would rally the necessary troops and convince the premiers that their power to override Section 28 was totally unacceptable. The Boss hastened to point out that the consensus reached had his endorsement, and therefore carried with it the support of cabinet.

He was more than a little astonished – indeed annoyed – that I would suggest such a plan. My protest would be seen as a breach of cabinet solidarity. Nonetheless, I pressed on. I would be discreet. My role would be strictly behind the scenes. I would not make a public statement. I would build on the momentum that had brought us this far. I had incredible confidence that the network of women in the country could take on the premiers. I outlined my plans, and the prime minister listened.

Though I would be an invisible minister, my offices would coordinate the campaign and communicate with the Minister of Justice, Jean Chrétien (who was less than enthusiastic). The network was already in place. It was a matter of convincing the premiers that they had underestimated the importance of Section 28 to the women of Canada. We had powerful forces in every province, women who were connected to every political party, and they would not hesitate to use that power.

The prime minister was more than a little sarcastic when he replied, "What makes you think you and these women can do what years of federal-provincial negotiations have failed to do?"

With icy anger, I then explained to him exactly how we would pull it off. There was no doubt in my mind that we would win the fight. If my role became known – and therefore a breach of cabinet solidarity had occurred – my resignation would be expected. So The Boss reluctantly agreed to my plan.

Ten days later, Jean Chrétien (who took all the credit) announced in the House of Commons that the provinces had agreed unequivocally to Section 28. The Boss never made reference to the issue again. (However, it did not escape my attention that the nomination of Bertha Wilson to the Supreme Court followed fairly swiftly thereafter.)

There were many doubters around the table that day. Was the prime minister one of them? As we left that cabinet meeting, we met face to face. He winked.

▶ LOUISE DUHAMEL
Assistant press secretary, 1980–84

Mr. Trudeau taught me to stand up for myself and for what I believed in. He taught me this not so much with words but through his own actions, both political and personal. My favourite story about him reflects, in my view, the very core of his strength of character and of his individuality. This is the Trudeau I liked the most: the rebel who would not conform, or compromise himself, just to fit in.

I was assigned to escort Mr. Trudeau to the 1982 Press Gallery Dinner. This was the time of federal-provincial conferences, knives in the night, and preparations for the Queen's visit on the occasion of the official patriation of Canada's Constitution and the adoption of the Charter of Rights and Freedoms.

CBC Television's *The Journal*, with Barbara Frum and Mary-Lou Finlay, had started airing in January 1982, right in the middle of one of the biggest fights the provincial governments ever had with the federal government: unilateral patriation of Canada's Constitution. Fed-bashing was everywhere, and the premiers were outraged at Trudeau's arrogance when he threatened to proceed on his own, without the provinces' consent.

Premiers Blakeney, Lévesque, Lougheed, Peckford, all ten of them used *The Journal*, and Barbara Frum, to air their grievances and outrage. She was a tough, hard-nosed journalist. She was confrontational, fast-paced, and she would cut off her victims in mid-sentence to shoot another well-directed, stinging question at them. It made for hard television to watch, but it was also good journalism.

As the succession of premiers she interviewed grew over the months before patriation, a pattern developed: she would battle with them for eight to ten minutes, and then she would kindly dismiss them with a "Thank you very much, Premier [fill in the name]," The interviewee's answer would always be "You're welcome, Barbara." It became her trademark and signature.

By the time the Parliamentary Press Gallery dinner was held, *The Journal* had been airing for three months, and the Press Gallery executive decided the theme of the dinner's show that year would be *The Journal*. To my surprise, after the dinner was over, Mr. Trudeau decided that he wanted to stay for the show, which usually started quite late, around 11:30 p.m. I sat beside him, in the second row, and watched this marvellous spoof put on by reporters. They had built an imitation CBC studio onstage, with a large screen, complete with two women reporters playing Barbara Frum and Mary-Lou Finlay, who interviewed other reporters acting as premiers.

As Mr. Trudeau watched all this, the reporters in the show imitated Ms. Frum's sign-off, and every "premier" they interviewed would end by repeating "You're welcome, Barbara" three or four times. Mr. Trudeau, who didn't get the joke, turned to me and said, in French, "Louise, I don't understand . . . what does the repetition of 'You're welcome, Barbara' mean?" I explained to the prime minister that it was the way she always finished her interviews. His reaction was to give me his famous "I'm not impressed" shrug.

Fast-forward two weeks later: the PM was giving his first interview to Barbara Frum. It was held at the end of the day, in the Commonwealth Room in the Centre Block, and my colleague Brian Smith and I were assigned to assist Mr. Trudeau.

Mr. Trudeau came in and sat down in one of the two Queen Anne chairs they had brought down from Toronto for the interview. Ms. Frum informed him he was in the wrong chair, could he change please. Needless to say, Mr. Trudeau was not amused! After three years with him as an assistant press secretary, I had become an expert at reading his body language, and I could tell it spelled trouble!

I knew the interview would not go well, but it went worse than I imagined. Barbara Frum was confrontational and aggressive, and he responded by being petulant, abrasive, and feisty. As they finished, Ms. Frum said, "Thank you very much, Prime Minister." The prime minister nodded and smiled. Then he started to get up from his chair to leave.

"Oh! No, no, no, Prime Minister," Ms. Frum said. "When I say 'Thank you very much, Prime Minister,' you have to say 'You're welcome, Barbara.'"

And, with both her hands on his shoulders, she pushed him back into his chair. There was a huge silence in the room, as if an arctic wind had just invaded the atmosphere.

I will never, never forget the steely look in Mr. Trudeau's eyes. At that moment, I learned a lot from him, and I learned a lot about him. He actually remembered the Press Gallery dinner show, and there was no way this prime minister was going to do the same as every premier (or anybody else for that matter) and participate in "signing" Barbara Frum's show! And there was no way he was going to say "You're welcome, Barbara" to a journalist who had just put him through the ringer. Pierre Trudeau was not going to follow the rules just because it was the thing to do to please somebody.

After she had pushed him down, she told the cameras to start rolling again, and she repeated, "Thank you very much, Prime Minister." This time, he nodded and omitted the smile. She started to ask him again to say . . .

"Well," he interrupted with that quiet, determined voice, his eyes just shooting darts at her, "I won't say it, and that's it."

He left the room with Brian Smith. And like prime ministers do, he left his assistant press secretary with the task of picking up the pieces.

▶ BILL DAVIS
Ontario premier, 1971–85

On the weekend leading up to the Charter of Rights and constitutional negotiations in November 1981, I agreed to meet with Prime Minister Trudeau at 24 Sussex. The purpose was to review strategy and critical issues. I assumed the PM had also met with Mr. Hatfield, the premier of New Brunswick, the other Conservative premier who was offering the federal government support in this initiative.

The prime minister had his associate clerk of the cabinet for federal-provincial relations, Michael Kirby, with him. I had brought Hugh Segal, Ontario's associate secretary of cabinet for federal-provincial relations with me. At around three in the afternoon, we gathered at the back of the prime minister's home, in a sunroom that was decorated with African spears and masks (!). The prime minister met us at the door in a wide Peter Storm sweater, jeans, and clogs. Mr. Kirby, Mr. Segal, and I were all wearing jackets and ties.

As the meeting progressed, the sunroom began to dim, as the November sun began to set. There was no light on in the room, and the prime minister and I continued talking in a progressively darkening room. This was not a problem for us, I hasten to say, as we both had staff to refer to the notes and keep minutes. The fact that it was getting darker for *them* didn't bother Pierre or me. In fact, as both Segal and Kirby were straining to see their briefing books and keep notes, Pierre winked at me, as if to say, "Let's see how long it takes for one of them to break."

Mr. Trudeau's staff were always far more reverential of him than were my staff of me. Finally, Segal broke the Silence of the Darkened Aides.

"Prime Minister, I am sorry to interrupt," he offered. "We don't work in the dark at Queen's Park as well as the federal government does here in Ottawa. Could I turn on a light?"

"By all means, Mr. Segal," the prime minister responded. "What took you so long?"

Chapter Nine

Longer Views, Differing Angles

▶ CONRAD BLACK

Chairman of Argus Corporation, publisher, and historical author

*P*ierre Trudeau first came to national prominence when Prime Minister Lester Pearson relied on him to respond to Quebec's bold request for a comprehensive redistribution of powers between the federal and provincial governments.

It was at the federal-provincial conference of 1968 that Premier Daniel Johnson first laid down this gauntlet. At the earlier Confederation of Tomorrow conference convened by Ontario's premier, John Robarts, in the autumn of 1967, Johnson had revealed a sweeping, but sensible, recitation of his proposals for constitutional reform and concluded by saying that for decades his predecessors of both parties had been asked what Quebec wanted.

"This is what Quebec wants. What does Canada want?" It was an effective performance.

Several months later, Trudeau, as the new minister of justice of Canada, responded that what was important was not the distribution of powers between governments, but the entrenchment of the rights of all citizens. At the time, I thought this was a brilliant stroke, and I still do. It certainly astonished Johnson, who was a man of great political agility. Presented in the spare, ascetic style Trudeau employed on important

occasions, it appealed to the idealistic bedrock of the nationalist movement of Quebec, and to the logic of most English-speaking Canadians.

In a stroke, successive Quebec leaders – Duplessis, Lesage, and
Johnson himself – seemed mere office-holders, seeking greater prerog-
atives and jurisdiction for themselves, while Trudeau appeared the
champion of the rights of man. Trudeau was Jean-Jacques Rousseau
crusading for universal rights; Johnson was another politician apparently seeking more for himself.

On the basis of this exchange, which became quite acerbic, Trudeau
started his quick rise to the succession to Pearson and continued his
long struggle with the nationalists in Quebec. When Johnson died in
September 1968, the nationalist torch in Quebec, which had been held
for decades by conservatives – Mercier, Bourassa, Groulx, Duplessis, and
Johnson – passed to René Lévesque and the Left.

The conservative nationalists, of course, had a natural brake on their
ambitions: they believed in the church, the courts, and even, up to a point,
Confederation. Lévesque's new siren song, on the other hand, assured the
absorption of most Quebec nationalists into a separatist movement.

Trudeau foresaw that this might happen, though he had no reason
to imagine Johnson would die at the age of fifty-three, but Trudeau
was quite content to do battle with the separatists directly, rather than
dealing with non-separatist nationalists, such as the Union Nationale of
Duplessis and Johnson.

This struggle continued for years, until the great referendum of
1980. Trudeau promised to repatriate the amendment of the Canadian
Constitution and entrench the rights of all citizens in the Constitution
if Quebec rejected Lévesque's option of sovereignty and continued association with Canada. Trudeau saw (as he coolly and presciently told me
several times) that Quebec would never vote for independence, unless it
could be sold as the joys of independence with the continued security of
federal protection.

In this, the most vital question he had to face in his public career,
Trudeau was correct. He narrowed the issue to a struggle between federalists and separatists, disposing of the Bob Stanfield–Dalton Camp
formula of "Two Nations," and the ambiguous Union Nationale formula
of "Quebec First," in favour of a straight contest between the conflicting

options. Johnson used to say Quebec would administer "every kick to Ottawa except the last one." Jacques Parizeau, with refreshing candour, acknowledged that, in presenting an endless sequence of demands for constitutional concessions, Quebec was trying to "tear the Canadian flag so far that it would be easier to tear it the rest of the way than to stitch it back."

Trudeau did not shrink from the confrontation that would be necessary to stop the insidious process of yielding jurisdiction to Quebec, enduring the cries of relief from the other provinces – and then their solemn assertions that, since all the provinces must be treated equally, they must have the same rights as Quebec.

In my social contacts with Trudeau, which were not extensive but did include seven or eight lunches or dinners between us or with one or two others present, I tried to press him gently on whether he really believed what he was saying. He was too cagey to acknowledge that he did think jurisdictional divisions were important and that he had been a little flamboyant in championing the rights of man over the impersonality of layers of government. He was a contrarian, and as his public demeanour often demonstrated, he was even suspicious of groups that were too admiring of him. He resolutely defended his position, but with that slightly ironic countenance the Canadian public came to know. He was much more endearing in person than on television, and he possessed the sort of high intelligence that was stimulated, rather than affronted, by a good verbal joust.

I was always opposed to Trudeau's steady move to a more leftist, interventionist state, and his attempt to distinguish Canada from the United States because of its more ample social programs, and more socialistic government generally. But the greatest challenge he faced was to prevent the secession of Quebec, and the combination of promotion of biculturalism ("*Maîtres chez nous mais pour tout le Canada*," he said at the convention that elevated him to the Liberal leadership in 1968), the outright acquisition of Quebec votes for federalism with transfer payments, and the ruse of replacing a preoccupation with jurisdictional divisions with the elevation of individual rights achieved this most important of all goals for his long tenure as prime minister.

I had read almost all of what he wrote in *Cité libre*, and, while his antagonism to Duplessis was excessive (as he privately admitted when I knew him more than twenty years later), he was an elegant writer (which made his last book the more disappointing for its banality). Once he was familiar with the burdens and restraints of high office, it was difficult to separate Trudeau the sly political tactician from the upholder of the principles he had championed as an academic and journalist.

Yet he dealt effectively with the greatest problem of his time, which was a mortal threat to the country, and because there was no one else on the federal scene who would have been credible trying to do so, I think Trudeau must be judged a successful, as well as an important prime minister, whatever his other policy shortcomings. Apart from that, I always found him a delightful conversationalist and a gracious host, though perhaps slow to reach for the bill in a restaurant, even when we were there on his invitation.

▶ MALCOLM FRASER
Australian prime minister, 1975–83

*P*ierre Trudeau was out of the mold of other Canadian prime ministers. In some ways he came from a different world; in others, he followed the tradition of Lester Pearson. He lived and governed alongside a giant. He was able to keep that giant as a friend. He attended meetings in Jamaica with another friend, Michael Manley – at the time not a friend of America's.

He contributed to discussions with Helmut Schmidt that brought the German chancellor closer to understanding the problems of the Third World. He could advocate improved relations with Cuba, enjoy Fidel Castro's company, and still keep his giant neighbour as a friend.

Many Canadian prime ministers have understood the need to dance with two partners, conventionally with the United States, unconventionally with the broader world. Pierre probably did more than the others to advance a global comprehension of Third World problems, but he was unable to persuade the G7 that those problems demanded action and not words. The problems that beset Trudeau's world and which occupied so much of his mind, and time, are still our problems today.

Canada has lost Pierre's skill, is even closer to the giant neighbour, being a member of NAFTA, but has managed to avoid the illicit pressures of joining the "Coalition of the Willing" in the Iraq war.

Canada, more than most countries, has had to fight for identity. There is the internal fight to which Pierre contributed so much and the external one, the economic and cultural pressure of the United States.

Pierre will be remembered: an unusual man, a great humanist, a great patriot.

▶ RICHARD O'HAGAN
First met Trudeau in 1965; communications adviser, 1975–79

*T*hat Pierre Elliott Trudeau was an uncommon man is not in dispute. It is his ranking as prime minister that is subject to debate: to some, he is great; to others, he is the greatest; still others take the opposite view, some vehemently so. In fact, it is a debate that will outlive many of us. I doubt that Trudeau himself would have been much impressed by discourse centred on his historical ranking or status. Divided opinion, he would have said, was a natural consequence of taking stands. He would certainly not claim to have been right, or necessarily wise, in all matters. He had a certain idea of Canada, and he acted upon it. How else, he would ask, should a self-respecting politician behave?

But Pierre Trudeau, as most of us now recognize, was no ordinary politician. I first met him when he arrived in Ottawa in 1965, a newly minted MP – sandalled, cravat-wearing, Mercedes-driving. The then-prime minister, Mike Pearson (for whom I worked), knew at once that he had a promising new talent in his ranks. He also knew – perceptive as always – that this star-in-the-making needed to be introduced carefully into the partisan political life. Parliament had its own hazards, and so did the environment around it; Pearson had in mind the media particularly.

The prime minister asked me to meet Trudeau and chat with him about what he might expect as a new (and distinctive) face on the Ottawa scene. I wondered how our budding star might react to such tutoring, but he was modest, attentive, and appreciative. He was already,

The newly minted MP
with Mike Pearson.

of course, much discussed, and the object of intense interest. So my wife, Wanda, and I arranged two or three smallish supper parties at our home as a way of acquainting him with some of the more influential denizens of the Parliamentary Press Gallery, along with selected others. Some had known him slightly, others not at all. The parties were a success and Trudeau entered fully into the spirit of the occasions; without abandoning his natural reserve, he was engaged and charming. I had wondered how ready he would be to give up a Saturday night at home in Montreal for social duty in Ottawa. But there was no hesitation. He had already shifted gears to accommodate a new phase in his life.

He was a celebrity, yes, and a highly individualistic one. But he also demonstrated that he was a quick study and took his parliamentary responsibilities seriously. Mr. Pearson would appoint him to the Canadian delegation to the UN, and make him his parliamentary secretary. The leap into cabinet as minister of justice would come in 1967.

I left Ottawa for Washington toward the end of 1966, as senior public-affairs officer at the embassy. A year or so later, my erstwhile student of Ottawa's peculiarities, continuing his rapid advance, would become prime minister, the role in which I would begin seeing him on his official visits to Washington. His cachet there (with everyone except possibly President Richard Nixon) made him a magnet for columnists, TV interviewers, and ambitious hostesses.

I was summoned back to Ottawa in 1975, first to work in the secretariat that administered the controversial wage-and-price controls, and then into the Prime Minister's Office as senior communications adviser. Those were not easy times for him; his marriage was coming apart in a highly public way, and things were not going well politically. Yet the lasting memory I have of him – astonishing in the circumstances – is that of a composed, measured, and focused head of government.

Just before his electoral defeat of 1979, I left the PMO for a job in business. Then miraculously, in 1980 the Liberals were re-elected and he was prime minister again. This was the year of the first referendum on Quebec independence; he campaigned hard and, for the separatists, he became enemy number one. We were not out of touch, although I saw rather less of him in his last four years in office. Oddly, it was in the more relaxed and mellowed years of his retirement that our relationship took on a different cast, and if anything grew stronger. I was proud to be seen by him as a trusted confidante.

Pierre Trudeau was *the* Canadian public figure of his time, unmatched in profile, scintillation, and provocativeness. That says a lot, since "his time" was a period that embraced such outsized personalities as John Diefenbaker and Brian Mulroney, not to mention Jean Chrétien. His prescient mentor and predecessor, Lester Bowles "Mike" Pearson, did not fully qualify for this category, his appeal flowing more from an understated modesty, although he was Canada's first – and still its only – genuine diplomatic star. Trudeau's star power was of an altogether different magnitude overshadowing all the others. He was a surpassing celebrity, recognized worldwide, the only one we've had so far.

Since he was so emphatically a man of the twentieth century, it was somehow fitting that Pierre Trudeau's life ended before the millennium itself ran out. In the course of his public life, he was much reviled, even detested – and this was not just in the West, where he seemed to have a gift for raising hackles, or among his own compatriots in Quebec, but across a wide spectrum of Canadians. His personal style contributed to those reactions: plain speaking, salted sometimes with defiant, combative

*Just a regular jean-clad guy
on Parliament Hill.*

gestures. And the causes he promoted – bilingualism and an integrated Canada with a strong central government – were not popular everywhere. But as a classic outsider, new to partisan politics, the legislative process, and public governance, he managed to do a good many things his way: he brought home the Constitution and entrenched a charter of rights and freedoms, among others. And well into retirement he continued to fight for his idea of Canada. And more than we realized, that resonated.

We didn't seem to know how deeply we felt about him, how much we respected him, until his death, a landmark event in our national evolution. He was *sui generis*, and some think we will never see his like again. Yet, I suspect Trudeau himself, with his characteristic modesty, would caution against such a prognosis.

▶ JEAN CHRÉTIEN
Cabinet minister, 1967–86, and prime minister, 1993–2003

*L*ong before I ever met Pierre Trudeau, I had known of him as a union lawyer and controversial intellectual, whose financial independence and lack of political ambition allowed him to always speak his mind. Though I admired him as a writer, I assumed he was trouble – not a trouble-maker, perhaps, but close – and I didn't think he would have an easy time getting elected as an MP. I even expressed that reservation to Prime Minister Pearson when he warned me that the entry of Jean Marchand, Gérard Pelletier, and Pierre Trudeau into federal politics in 1965 might delay my own appointment to the cabinet. As it turned out, though Pierre wanted to be elected in a French-speaking constituency, everyone thought he was too provocative, and he had to be more or less imposed on the English-speaking riding of Mount Royal.

In those days, the Quebec caucus of the Liberal Party was divided in the minds of the press and the public between the Old Guard and the New Guard. It was a silly sort of classification, but there wasn't much we could do about it. One day, I was asked to nominate a member of the so-called New Guard to be chairman of the caucus. We lost by one vote, because Trudeau decided to abstain. I wasn't too happy when I went to explain the situation to him.

"But, Jean," he said, "I didn't know either of these guys. I listened to their speeches and the one seemed just as good as the other. I didn't care who won. There was no difference, so I didn't vote."

Boy, I thought, does this guy ever need to learn a bit about politics.

Within a year, at a press conference following a meeting of federal and provincial finance ministers, he pulled me over to stand immediately behind Mitchell Sharp, so that both our faces would be on TV and in the newspapers to show that Quebeckers were involved in the important economic issues of Canada.

"You sure learn quick," I told him.

Even though he enjoyed a rapid rise as Pearson's parliamentary secretary and then minister of justice, no one saw him as a future leader of the party until after his famous line: "The state has no business in the bedrooms of the nation." And there was his dramatic clash with Premier Daniel Johnson on television in early 1968.

Before the 1968 leadership convention, I had already committed to Mitchell Sharp. I had assumed that, if there was going to be a candidate from Quebec, it would be Jean Marchand.

Trudeau came to ask, very humbly, for my support.

"I'm sorry, Pierre, but it's your own fault," I told him. "You once told me, when we were working together with Mitchell, that you thought he would make a very good prime minister if he could ever learn to speak some French. Well, Mitchell has learned to speak some French, so I'm just following your advice."

I did assure Pierre, though, that he could count on my support on the second ballot if Mr. Sharp was doing badly. When Mitchell decided to drop out before the convention, I was delegated to phone Pierre at his mother's house to organize a meeting between the two camps. Mitchell's support proved pivotal, because it sent a signal that Trudeau was now acceptable to the so-called party establishment.

Pierre's nonconformist style, his newness, his outspokenness, his intelligence, and his athletic skill, everything about him struck a chord with the Canadian people, and the wildfire was unbelievable. But, unlike some other one-day wonders I've seen during my career, *his* wildfire was based on substance. Sudden popularity cannot be sustained if its basis is weak, and big expectations are always in danger of producing big disappointments. But, in Trudeau's case, his strength was the real thing.

Though Pierre could be extremely charming, small talk wasn't one of his strong points. Once, I remember, we were on a plane together with nothing to do but sign documents, and I tried to get a conversation going.

"It's still raining outside," I said, peering out the window.

"Of course, if it's raining, it's outside," he replied. And that was the end of that conversation.

Another time, however, when we were sitting beside each other in the House of Commons, he surprised me by saying, "You know what I did last night?"

I couldn't imagine, and it was totally unlike him ever to talk about himself in such a proud way.

"I did a backflip on a trampoline for the first time in my life! I just had to tell someone."

I can't say I became a close confidant of his, in part because of the difference in our ages. But I liked him, I respected him, and we worked well together. When he gave me the job of minister of Indian Affairs, I rarely bothered him with problems and he never interfered, despite his great interest in native issues and the North. At one point, he even called me to ask why I hadn't talked to him for a year.

"If all my ministers were like you," he said, "being prime minister would be so easy. I just give you a job and you do it."

In cabinet meetings, Trudeau would listen to everyone and take all their opinions into account. He loved intellectual seminars, logical arguments, and lengthy meetings. He was the most patient with those he respected the least. If he was quiet and polite, he wasn't paying you a compliment. As soon as he started arguing back, you knew you had his attention for the rest of the day.

If necessary, I was never afraid to contradict him. At one point during the 1980 Quebec referendum, he made a public statement saying he was worried about the results. I was confident that the federalists were going to win, because I was on the ground in the province almost every day, and I told the press that Trudeau had no reason to worry.

We had lunch together the day he was to make one of the most important speeches of the campaign at a huge rally in Montreal.

"You know, Pierre," I said, "it turns out that I'm pure and you're not. According to René Lévesque, your Scottish blood is stronger than your French blood, but I don't have that problem: I'm 100 per cent pure French."

He got so angry at Lévesque's remark that it pushed him to give what was perhaps the best speech of his life.

Many people on both sides of the issue thought that Pierre only wanted to put down Quebec. That was a terrible misinterpretation of what he was trying to do. He believed in the values of Canada and wanted to preserve them. That meant promoting French Canadians, not crushing them. It meant official bilingualism, "French Power," and national unity.

It also meant the patriation of the Constitution and the Charter of Rights. In that case, Pierre certainly had no desire to isolate Quebec. The critics usually forget that Manitoba, as well as Quebec, initially refused to sign the deal, though for different reasons. Or that Premier Lévesque had cornered himself, by trying to cut a pact with the other premiers.

After I became prime minister myself, I used to talk regularly with Pierre, and we'd meet from time to time for dinner. He was good about never telling me what to do, because he understood the difference between being in power and being out of power.

"Jean," he once said, "you have been elected and I know you will do a good job, so you don't need my advice."

But I occasionally sought his advice. He had a way of asking questions that let me know his perspective. During the debate over the Clarity Act, for example, when everyone in Montreal was telling him it was going to end in disaster, he simply asked me if I was sure it was going to work, even if it was the right thing to do.

"Don't be worried, Pierre," I joked. "If it doesn't work, I'll come and practise law with you."

I was flying from Guatemala to Jamaica for a meeting of Commonwealth leaders when I learned of Pierre Trudeau's death. I knew he had been in bad health and wasn't fighting it any more.

"God has decided that my time is up," he had said to me when I saw him a few months earlier. The news came as a shock, nevertheless, and people could see from the tears in my eyes that I wanted to be alone with my thoughts for a while.

The outpouring of grief at the time of his death was enormous. And though it is too early to tell how history will judge him, I'm sure that he will be recognized as a great Canadian: interesting, exciting, stylish, courageous, an intellectual, an athlete, a man of the world and yet an ardent patriot. He was what most Canadians wanted to be, and he represented the values that he enshrined in the Constitution.

▶ JEAN CASSELMAN WADDS
Progressive Conservative MP, 1958–68;
High Commissioner to the Court of St. James, 1979–82

I had been in Parliament several years when Pierre Trudeau appeared on the political scene. He was said to be brilliantly clever, the choice of the revered Liberal Lester Pearson. He sat directly opposite to me in the House of Commons, dressed informally. I had grown up in the era when members of Parliament wore striped trousers, morning coats, and highly polished black shoes. Trudeau's brown sandals and open-necked coloured shirts were different, but we paid little attention to the statement they made.

With the 1968 election, Trudeau became prime minister and the un-Canadian Trudeaumania filled the media. But we Conservatives were still high on the great Diefenbaker years. We were only on the edge of the changes that Trudeau exemplified, and not overly impressed.

In late 1979, Prime Minister Joe Clark gave me the honour of representing Canada in Britain, as the Canadian High Commissioner to the Court of St. James. I was busy familiarizing myself with the personnel and the workings of the office when the Clark government fell.

It was a unique situation. While waiting to see what would come next, I was told, confidentially, that Prime Minister Trudeau had said: "Wadds is to stay in London." I liked the message, and I also liked the way it was done – no delays, no indecision, and no hollow promises. I came to see this as the Trudeau style.

Repatriation of the Constitution and other international matters brought the Canadian prime minister to London from time to time, and part of my job was to meet him at the airport. The first time was the only time, for Trudeau said, "Jean, this is a great waste of your time. There is no need for it."

He had Justin with him, aged eight or nine, and here I saw the warm and human side of the prime minister. Never have I seen a parent so gently, firmly, and effectively handle a child. There was no confusion. Justin sat between us as directed and was quiet as directed, because he was given the reason: his Dad and I were going to talk business.

Justin had one question. His camera had jammed and he had missed some much-wanted pictures. There was no fuss. Trudeau said, "Don't worry, son, you'll have those pictures in your mind's eye forever."

One of Trudeau's visits included lunch with British Prime Minister Margaret Thatcher at 10 Downing Street. To see these two colourful leaders converse was like watching a mental ping-pong game. Sentences were scarcely finished as these two unusual minds exchanged opinions quickly, clearly, with no wasted words.

The reason I am relating some of my meetings with Trudeau is because of one in Ottawa. I had come back for a briefing meeting and was told that the prime minister wished to see me. There were many news cameras at his office, and I could see that he was having a busy day, but he insisted on putting on his suit jacket to welcome me. Then to my surprise he said, "I hear you are doing a splendid job in London, but also I hear you are working very hard. Please do not endanger your health."

In this age of bitter, unpleasant (and even violent) words between politicians and diplomats, I treasure those words of caring and civility, delivered with Pierre Trudeau's proverbial charm. May these qualities be found again, and more often, in our future leaders.

▶ JOE CLARK
Defeated Trudeau in the 1979 election, and then was defeated by him in 1980

*I*n the tradition of the House of Commons, the prime minister and the leader of Her Majesty's Loyal Opposition sit directly opposite one another, "two swords' lengths" apart. Pierre Trudeau and I sat across that aisle from one another for seven years, through the victories and defeats of both our governments, through the fierce debates of his National Energy Program, and the unilateral patriation of the Constitution. Sitting across the aisle from one another was about as close as we came.

The simple operation of Parliament requires regular consultations between the offices of the prime minister and the leader of the Opposition, but those were generally handled by others. Offhand, I recall only two major occasions when those consultations were personal, between Mr. Trudeau and myself, and they were both unsatisfactory.

He had sought my support for his constitutional initiatives in 1982, but our different views of the nature of Canada were too deep to allow agreement.

Earlier, in the winter of 1979, I had briefed him on the American hostages, whom we were trying to move secretly out of Iran, and was surprised when he raised related questions in Parliament while we were still trying to move the hostages out.

Parliament was a place of business for him, not at all a "club," and, I thought, not particularly a place he wanted to be. He did not, as John Turner would, linger in the House after Question Period to debate, or seek to build friendships across the floor.

Pierre Trudeau was an accidental parliamentarian. He came to Ottawa to be in government, not to be in Parliament. Many of his natural talents played well in the House of Commons – his intellect and quickness, his gift for repartee, his interest in a serious debate, his affection for some of the strong and talented people who sit in any Parliament. Through nearly twenty years in the House of Commons, I don't believe he sat a single day as an ordinary "private member" and, when his power was over or ending, he got out as quickly as he could.

Outside Parliament, in both social and formal settings, he was, almost unfailingly, friendly, polite, even gracious. When I defeated him, in 1979, he gave me advice on organizing a government, and working with the public service, that was frank, sensitive, and much more helpful than he had to be. When he defeated me, in 1980, in our first telephone conversation, he moved quickly from the formal script of consolation and congratulation, to note how hard it must be to lose a government after so short a time. There was no victor's bite to that comment. They were the genuine and sympathetic words of a man who knew losing as well as winning.

As I reflect on them, our most personal connections were as parents, not party leaders or parliamentarians. His sons, and our daughter, were raised in the public eye. That's an artificial neighbourhood, where your guard is always up, and it is, I think, particularly hard on children. His instinct, with our daughter, Catherine, and other "public" children, was

Two polite, gracious men – new PM Joe Clark with newly ex-PM – in 1979.

to bring their guard down, to be personal, informal, the opposite of artificial. I have seen him brush past MPs and bureaucrats with whom he worked closely or whom he knew well, too busy for courtesy. I never saw that happen with children. He took them seriously, and went out of his way to engage them.

We have a photograph of a visit to Ottawa by Queen Elizabeth II. Maureen was out of town that day, so Catherine stood with me in the receiving line, a six-year-old pressed up against venerable vice-regals, Madame Léger and the Micheners. Pierre Trudeau was escorting Her Majesty down yet another line of dignitaries. He paid appropriate deference to the former governors general, and then said: "And this, Your Majesty, is Catherine Clark." He made it seem as though the Queen had come to see the six-year-old.

I think prime ministers can't function without a sense of humour. While our parliamentary confrontations did not reveal much of that humour on the part of Pierre Trudeau, other experiences did. When I had just been elected leader of my party, my strategists and I were contemplating how "Joe Who" might sweep the country, and particularly how we would deal with the small problem of the charismatic incumbent.

Not impressed with the speechwriting, a trio of unengaged listeners
– Justin, Michel, and Sacha – at Rideau Hall ceremony.

He was the sophisticated pirouetting prime minister, the intellectual, the "Northern Magus," the philosopher-king, Mr. "Just Watch Me," and I was this gangly, callow kid from somewhere out back of the beyond, who had to beat him.

The House of Commons was a fair fight, and we thought we could win on the issues. But the currency of television elections is "charisma," where my inventory of natural advantages was sparse. Among those advantages, however, was height. I was three to four inches taller than Pierre Trudeau. But everyone thought the opposite. The Magus was thought to tower over the kid. My hard-pressed advisers concluded that, if we could prove that this one caricature was wrong, that might help level the fighting field.

So, on the night of a packed reception in the Château Laurier for then-U.S.-vice-president Walter Mondale, I ventured forth, with a passel of photographers, to have my picture taken towering over Pierre Trudeau. He immediately knew what was up and, whenever my photographers and I hove into sight, the prime minister of Canada would skitter off to another side of the room. I don't know what Walter Mondale thought of the evening, but for Mr. Trudeau and myself, it was a diverting game of urban tag. He won. We didn't get our picture.

Years later, in the mid-1990s, he and I were in Atlanta, Georgia, together for a meeting of the Council of Freely Elected Heads of Government, an organization established by former president Jimmy Carter. A special bus shuttled its weighty load of former presidents and prime ministers back and forth between our hotel and the Carter Center. Maureen and I had to leave Atlanta early, to catch a plane, so, on the final morning, we brought our luggage from the hotel to the shuttle bus. We were on the elevator – just Maureen, myself, and our two heavy bags. I had, famously, lost luggage on an international trip some years before, so we had become quite proprietary about our suitcases.

The elevator stopped at a lower floor, and Pierre Trudeau got on. He was in his seventies then, and that Atlanta meeting had been the first time I had thought of him as frail. He shouldn't have been lifting heavy luggage, and he knew it, but the gentlemanly thing to do was to help Maureen with her suitcase. So he did. A few steps into the lobby, she hailed a porter. To everyone's relief.

Minutes later, as the bus left the hotel, it bumped over a curb. Audibly. Pierre Trudeau turned in his seat and said: "There go your bags, Joe," both an acknowledgment of the porter's intervention, and a deft double entendre.

About a decade after his "walk in the snow," the National Archives opened an exhibit featuring former prime ministers. The 1993 election had left the country divided into regions, and the electoral system dangerously uncompetitive. Strolling through the archives, Mr. Trudeau and I came to the famous campaign poster that helped bring Sir John A. Macdonald back to office. It read: "The Old Man. The Old Flag. The Old Party."

Pierre said: "Do you think I should try it again?"

▶ GORDON GIBSON
Assistant to Trudeau, 1968–72; B.C. Liberal leader, 1975–79

During my time with Trudeau – from the beginning of the leadership campaign in 1968 until 1972, when I left to run as a candidate – he was always very kind to his staff. It is quite true he didn't suffer fools gladly, but there weren't many fools in the PMO those days, or so we flattered ourselves. He also made full allowance for those who, by virtue of their background or talents, couldn't keep up with his intellect, but he could be merciless with supposedly important people who didn't measure up to his standards. This included his ministers.

I recall an occasion in so-called political cabinet (dealing with party business, but a strange phrase since all cabinet meetings are intensely political) when a minister from British Columbia accurately but awkwardly put forward a view that Trudeau didn't like, but which the minister correctly said was held by a great majority of British Columbians. Instead of just accepting the view as useful information, which it was, Trudeau sliced the poor man to ribbons in front of his colleagues for his stupid position.

He gained a reputation for intellectual arrogance, which I think was more the simple demonstration of his mental horsepower than anything else, but the reputation stuck. It didn't much matter – few were prepared to challenge him in any contest of ideas or words, from the media or elsewhere. He could criticize others for demagoguery – I remember him saying that of former NDP leader David Lewis – but was quite capable of using such tactics himself, with such sophistication that he usually got away with it.

Trudeau had quite a reputation as an athlete, and no doubt he kept himself in good shape. But there was something the public never knew – he was not long on energy. His days were carefully planned for the conservation of energy.

After I left the PMO and was elected as a provincial MLA in British Columbia, my view of the majesty and omniscience of Ottawa as the best government for the people was very much changed. Ontarians don't see this, as they own both Ottawa and Queen's Park, but for people in what are condescendingly called "the regions," it is quite a different story. For us, Ottawa can be remote and aloof.

Thus, when Trudeau began his power play vis-à-vis the provinces on constitutional repatriation after his re-election in 1980, I lined up on the other side, notwithstanding the fact that I had run for him as a candidate in the election earlier that year. My recent experience as leader of the provincial Liberal Party had given me a different perspective. (I do not want to make this leader status sound too important. I was a caucus of one in the legislature. There were never any problems with splits over policy, and the main parties were quite friendly to a third party that posed no threat. It was an absolutely wonderful experience, and I think I did speak for B.C. Liberals, in a party that, at that time, was not divided as between feds and provs.)

These were years when Trudeau was engaged in two great fights of his life – with René Lévesque (a wonderful man) in the 1980 Quebec referendum, and with the provinces generally on patriation and constitutional amendments. He did not need a former loyalist from the West on the other side, but I certainly was, and aggressively so. I wrote to every Liberal senator, with a copy to every Liberal MP, saying that it was essential that the amendments be held up by the senators (as representatives of regions) pending a nationwide referendum, which, I argued, was the only legitimate way of validating such an important move. Trudeau was not amused. We did not speak for several years.

When we next met, in 1988, it was at a twentieth anniversary party of his winning the Liberal leadership in 1968, which of course had been an absolutely amazing and exciting time that none of us assembled would ever forget. When we shook hands on that occasion, he suggested we should "bury the hatchet" (he was always good at idiomatic speech) and of course I agreed, though it was never the same, naturally.

But I will always remember that evening. Think of it as a meeting of old soldiers, remembering a great battle. It had indeed been a "famous victory," and there was a lot of emotion in the air.

Trudeau spoke – apparently extemporaneously, but he always thought these things out in advance – for about forty-five minutes. It was a remarkable talk, divided roughly into thirds – on domestic policy, world affairs, and political philosophy – but I remember none of the details save the ending.

He wound up by saying that we had all had a wonderful run together, and thanked everyone for that. He noted that we had worked hard and been very successful, but we should remember that no one fully controls these things. Because in politics, he said, "the greatest thing is timing. And in timing, the greatest thing is luck." I recall the words clearly, because they so surprised me.

He was right about luck of course, but to hear these words of humility from a man so famed for the above-noted intellectual arrogance was something that much struck me, and I will not forget it.

History will judge Mr. Trudeau as a prime minister. The record was undoubtedly mixed. But after a reasonably long life of encountering many people, I have no doubt of one thing. He was a very great human being, and it was a privilege to have known him.

Chapter Ten

Citizen of the World

▶ JOHN KENNETH GALBRAITH
Economist

Pierre Trudeau was perhaps the most delightful person I ever met in the world of politics; any meeting and conversation with him was a pleasure. The meetings included several here at Harvard, and others in Quebec winter resorts, Ottawa, and elsewhere in Canada.

Much of our conversation had to do with the economic problems of the time and the solutions variously offered, but we gave wide-ranging attention to other matters, including, in particular, the low level of accomplishment in politics and especially in economic policy. We shared a consistent view of the inadequacy of those qualified simply by their possession of money or motivated only by the hope of pecuniary reward. In this we combined pleasure with, inevitably, a sense of our better view. Neither of us was ever overcome, or rendered silent, by personal modesty or caution, and we did share our views as to solution, something on which we found general agreement.

I think it fair to say that we were more likely to concentrate on Washington than on the less spectacular inanities of Ottawa, but neither did we neglect.

But this was not all. I had friends in Canada, some of them related to my own Canadian origins, rather more from my continuing interest in the Canadian scene. More impressive was Pierre's pleasure in his large group of American literary, theatrical, artistic, and, of course, political friends. We met with this coterie of intimates in Cambridge and Washington, but most frequently in New York. It was never a surprise if, at any of the social occasions in New York that my wife, Catherine, and I much enjoyed, one of our first encounters was with Pierre Trudeau. These encounters displayed an important side of the Trudeau character: the wish to separate politics from personal enjoyment and grace, and not to allow political considerations to dominate. Still in my mind is a comment, made about his personal enjoyment, that could perhaps have been adversely repeated: "Better a weekend in New York than a week in Montreal."

Others have told, or will tell, of Pierre Trudeau as a political leader. I found him on our various encounters in relentless pursuit of political solutions and consideration of the intelligent course of political action. It was this that brought us together. My professional reputation is as an economist; we discussed the intense political problems of the two countries within the sphere of economics and involving the questions of economic policy and action as it affected the two countries. A recession in the United States could have, equally, an effect in Canada, and Canadian misfortunes could have an adverse effect in the United States.

Of all the politicians I have encountered over a lifetime (and there have been many), there have been few – if any – economically more perceptive and given to affirmative policy than Pierre Trudeau.

Ending a comment like this there has often been the same concluding line: "We will never see his like again." Remembering Pierre Trudeau, I can only hope that there may be more good neighbours following his contribution to economic well-being, political tranquility, and shared cultural achievement. With all this I agree and indeed emphasize but there is more: there will, indeed, never be anyone like Pierre Trudeau.

▶ JONATHAN KOLBER
Israeli-based business executive, who, with his parents, Leo and Sandra
Kolber, made several adventurous foreign trips in the late 1980s

I recall an incredible journey from Islamabad in Pakistan through the Hunza valley, up the ancient Spice Road into China. A group of us (Senator Jack Austin and his wife, Natalie Freeman, my parents, Leo and Sandra Kolber, and me and Pierre) were guests of Pakistan's president Zia al-Haq, who felt he needed to thank Pierre for a key UN vote in which Canada was one of his few supporters. Zia wanted us to helicopter all the way (security, you know), but Pierre would hear nothing of it. He was on his own version of a *National Geographic* special and didn't want to miss out on any of the effects!

That didn't mean, of course, that when we got stuck at Gilgit in the Hunza valley, that Zia's security concerns didn't override Pierre's wish for a natural experience. You see, a small glacier had melted and turned into a very large pond (or smallish lake), making the road impassable. Well, in came a platoon of Pakistani army-corps engineers to save the day! Helicopters and trucks arrived and, within three or four hours, had constructed a wonderfully sturdy pontoon bridge across the melted glacier. We enjoyed the luxury of it and didn't mind being spoiled in the least. The most bizarre part of the adventure occurred when we reached the other side and, instead of being greeted by the early predecessors of al-Qaeda in an isolated and godforsaken place, we were warmly applauded by a small group of French-Canadian adventure travellers. A surreal experience.

When we arrived in Tashkurgan, having crossed the Khunjerab Pass at five thousand metres and feeling a little dizzy, we were put up in a rest house for the night. (Personally, I felt as if we had been propelled back three hundred years to a Marco Polo nightmare.) We each were given our *own* rooms (a huge treat), which were not really heated, and it was freezing. And we were to sleep in tapestry carpet-like blankets, piled up six high to keep us warm. There was, of course, no way to shower (we would wait two more days to arrive in Beijing for that). And guess what? No toilets.

We were given ancient-looking chamber pots in our rooms. Pierre was not happy about this, and I volunteered to reconnoitre. I discovered that the rest house was being expanded and, at the end of the corridor, a "modern wing" was being built. By forcing apart two timber planks, I could sneak into the other side. With Pierre following me holding a flashlight, both of us in our pyjamas and heavy overcoats, we discovered a yet-to-be-completed Western toilet, in a kind of closet.

The only problem was, it was behind a locked door, but the toilet was beckoning to us through the cracks in the door. So, at 2 a.m., all alone in this dank, dark, cold rest house, Pierre gave me the order:

"Break the bloody thing down, Jonathan, we've got to get to the toilet!"

So I did.

▶ IVAN HEAD
Counsel on Constitution, 1967–68; special adviser, 1968–78; president of International Development Research Centre, 1978–91

*I*nternational state visits at the head-of-government level are necessarily shaped by protocol and ceremony, particularly when it comes to welcoming ceremonies at airports. In the early 1970s, these circumstances were invariably enhanced in visits to the capitals of major countries in Asia. One explanation for the extraordinarily colourful welcoming arrangements in those days was the understandable desire of the host government to indicate to its own citizens that it was receiving foreign dignitaries in a fashion that showcased both the hospitality of its culture and its competence as an – often – recently independent state. Another explanation for the (sometime) variation in lavishness was the importance of the visitor and the country that he or she represented.

All these circumstances combined as Prime Minister Pierre Trudeau travelled through Asia in those years. Stepping off the Canadian aircraft in Beijing, Jakarta, or New Delhi, he was received in an atmosphere and greeted with a spectacle that approached the complexity of the opening ceremonies of the Olympic Games. There would be a red carpet, of course, and a military band that often (but not always) played "O Canada" in a

Flowers for all of us.

rendition as stirring as any heard in Ottawa. There were dancers as well,
garbed in striking local costumes, often garlands, and, always, dozens of
flags – Canadian and local – flew from a forest of flagpoles on the
boundaries of the tarmac. Seldom did the prime minister's accompanying party feel more proud to be Canadian than when they participated
with him in these solemn yet joyful events.

In January 1971, en route to and from a Commonwealth Heads of
Government Conference in Singapore, the prime minister accepted the
invitations of several Asian Commonwealth governments to break his
journey and to engage in discussions with the host prime ministers. One
of these stops was India, where Prime Minister Indira Gandhi had proposed an elaborate program that included, in addition to several rounds
of formal talks, visits to landmarks such as the Taj Mahal, official lunches
and dinners that permitted policy speeches to be delivered by the two
principals, and a cultural concert. We began the visit in Agra, and from
there we travelled to Varanasi. The official portion of the visit com-
menced with our arrival at New Delhi airport, where the tone of the
occasion was to be set. Set it was, but with two unscheduled incidents
that were entirely unexpected – by the welcoming party or by many
members of the Canadian delegation.

As our aircraft pulled up to the red carpet within seconds of our scheduled arrival, it was clear that the welcoming party was immense in size. Prime Minister Gandhi stood at the bottom of the steps ready to receive Mr. Trudeau. Strung out behind her was a long line of Indian officials. To one side was a large Indian military band, and close to it a contingent of splendidly uniformed soldiers, ready to be inspected by their distinguished visitor. Colourfully garbed dancers seemed to be everywhere. Close by, as is often the case on these foreign travels, were staff members of the Canadian High Commission, plus other members of the local Canadian community, accompanied by dozens of cheering Canadian children all waving tiny Maple Leaf flags. Further back, well away from the waiting motorcade, were hundreds of persons, mostly Indian, lined up as witnesses to this special event. There was no doubt that the Trudeau reputation had preceded him to India. We would soon witness scenes reminiscent of the 1968 election campaign, though set against an exotic background.

The first unexpected incident occurred within moments of Mr. Trudeau's descent of the steps. The two prime ministers were to shake hands and exchange friendly greetings (this was not their first meeting). Mrs. Gandhi would then, as is the Indian custom, place a large garland of flowers around his neck. Before any of this could happen, however, and to Mrs. Gandhi's total surprise, Pierre Trudeau produced from behind his back two flower garlands that he had brought with him for this purpose from our previous stop in Varanasi, and placed them about her shoulders. As the Indian press photographs verify, she was delighted, and roars of approval went up from the crowd of onlookers. This man was as unpredictable as they had been told. Following the formal ceremonies, Mr. Trudeau then walked from the carpet over to the cheering Canadians, as was his habitual custom on these occasions. He chatted with them, shook hands, signed autographs, posed for photographs, and demonstrated how gracious and informal a Canadian prime minister could be. Then came the second incident.

As Mrs. Gandhi directed him toward the waiting limousines, Pierre Trudeau heard his name being called from the members of the public held back by rope barriers. He turned his head toward them, then broke out in a smile and jogged over with obvious enthusiasm to embrace several men in clerical garb, and entered into an animated conversation with them. This, too, was a totally unexpected occurrence, one that concerned the security and protocol folks – and completely mystified the rest of us. Who were these people, how did the prime minister know them, why would he hold up his hostess and the carefully prepared schedule for several minutes of lively exchanges? Finally, realizing how much time had passed, and not wanting to embarrass Mrs. Gandhi, the prime minister said farewell and returned to his assigned car. Only after we had arrived at our quarters in the magnificent Rashtrapati Bhavan of Mogul splendour were we able to interrogate him.

Those were Canadian missionaries, he told us, men who had welcomed him into their small communities more than two decades earlier, when, as a young man, he was travelling across the continent in modest fashion, hitchhiking and on foot. He had never forgotten their kindnesses to him when he had appeared on their doorstep in ragamuffin clothing, seeking a place to sleep. He had not been in touch with them in that long interval, but they had clearly not forgotten their young visitor and the long, searching conversations in which they had all engaged over a period of many days.

When they had learned of his forthcoming 1971 visit, they travelled the considerable distance from their mission in Bengal, not sure whether they would be able to get close to him, not confident that he would recognize them in their homespun attire, with their changed appearances after so many years. But recognize them he did, and joyfully. Quickly, arrangements were put in place for these priests to be included in the formal dinner that Canada would offer in honour of Prime Minister Gandhi. On Pierre Trudeau's instructions, these Canadians in this faraway place would be accorded the same courtesies and the same kindnesses that were extended to the most prominent persons on the official guest lists. These were his friends from long ago, all the more welcome because of their unexpected presence.

Incidents of this sort, in one form or another, cropped up often in the official travels of Pierre Trudeau. Always was he sincerely delighted to encounter acquaintances from the past, always was he gracious and modest in his encounters with them, always did he exhibit genuine glee in departing from rigid formality (but always in good taste and

Canadian Press, Peter Bregg

With Ivan Head, his close adviser and friend.

high spirits), and never did I see any element of impatience, arrogance, or indifference.

These are my memories of the real Pierre Trudeau, the kindly human being who functioned instinctively and openly with others, whatever the occasion, whatever their age or nationality, whenever the opportunity arose. These occasions remain vivid in my memory every bit as much as his stirring public appearances and his skilful negotiating accomplishments.

▶ RAYMOND BARRE
Prime minister of France, 1976–81

I met Pierre Trudeau several times when we were both prime ministers, and I thought he was a sensible man, especially when we discussed relations between Paris and Ottawa. He came once to France on a private visit in the late 1970s and I visited him in Ottawa. It was very moving to watch him managing his charming sons.

Once when I was visiting Canada, long after M. De Gaulle's famous speech in Montreal, I was at the Montreal airport to fly back to Paris. In those days, the fact was underlined that the Canadian federal government would be the official government to welcome me and see me off. A few days after I got home, Pierre sent me a caricature from a French Montreal newspaper. It showed me getting on the plane, and the comment read: "Vive le Raymond Barre libre."

⟩ ROY McMURTRY
Ontario attorney general, 1975–85; High Commissioner to
London, 1985–88

I recall that Pierre Trudeau was still very much on the mind of Margaret Thatcher when I arrived in London, in April 1985, as the Canadian High Commissioner. This was almost eight months after Brian Mulroney had become prime minister, and her last contact with Pierre had been at the G7 Summit the year before.

Prime Minister Thatcher was still angry about the fact that Pierre and President François Mitterrand had adopted the habit of conversing with each other only in French in her presence. Her angry recollection (to me) was exacerbated by the fact that a particular clause in the summit communiqué, that only she and President Reagan wished included, was indeed included, but only in the English version and not in the French. For Mrs. Thatcher, this was but one more example of an ongoing French conspiracy between Paris and Ottawa.

⟩ GERALD FORD
President of the United States, 1974–77

*W*e had a very personal friendship that began at a G7 meeting in 1976, when I insisted Canada be included in the group. At that time, when I

Kristin Bennett

Who needs bodyguards?

proposed Canada become a partner, the French rejected the idea because they wanted a European country (Italy) to join instead. But I insisted, and Canada became a member.

Occasionally, after he retired, Pierre came to visit Betty and me in Colorado to spend a few days skiing. He was a better skier than I; I'm in the middle of the pack. I always had two people from the secret service with me when I skied. Pierre had no security.

Pierre and I had our philosophical differences, but I like to think we complemented each other.

▌ JAMES CALLAGHAN
Prime minister of Great Britain, 1976–79

*P*ierre was always so natural in what he said and did. I remember vividly one occasion when we were all together at the meeting of the Commonwealth Heads of Government. The meetings took place at Lancaster House, the former home of the Dukes of Sutherland, which has a most impressive staircase. This must have been thirty years ago, so Pierre would have been in his mid-fifties. But there he was: sliding down the banister rail, which scandalized some of those watching, but delighted the rest of us!

We met at regular intervals, over many years, in a number of capital cities. I remember once my wife and I were invited to stay at Harrington Lake for a weekend with him and his sons. As gifts, we had brought the boys small models of the Concorde, which they enjoyed immensely. One of the boys, I don't recall which one, managed to launch his plane directly at my nose, which hurt!

▶ BRENDA NORRIS
Met Trudeau in 1968, when they sat in adjoining boxes during the 1968 Liberal leadership convention, and saw him often over the years for meals and social events.

*I*n June 1997, I was in London to see my new grandson, and I took the Chunnel Train over to Paris to spend a few days with Donald Johnston (former president of the Liberal Party, cabinet minister, and then head of the OECD in Paris) and his wife, Heather, in their beautiful flat on the rue Henri Martin. Don's chauffeur collected me at the station, and when I walked into the drawing room, there was Pierre silhouetted against the French doors and reading what I later discovered to be *The Decline and Fall of the Roman Empire* by Gibbon. We were to be fellow house guests for the weekend.

Friday evening, Don gave a rather formal but very interesting dinner party for Pierre, during which – I might add – there were several quizzical glances shot in my direction. I didn't bother to inform the group that I was a happily married mother of four and grandmother of eight. Anyway, those who knew Pierre well would have known I was far too old for him!

Saturday afternoon we all went to the finals of the French Open ladies' doubles tennis at Roland Garros Stadium. A beautiful girl in a backless sundress sat in front of us and climbed over us at least five times for a Sprite or a Coke or whatever. She was with a very good-looking man, and it was evident that tennis was not the main attraction of the afternoon for her. On her last trip for yet another snack, her gentleman friend whipped out a cell telephone and, although we presumed he was French, he proceeded to tell the person on the telephone (who was clearly his wife) how much he loved her, and that he would be home soon – all in English. Pierre and I burst out laughing, and I said, "Only in France."

"Or Quebec!" Pierre replied.

The weekend was magic. We lunched in the Bois de Boulogne at Don's very chic tennis club, "Le Tir aux Pigeons," where families were having Sunday lunch. The little girls who played around after lunch wore pretty dresses almost to their ankles, while their mothers in miniskirts supervised them. Pierre cast an appraising eye.

Our last night, we took Don and Heather to dinner at Chez André on la rue Marbeuf. The restaurant was my choice, and I was rather nervous, but we sat outside on a soft June night surrounded by charming Parisiens and had a superb and not too expensive (!!!) dinner. Pierre said, "I must congratulate you on your choice of restaurant." I was delighted to hear that, knowing his reputation for dining in fine restaurants all over the world. It was an unforgettable evening.

With Don Johnston and Brenda Norris
at Chez André, in Paris, 1997.

The following morning at breakfast, I pulled out a clipping on Paris restaurants from Britain's *Spectator* magazine that I had brought with me and had forgotten to consult. The critic listed several restaurants and then said, "But my favourite restaurant is Chez André." I read this to Pierre, because the critic had ordered exactly the same dinner that he had chosen, and when Pierre saw the price, he remarked, "That is less than I paid."

I have many memories of Pierre over the thirty-five years that I knew him, but our weekend together in Paris is the one that I shall always cherish. Who could ask for a more charming and amusing and gallant escort than Pierre Trudeau?

▶ DON JOHNSTON
Trudeau's lawyer; friend (since 1957); cabinet minister, 1980–84

*I*n early 1994, at the swearing-in of the Chrétien government, I invited, among other friends, Trudeau, Mordecai and Florence Richler, journalist E. Kaye Fulton, Elizabeth Dickson, my former legislative assistant, and my wife, Heather, to a reception in Ottawa, as I was still president of the Liberal Party.

Later, the seven of us repaired for dinner at Mamma Teresa's, and after all the political chat had flared out, the subject of Sable Island came up. Why had none of us been there before? Trudeau – whose vast knowledge of Canada (and the world) was legendary – admitted he had never been there. Sable Island, for those of you not at this lively dinner, lies about three hundred kilometres southeast of Halifax. Mordecai admitted as well that he'd never been there, though he did not manifest any great enthusiasm for putting it on his *must visit* list.

Kaye Fulton and I had some acquaintance with Sable Island. A decade before, I had been asked in my capacity as Minister of Science and Technology to visit one of the submersible oil rigs operating off the island. Kaye, then of *Maclean's* magazine's Halifax bureau, said she would love to tag along. So off we went by helicopter. Since the oil rig was not that far from Sable, I asked the pilot if we might fly over the island on the way out.

We were enchanted. Seals lounged on the beaches. Seeing the untrammelled (and undeveloped) sand dunes, the sparse vegetation, and, mostly, the wild herds of horses made each of us conclude we would dearly love to set foot on that barren terrain.

So, back at Mamma's, Elizabeth Dickson and I extracted a promise that all at the table would join an expedition to Sable, if possible – given it was a protected piece of federal property with limited access.

We went to work to make the trip happen, and finally secured permission to land, and a date: the fourth of July, 1994 (!).

We all met up just south of Halifax. Our base camp (to give you an idea of our collective notion of the Sable safari challenge, and the opinionated and well-travelled group we were) was at Heather's family summer spread on Mahone Bay. After drinks and a sumptuous dinner at Mimi's Ocean Grill, and a cruise around Mahone Bay the following day, we intrepid adventurers were ready to set out in a rather rickety old aircraft, for our one-day safari to Sable Island.

Weather around Sable is quite unpredictable, but on this American Independence Day, it was magic, with clear skies and little wind, which eventually allowed us to settle gently onto the beach. From the air we had a glorious view. The sea glistened in colours from deep cold blue to emerald green. We could see the seals dotting the beaches, the wild horses gambolling among the dunes.

With a picnic lunch and lots of energy and curiosity, we set out to explore, though we were warned not to try to make any contact with the feral horses. This protective warning, of course, brought out the impish, rebellious nature of the former PM. From his youth – throwing snowballs at Lenin's statue in the Soviet Union – to the last of his days, Pierre enjoyed challenging what he saw as authority "overreach." However, the horses ran their own country here and seemed quite content observing us – and him – from a distance. Pierre never got closer to them than a couple of yards.

We were then invited to the weather station to meet the people who ran it and to watch a weather balloon being released. A young man rushed forward to Mordecai with a copy of *Soloman Gursky* for his autograph. I don't know what Pierre thought, since his own memoirs headed the bestseller lists at the time. Mordecai was pleased with the book's

*(Top) The opinionated group at Mimi's Ocean Grill. Left to right: Mordecai
Richler, Heather Johnston, Pierre, E. Kaye Fulton, and Florence Richler.
(Bottom) A reflective sailor cruising Mahone Bay, Tilley Hat
in hand, with Florence Richler in foreground.*

breadth of circulation, even though he was accused of having planted the book in advance to impress us all.

As the afternoon advanced, we could see a fog bank rolling in from the western front, so we quickened our departure. The alternative might have been a very long stay on the island, which was frequently fogbound. Pierre agreed, reminding us were just visitors there.

The Sable trip with Pierre was a moving and splendid experience engraved in all our memories, and just another reason I miss him so much.

▶ JONATHAN MANTHORPE
Foreign correspondent

*I*t doesn't matter now who told me Pierre Trudeau was in town. It was March 1992, and I was in a hotel in Cape Town, banging out a story about the parlous state of negotiations aimed at achieving majority rule in South Africa, when the call came. Trudeau was travelling through South Africa with Senator Jack Austin, his wife, Natalie, and Nancy Southam. I immediately called Nancy at the hotel where I had been told the party was staying.

"How did *you* know we were here?" said Nancy with more than the usual touch of accusation in her tone. I pointed out that her family paid me moderately well to know stuff like that. "Well, you'd better come around and have a whisky then," she said, grudgingly.

Trudeau's presence in South Africa had come to the notice of several other people as well, as I learned over whisky with Nancy. Both Nelson Mandela and the country's president, F.W. de Klerk, wanted to see Trudeau. Their eagerness was understandable. Trudeau was an expert on international law, as well as one of the world's most famous ex-prime ministers. His special renown for trying to weld Canada's two founding cultures into a workable whole was clearly an experience of value to South Africa at that moment.

The group's itinerary was overseen by the Canadian embassy and included a request to hear South African music. The embassy had bowed

to this wish by including a reception at Kippie's, a jazz club in a repro-
duction Edwardian toilet in Johannesburg's old market district. I didn't
like the place. It always struck me as a failed attempt to create a little
ersatz multiracial enclave acceptable to the apartheid regime, in order to
fool tourists.

Maybe it was the whisky, but I said I would happily take Trudeau and
his companions to a real South African jazz club in Soweto, the vast
black township of some five million people and the second-largest city
in Africa. Then I went back to my hotel and forgot about it.

The following morning my phone rang. There was silence for a
moment and then a friend at the Canadian embassy in Pretoria said
wearily, "Jonathan, why are you trying to kill our former prime minister?"

It seems Trudeau really liked the idea of the visit to a Soweto jazz
place and had insisted it be put on his agenda. The more embassy officials objected, the more they said it was too dangerous, the more
Trudeau dug in his heels and demanded to go.

I spluttered to my embassy friend that I was going to take them to
the Blue Fountain, the famous shebeen illegal-drinking den run by "The
Godfather of Soweto," Godfrey Moloi.

"There's never any political trouble around the Blue Fountain," I
said. "Godfrey won't allow it."

The retort was not as weak as it sounded. The narrow focus of the
television camera always gave an overly intense picture of the anti-
apartheid violence in this sprawling township. There might indeed be
bloody confrontations between local people and the police in one area of
Soweto, while in the rest of the townships life went on calmly. And around
the Blue Fountain there was never any trouble. Moloi, a jazz saxophonist
and former gangster who had worked out that brains were more powerful
than muscle, had no time for politics. He branded anti-apartheid cam-
paigners "a bunch of loafers and drunkards." That may not have made him
popular with the activists, but Moloi, through his generous sponsorship of
scores of local causes, was too popular for anyone to touch.

Heated negotiations were conducted over the next few days between
Trudeau's party, then in transit to Johannesburg, and the Canadian
embassy. When I arrived in Johannesburg a couple of days later, I learned
the embassy had reluctantly offered to provide two cars and drivers who

knew Soweto, but that was it. They took no official responsibility for whatever evils befell us.

Meanwhile, I told the story to a colleague, John Battersby of the *Christian Science Monitor*, with whom I was working on a story and who knew Moloi better than I. John was eager to be included in the night out and undertook to talk to Moloi.

On the appointed evening, I met Trudeau, Nancy, and the Austins for dinner at their Sandton hotel before we set off. I hadn't seen Trudeau for over ten years, since I had worked for him in London as a special adviser on the "patriation" of the Constitution. Our drive out to Soweto was, as expected, uneventful.

When we walked into the garish Blue Fountain beer hall, Moloi rushed out of his office to greet us. The hall was, as usual, bustling with regulars propping up their habitual tables or corners of the bar. What was striking was that everyone recognized Trudeau, and that no one was surprised the former Canadian prime minister would wander into their watering hole in the middle of the dusty and poverty-wrenched township. Several of the guys at the bar called out, "Hey there, Pierre," and others came over to pump his hand.

The irony and minor disappointment of the evening was that it was not a night for live jazz groups at the Blue Fountain. My promise of, and Trudeau's lust for, the true beat of South Africa came to nothing. Well, not quite. There was plenty of taped music by local bands, dancing, and general jollity. Everyone went home happy.

▶ MATTHEW W. BARRETT
Former chairman and CEO of the Bank of Montreal

I arrived in Montreal, aged twenty-three, from London, to continue my career at the Bank of Montreal. It was Centennial year, 1967, and – as I was soon to discover – it was a year brimming with hope and confidence. It was as if Centennial year and the Expo 67 celebration were backdrops to yet another Canadian event, the following year, that would catch the attention of the world: the election, on a wave of euphoria, of Pierre

Elliott Trudeau as prime minister. I was not (yet) a Canadian (I carried an Irish passport), but that didn't prevent me from being caught up in the excitement generated by this extraordinary new figure on the political scene.

Like everybody else, I was accustomed to a more prosaic kind of politician. To the extent I paid attention to politics at all, that had been my experience, in Britain and in Ireland. As everybody agreed, Trudeau was a breath of fresh air. But before many months had passed, a question began to be raised: was he too good to be true, this attractive, intellectual man of action? The answer would not be overly long in coming; in fact, the Liberals and Trudeau were reduced to a minority at the next election, in 1972.

However, Pierre Trudeau was never far from my consciousness. While he appealed to my romantic side, I was immersing myself in management and economic issues. And though it was not part of my responsibility to worry about public policies and their implications – my duties were much more mundane than that – I was sufficiently aware to be made uncomfortable by some of Trudeau's economics. I respected his social policies and certain of the things he attempted to do internationally, but his economic policies (the unforgettable National Energy Program foremost among them) gave me serious pause. And yet, like so many others, I found him captivating.

On a personal level, I first made Trudeau's acquaintance at Bank of Montreal social functions in Montreal. This was after his retirement, when the bank's then-chairman, Bill Mulholland (who had a special regard for Trudeau), would invite him to dinners and concerts. On those occasions I found him unfailingly gracious, interesting, not at all intellectually arrogant or self-centred as he was often painted.

My most substantive contact with him would come in September 1997, when I invited him to be a special guest of the bank at meetings of our board of directors in China. These meetings, which had already been deferred once because of events in China, were to be held in Hong Kong and Beijing, with a side trip to Sian, home of the famous excavated clay soldiers and horses.

Some months in advance of this trip, I was in China on business and, in the course of conversations related to a rescheduling of our visit, I was

*Prime Minister Trudeau gets a little assistance with
his chopsticks from Chinese premier Chou En-Lai.*

reminded (not for the first time) of the high regard in which Mr. Trudeau
was held by the Chinese leadership. This arose, in part, from his demonstrated interest in Chinese civilization and culture, but also because of the
"face" he had given the Chinese when Canada, at his initiative, led the way
in giving recognition to the semi-isolated Communist regime.

It was then it occurred to me that I should invite him to participate
in what for us was a historic occasion. I immediately telephoned Canada
from Beijing to have Mr. Trudeau sounded out. He was not only open to
the idea, but he became a star member of our delegation.

Not every director of the bank, I might point out, was enthralled
with my idea. People who sit on the boards of banks and big corporations are not without ego themselves, and Mr. Trudeau would clearly
represent a competing attraction. More important than that, though,

among some of the directors there was still a residual bias; they were, for the most part, conservative by definition, and Mr. Trudeau's economics, which I suspect many of them would have been happy to characterize as "voodoo," had left them distinctly cold. But, in the end, they acknowledged that his presence would be a benefit to the bank, and they made him welcome.

For my part, the Pierre Trudeau I found myself travelling with was very different from the Pierre Trudeau whom we had all known from a distance when he was at the peak of his form. He clearly was not well, though his ailment was not readily apparent. He walked with a certain hesitation, and there was just a hint of vagueness in his manner that gave rise to speculation in our travelling circle that he might be suffering from a degenerative disease. But so far as I was concerned, he was open, charming, and willing to contribute in any way possible to the success of our mission.

Because he was such an object of respect in the eyes of the Chinese authorities, he was particularly sensitive not to upstage me as chairman and chief executive, nor to allow the fundamentally commercial purposes of the trip to be in any way overshadowed by his presence. This, in its own fashion, was an eloquent answer to those who suggested he had no appreciation of business.

In our private conversations, Pierre did not attempt to disguise that he was not his old self. He made no specific allusions to his condition, but seemed continuously conscious that his memory and recall, his ability to articulate, were deteriorating, and that he could not "perform" either to his own standards or to the expectations of his arbiters. It was a poignant note he struck, and it could not have been easy for him to make that disclosure; I was far from one of his intimates, yet I felt a sense of humility that he should regard me as empathetic enough to be honestly told such things.

There could be no doubt about the value of his participation. In practice, however, it was for the most part frankly ceremonial, although at lunches and dinners he was an engaged and, by and large, contributing participant. We were able to ensure that he was not asked to respond to toasts or tributes, apart from his own gestures of acknowledgment. When we met with Zhu Rongji, Vice-Premier, State Council, People's

Republic of China, and with Jiang Zemin, President, People's Republic of China, at formal public receptions in the Forbidden City, Trudeau asked me to help animate and maintain the dialogue.

When the trip was over and Trudeau took his leave – he was on his way to Japan – we both knew it had not been easy for him, but we also knew that, within the limitations of his health, he had played his part. I also sensed that for him this was an important trip to a part of the world about which he had deep feelings, which were reciprocated in kind by his hosts. To that end I could count myself an honest broker, having served the interests of the bank, while giving one of our most absorbing public figures an experience to help carry him into his declining years.

Chapter Eleven

The Light Side

▶ TERRY MOSHER (AISLIN)
Political cartoonist

Keep in mind that this is necessarily a look at Trudeau from a distance. I didn't know the man personally. Indeed, the only time we actually spoke was at a Montreal function in the mid-1980s. It was one of those meet-the-author events, of which I now have little memory, my having been an avid drinker at the time. I do remember spending much of the evening helping Hugh MacLennan (of whom I was very fond) steer clear of the people he wanted to avoid. At one point we bumped into Trudeau, and he and I had a brief chat about the best sketchbooks available. Apparently his sons were showing an interest in drawing. Thankfully, unlike many other politicians I've encountered, he didn't want to talk about what I had or hadn't done with his chin. From a political cartoonist's point of view, *not* knowing the subject personally is better. Otherwise, you risk actually getting to like the person, and that undermines your effectiveness.

Pierre Trudeau once famously said: "Just watch me." So I did – along with every other Canadian.

In the mid-1960s, Gérard Pelletier, Pierre Trudeau, and Jean Marchand were enticed to go to Ottawa by then prime minister Lester Pearson. The idea was to give Quebec a more credible face in the federal government. The trio became known as the three wise men.

I started drawing political cartoons for the *Montreal Star* in 1967, the same year Pierre Trudeau became prime minister of Canada. In the first flush of Trudeaumania, other cartoonists often drew him as an aging flower child. I took a different approach, often portraying him as a very determined and calculating character. A case in point is this cover for

Time magazine, in which he is holding Canada together, but a Canada whose mouth he has sewn shut.

My suspicion that Trudeau was a far more resolute character than commonly believed was borne out during the FLQ crisis of the early 1970s.

During that period, Old Montreal's Nelson Hotel became the unofficial headquarters for a collection of rounders and quasi-revolutionaries who held daily press conferences during the October Crisis. My friend Nick Auf der Maur and I would drop in to check out the action from time to time. At one point, I was introduced to FLQ lawyer Robert Lemieux. When I mentioned that I was working on a caricature of him for the following Saturday's *Montreal Star*, it was "suggested" that I show him the cartoon and get his approval first! Obviously I declined. I said that I had never asked Trudeau's permission. That was a mistake. One didn't *say* Trudeau's name around the Nelson, so much as hiss it.

Pierre Trudeau was accused of many things, but never of being a fool. Quickly grasping the pandemonium in Montreal, he declared the War Measures Act on October 16, 1970. Despite the ever-present rose in his lapel, he was never again depicted as some hippie flower child. Here's a cartoon I drew for *Maclean's* at the time entitled "Captain Canada."

In the early Trudeau years, the leader of the Opposition was Robert Stanfield, a competent and generally well-liked politician, who was not crafty enough to beat Trudeau over three successive federal elections. I drew this cartoon of Trudeau and Stanfield as a dancing couple for the cover of an 1972 election handbook produced by *Maclean's*. Note the positioning of the knees.

Despite these consecutive wins, campaigning across the country was never one of Trudeau's favourite activities. He was not a populist by nature, as shown in this cartoon drawn during the 1974 election.

I am often asked as a political cartoonist whether there are elements of a subject's life that are out of bounds. My own rule of thumb is that a politician's personal life is of no interest to me unless it begins to have an effect on their public performance. Even then, the issue has to be handled carefully.

In April 1971, Pierre Trudeau married Margaret Sinclair in storybook fashion. Just a few years later, the storm clouds rolled in when Margaret went off to Toronto to hang out with the touring Rolling Stones. I drew a cartoon of the new Opposition leader, Joe Clark, sitting at the breakfast table with his wife, Maureen McTeer. Maureen is wondering how the press would react if she were to run off to Regina with Tommy Hunter . . .

"I WONDER HOW THE PRESS WOULD REACT IF I SUDDENLY DASHED OFF TO REGINA WITH TOMMY HUNTER?"

The Trudeau marriage disintegrated. Several years later, I drew Trudeau asking testily which damned Margaret was on the phone: Trudeau or Thatcher?

Joe Clark and the Tories were elected to run the country in June 1979. Bungling a non-confidence vote on his first budget, Clark was forced to call another election, which he lost, having served just 272 days as prime minister. Trudeau and his Liberals were swept back into power in imperial fashion, inspiring this cartoon that appeared in the *Gazette* the morning after the 1980 election. Back before we knew it, it was as though Trudeau had just stepped out for an evening's entertainment.

Pierre Trudeau won that 1980 election by keeping a detached and calculated distance from the Canadian public, as shown in this cartoon. (Interestingly, Trudeau bought the original of this piece and gave away signed copies to all his key campaign workers.)

The particular significance of Trudeau's having regained power at that moment was that he was around to play a role in Quebec's 1980 Referendum, a bit of serendipity for Canada as it turned out. There are those who believe that if Joe Clark – seemingly always anxious to placate Quebec – had still been prime minister, the crafty René Lévesque would have prevailed. Instead, Lévesque had to deal with Trudeau, leading to this next cartoon. It appeared on the front page of the *Gazette* the morning after Lévesque's referendum loss.

The piece proved so popular that it was used as the cover illustration and title for the next volume in my series of collected cartoons, which was published in the fall of 1980. In Ottawa to do some publicity for the book, I was scheduled to be interviewed on television by – of all people – Margaret Trudeau. Before we got started, Margaret took a look at the cover and marched off the set, indignantly muttering about the drawing being obscene! I guess she didn't see that the cartoon was actually very complimentary to her former husband. (The interview did eventually go forward, but with another host.)

Subsequently, Doris Giller, then the *Gazette*'s book editor, bought the original for her husband, Jack Rabinovitch. This means that I still get to see the cartoon – which hangs in Jack's kitchen – when I visit him in Toronto.

Pierre Trudeau once told Mordecai Richler in confidence that, if Canadians had any idea how much money his government was actually funnelling to Quebec, they'd probably ride him out of Ottawa on a rail. This might explain why the following was one of Pierre Trudeau's favourite political cartoons, according to his good friend Stratton Stevens. The cartoon is entitled "Put Up and Shut Up!"

Next to his successful battle against Quebec separation, Pierre Trudeau will probably be remembered most for having repatriated the Constitution from England.

There was a great deal of politicking involved . . .

THE CONSTITUTION

... without, of course, Quebec's participation.

In the end, Trudeau prevailed. Canada had its Constitution, even if not everyone was happy about the outcome.

The Constitution

Although a flamboyant personality, Trudeau was so frugal in his personal life that he gained a reputation as a cheapskate. On the other hand, when it came to public finances, his government's spending practices bordered on the irresponsible.

In 1984, when Trudeau finally resigned for good, I drew this cartoon of him, twisting Richard Nixon's quotation about the press not having him to kick around anymore.

Globalization may well be the hallmark of the twenty-first century, bringing with it an erosion of individualism and our sense of place. How significant it is then, that three powerful personalities who were born in Montreal and made international reputations as Montrealers, all died there in 2000: Jean Drapeau, Maurice Richard, and Pierre Trudeau. All had different careers and were perceived very differently, depending on one's political bent and newspaper of choice. Nonetheless, all three were identified by their "Montreal-ness." The passing of Pierre Trudeau, such an elegant, dashing, and vigorous individual, was a particular shock. We reflected perhaps the more on our own mortality.

Here's one final thought: drawing Pierre Trudeau was a challenge. As a political cartoonist, I always have to look beyond the supposed rules of physiognomy that determine how human beings react and engage with each other. On the surface, you see, Pierre Trudeau was a short fellow with a receding hairline and a weak chin. And yet, with a simple glance, he could stop gorgeous and sophisticated Montreal women in their tracks. The power shone through his physical appearance. The trick was to capture Trudeau's confidence, intelligence, arrogance, and even that charming shyness that sometimes came through. We'll never forget that shrug.

Chapter Twelve

Women

▶ JENNIFER RAE
*First met Trudeau when serving as director of PR and publicity for his
1968 leadership campaign*

*I*t was February 1968, and I had arrived back in Ottawa after some time
away, on an impulse. My brother John had called me in Mexico City to
say, "Come to Ottawa. There's work to be done on Pierre Trudeau's campaign, but you have to catch a plane and get here quickly."

That was the beginning of a multi-week rollercoaster.

Every political campaign has an all-encompassing intensity, but
the "P.E. Trudeau Campaign for Liberal Leadership" had a heightened
acuteness to it, because we were the improbable patchwork of "gifted
amateurs," brought together by Trudeau's irreverent, fresh approach.
The country was idealistic and smitten by his charm and I – always a
sucker for charm – was captivated.

Gussy Turner, my best friend since age three, and Alison Gordon, my
great friend at Queen's University and in London, had joined the throng
of people wanting to see Trudeau as prime minister. Ali and I ran the PR
and Publicity department; Gussy and Suzanne Depoe oversaw the hospitality suites. We all worked ourselves to the point of exhaustion.

Throughout the campaign, I saw Trudeau routinely at public events
and at meetings. He was incisive at getting to the nub of an issue, and

vigorous in his questioning. He was disarming in his lack of ambition or guile, and in his penchant for flirting with every woman from three to ninety-three.

On the night of April 6, his victory, Pierre arrived at the celebration at his campaign headquarters and warmly greeted all of us. The room was hot and overcrowded. We were boisterous and giddy, mixing laughter with tears. Pierre and I talked for a minute. Then, later, just before he left, he said in my ear, "Will you go out with me sometime? Can I call you?"

Our first date was a few days later, on April 11. We drove to Montreal and had a lobster dinner; I returned to Ottawa by train the next day. I was twenty-four. He was forty-eight. We saw each other frequently for the next several months. We went to movies, out to dinner, occasionally to cocktail parties, formal dinners, and public events like the Montreal Grand Prix. But the venue of choice was Harrington Lake, his refuge, where we could hang out and relax.

He was inclusive and welcoming to my friends. He was inventive, passionate, and generous-spirited as a lover. But he was not exactly lavish with money. If we went to a movie, he rarely had cash and would borrow money from me, or his chauffeur. The only "present" he gave me during our relationship was an old pair of used tennis shoes, obviously belonging to another girlfriend, which he fished out of the trunk of his car with a flourish.

"Here," he grinned. "About your size; these should do."

By contrast, he was unstintingly expansive with his ideas and in his relentless prodding to make me question and think things through, reinforcing a life-long lesson from my parents. In discussions, he was always probing.

"But, why, Jennifer, do you say that?" "Why do you think that?" "Why do you believe that?"

He encouraged me to be fearless, to take chances, to try new things.

"How do you know that you can't achieve that, if you don't even try?" he would urge.

He was charmingly boy-like, playful and mischievous, poking fun at stuffiness. But he was, at times, somewhat stuffy himself, and appalled by what he viewed as bad form. He was clearly not amused, for example, by my brother John's German Shepherd leaping on his famous trench coat with muddy paws. Nor was he happy with my inept handling of a canoe that overturned us, fully clothed, into the midnight waters of Harrington Lake.

It was about a year after we first met, February 1969, that "the oyster rebellion" occurred. We were at Harrington Lake, with a couple of people joining us for dinner. He wanted smoked oysters on wheat thins as an hors d'oeuvre.

We worked together in the kitchen. I prepared the plate, and sliced lemons into neat wedges. Without thinking, I squeezed one of the lemon pieces in a drizzle over the oysters.

"What on earth are you doing?" he asked, his face and tone showing that he was *really* angry.

I was flustered by the mistake but, more than that, puzzled by the depth of his displeasure. We had one of those awful, between-clenched-teeth-so-the-guests-don't-hear arguments. It turned out that freedom was the issue.

"The reason I am irritated," he finally explained, "is that each person has the right to decide whether he or she wants to have lemon juice on the oysters. You have taken that choice away."

Shortly after that night, I married someone else.

Then he married the beautiful Margaret. Our lives didn't intersect, but as the years went by, I followed Trudeau's career and life intently, sometimes getting a greeting from him through a friend, or a family member, who had seen him; occasionally actually getting to talk to him. We talked about our children – my four, his four.

When he spoke of his children, he had light behind his eyes.

It was evident they were the most important part of his life. During one of our brief talks, he told me proudly that he thought he had successfully imparted to them "the most important lesson."

That lesson was to question, question, question, to appreciate people's freedom to choose, and to choose well.

▶ BARBRA STREISAND
*Director, actor, singer, producer, composer, philanthropist,
activist, and friend of Trudeau's*

*P*ierre Trudeau was a graceful balance of contradictions. He was an elegant, private, and dignified man who was also charmingly bohemian. And it all flowed through him so naturally. He was always ahead of his time.

This thought occurred to me when the U.S. Supreme Court, quite amazingly, ruled that the State of Texas could not prosecute the sexual behaviour of two consenting adults. In achieving Criminal Code amendments on abortion and homosexuality in Canada, Pierre had said, "The state has no place in the bedrooms of the nation." It's hard to recall now just how bravely that echoed in the halls of power then. He was no stranger to setting new ideas in motion.

Both personally and politically, Pierre was a complex and fascinating man, with the wit and brilliance to charm us all. I so admired him for his iconoclastic and unconventional style, such as the day he so famously first wore sandals into the House of Commons.

There was a strange serendipity in our meeting. During a period when there was no significant other in my life, my friend, Cis Corman, and I were looking through *Life* magazine, jokingly checking if there might be a suitable candidate somewhere in the pages who would be right for me. There was a piece on Pierre, and he certainly captured my imagination. By the way, I've always believed that imagination can manifest itself in reality.

Some time later, in 1968 or 1969, I attended a party following the premiere of *Funny Girl* in London, and was placed at Princess Margaret's table, as was – to my surprise – the prime minister of Canada, Pierre Trudeau. He was everything my imagination promised and more.

I was fascinated by him, but when he asked me to dance, I told him I didn't like to dance in public and introduced him to Cis, who was his delighted dancing partner that night – with pictures on the front page the next day.

As my friendship with Pierre developed, he invited me to Ottawa to attend the opening-night performance of the National Ballet of Canada.

I brought Cis along as my chaperone. I knew I'd have a good time, since my lucky number is 24, and he lived at 24 Sussex Drive. Pierre held himself – and others – to strict disciplines. Very few things took precedence over his strict regime, and dinner guests all knew that they were to make their departure at 10 p.m.

For a while there, in his early years as prime minister, I remember he was quite the rock star. Women would run up to him asking for a kiss. But he never forgot his role as a statesman, and he took very seriously the power he had to change people's lives on a larger scale. He just had a natural ability to inspire others and to work toward a more just society.

Both during his time as head of government and later, he was a model of dignity and humanity, qualities the international community noticed by nominating him for the Nobel Peace Prize, and awarding him the Einstein Peace Foundation International Peace Prize. And what impressed me always was that he did it all with his own brand of flair and sense of justice that was the key to all he was and did.

He reminded me of the father I lost – intellectual, yet physical, loving sports *and* information, that great connection of mind and body. I'm very proud to have been a part of his life.

▶ GALE ZOË GARNETT
Writer and actor

*F*rom our first meeting, in December 1980, Pierre and I frequently shared memories of our fathers, both too soon dead (his when he was fourteen, mine when I was twelve). They were both adored, and both somewhat mythologized by the non-contradiction of absence.

"My father was outgoing, expansive, gregarious," he said once. "I am not. Never have been. I am a solitaire, really. When I do something big and playful, like that pirouette behind the Queen, I am, I believe, pretending to be my father."

I asked if this pretending helped keep Charles Trudeau on earth beyond his premature death. Pierre did that nose-wrinkling and triple-upward flutter of his hand, which I knew meant disagreement, if not

Pierre, Gale Zoë Garnett, and unidentified party guests in Montreal early 1980s.

outright disapproval. He then explained that trying to hold his father on earth would be "spiritually disquieting," but that occasionally pretending to be his father made him feel "happy, and a bit more gregarious."

I do not know if his own fathering was, in part, homage to his father. What is sure is that he adored his sons and his daughter, and joyously permitted himself to love them more openly and completely than he loved anyone other than his ever-missed father.

I met Michel first. I'd been invited, on March 17, 1981, for my first visit to 24 Sussex Drive. I took the train from Toronto to Ottawa. Knowing I'd be meeting the boys for the first time, I stopped en route at Ampersand, a now-gone toyshop in Ottawa's Byward Market, to get them some gifts (yes, I wanted them to like me).

At the house I was greeted by Heidi Bennet, the household coordinator. She made me welcome, and said the boys were still at school. I was shown "my" room, and then taken to what Heidi called "The Freedom Room," a book-filled study with comfortable chesterfields and two writing desks. Two large windows offered a wonderful view of the icy Ottawa River and an expanse of snowy back lawn. Someone had arranged a tray with biscuits and tea. I found a book about Hong Kong and was reading it when I became aware of another presence. A large-eyed tiny male person, in a striped shirt and jeans, was standing in the doorway, watching me.

"Hi. Are you Miche?"

"Yeah."

"Hi. I'm Gale. A friend of your dad's."

"Yeah, he said someone was coming."

"That's me . . . want to do something?"

"Like what?"

"Dunno. What would you like to do?"

"Well, I'd like to swim, but I have to wait for my dad to come home. We could practise reading."

"Okay. Your book or mine?"

"Yours. I already know mine, so it's not really practising."

So we read aloud about Hong Kong. Miche read well and was very visual ("Kowloon – that's two animals").

Justin and Sacha arrived home together. We were introduced and sat in the Freedom Room, discussing this and that. Then Pierre got home and, from the foyer, shouted "*Salut, mes enfants!*" Shouting "Papa! Papa!" the boys took off down the stairs and proceeded to climb all over him. They were all laughing, including Pierre.

That night Miche came downstairs in his pyjamas, along with his brothers, to say goodnight. His father had gone, for a moment, to take a telephone call. I had a tiny cardboard music box with a clown face on it, in my purse. I took it out and cranked it. Its melody tinkled out. Miche grinned.

"Want it?"

"Yes, please!"

I gave it to him. At which point Pierre returned to the dining room.

"Look, Papa!" Miche cranked the music box.

"Where did you get that?"

"It's Gale's. She gave it to me."

Pierre furrowed his brows and pursed his lips.

"No. It's not yours. It's hers. You must give it back."

I was bewildered. "It's all right, Pierre," I said. "I want him to have it."

"No. I don't want the boys to be cadging things from visitors."

"He wasn't 'cadging,' I really . . ."

"Please, Miche. Give Gale back her music box."

He did. We both looked miserable. Then Pierre had another tele-phone call, and sedition broke out in the dining room. I wound the music box into the waistband of Miche's pyjamas, and then rolled the band a few times, and pulled the pyjama-top over the whole business. Pierre returned again. My co-conspirator kissed his father goodnight, hugged me, and went off to bed.

Pierre said, "You must not let men bully you into things," meaning Miche and the music box.

"Does that include you?"

He looked at me, quite seriously. Then he smiled and touched my cheek. "Yes. Yes, it does."

All of "the Trudeau men" were and are legendarily athletic risk-takers. Pierre was about sixty-two when I watched him execute twenty somer-saults on the trampoline owned by Senator Bud Drury.

One twilight at 24, Justin, out on the lawn, somersaulted over and over, while his father and I discussed a film we'd both liked. Finally, as Justin headed into his fifteenth perfectly executed somersault, I said, "Will you say something to Justin about his trampoline work before he breaks his neck waiting for a word?"

Pierre opened the French doors and shouted: "Bravo, Justin! *Bien fait!*" Justin, sweat-shiny and red-faced, grinned hugely as he jumped down from the trampoline.

Not all the juvenile athleticism drew praise, however. We were at Harrington Lake having breakfast one morning when Pierre, eyes sud-denly wide with alarm, whispered, "Don't move." Oh God, I thought, we've been taken hostage. I said nothing, and did not move. Pierre slowly stood up and walked out the door. He went round to the side of the house, where Miche was hanging upside down from the second-floor windowsill of his bedroom.

"Please drop now, Miche. I'll catch you."

Miche dropped. Pierre caught him. And told him, again, that he was not to hang from the windowsill.

Pierre liked to have a sauna and swim after dinner. Once, during sauna-swim time at 24 Sussex, he asked if I wanted to "do the Finnish thing." He was not usually prone to esoteric kinky-sounding proposals.

"Do the Finnish thing?"

"Yes. Roll in the snow, after the sauna and before the heated pool."

So we did. The RCMP circled the house and would be at the pool area, he said, every ten minutes. So we rolled in the snow, which was great, then ran back into the house. I wondered what the RCMP made of the shapes and footprints in the snow. Perhaps it happened a lot.

I always carry a Swiss Army knife with me, and I remember one date with Pierre when it came in handy. We had gone, with the French ambassador, to see Yves Montand at the National Arts Centre. Afterwards, there was a dinner for M. Montand at the French embassy, and Pierre invited Mme Gabrielle Léger, the widow of the former governor general, to ride with us to the embassy. En route, Mme Léger realized that she'd caught a bit of her navy blue chiffon dress in the door of the car. Pierre opened the black limo door ever so slightly, explaining in French to the driver that a bit of the gown was solidly wound into the door's works.

"*Est-ce que je peux vous aider?*" I enquired. "*J'ai mon couteau de l'armée suisse.*" ("May I help? I have with me the knife of the Swiss Army.") I explained that I'd just have to cut the tiniest piece from the hem of the floor-length gown. Mme Léger thought this was a *bonne idée* and told me to do this. It was done. Walking up the stairs to the French embassy, with all sorts of people standing at attention, Pierre whispered:

"Do you always carry a Swiss Army knife in your evening bag?"

"Yes."

He shook his head, smiling. "Useful. Very useful."

Another time we met in New York. Pierre had been invited there to receive The Family of Man award, and I was also in that city, rehearsing a play. As my rehearsal did not end until after the award presentation, he asked if we could meet after the ceremony, at the Pierre Hotel, where he was staying the night. He was not certain how long the ceremony would be, so we agreed to meet in the small bar just off the main lobby.

I was quietly drinking a gin and tonic in the noisy bar when Pierre burst into the little round room. Behind him was a flying wedge of about seven American security guys (we always joked about the "John Wayne security" in the States), their heads and eyes rolling in all directions.

Pierre suggested everything would be "calmer" upstairs, and that it had been "a long day." We stepped inside the flying wedge. It was reduced to two men for the elevator. When we got to the Presidential Suite, the two men stationed themselves outside the double doors.

Once inside the Presidential Suite, I took off my shoes (as usual). Pierre opened the mini-bar. There was orange juice, Perrier, and Canadian beer. Atop the mini-bar was a bottle of Veuve Clicquot champagne on ice.

"Well, what would you like to drink?"

I looked at the champagne. Neither Pierre nor I drank very much, but I did want a glass of "the Widow."

"I'd like this," I said.

Pierre pursed his lips. "Fine. You have that. I'm going to just have an orange juice. If I drink champagne, I'll be too sleepy, and I do want to spend some time with you."

I looked at the large bottle. There was no way I could consume more than two glasses.

"Oh, I don't know. I won't be able to drink much of it, and the rest will . . . just go flat, and you won't be able to have any, and . . ."

He put his hands on my shoulders. He was smiling.

"I don't believe I will want any at all . . . and your frugality is good . . . but, if I were to want it, I can get more."

I flushed. Right. Budget Baby and The Rich Guy discuss the Champagne. I had two glasses. We had a good visit. I said goodnight to the John Wayne Twins when I left.

There were frequent examples of our different relationships to money and frugality. After he bought the Ernest Cormier art deco house in Montreal, we went one day to explore it and to clean out the crawl spaces (who says I don't lead a glamorous life?). The original furnishings were still in the living room. The windows went from the floor to the stratosphere.

"My sister said I shouldn't have bought this place, because no one will be able to clean the windows," he said, with a slight shrug.

And there was this amazing slightly pleated, pale-salmon-coloured wallpaper, made of the thinnest possible wood.

"What great stuff," I said. "It's a shame that it's peeling."

"Yes. It does need replacing. I'll send to Japan for it."

Right. Why hadn't I thought of that? To this day, when I wish to indicate that something isn't a problem, I say, "Not to worry. I'll send to Japan for it."

Years later, I told Pierre of my adopted euphemism. It made him laugh, though I do not believe he ever saw anything unusual in "I'll send to Japan for it," as a form of effortless problem-solving.

He was famously frugal (he stopped buying Perrier when the price went up a few pennies) but when his frugality collided with beloved gourmandise, gourmandise won. Caviar, pheasant, fine chocolate, and escargots (which the boys also loved, and would have with orange juice!).

One day, when I was visiting him in Montreal, we went to a fine Italian restaurant. When the bill came, Pierre produced a green American Express card. He was clearly delighted.

"Do you know these? They're marvellous. You can use them just like money." He was serious. And looked, for a moment, as young as Justin.

"Yes, I know. I have one."

The man had been PM for sixteen years. Years in which the rest of us had got our credit cards.

In the twenty years we knew each other, Pierre would say gracious and affectionate things from time to time. Some of it was courtly nonsense, things he thought a woman, any woman, would want to hear. Things in which the effort was the significant factor. The best thing he ever said to me was "Talking to you always cheers me up. I always feel better when I talk to you." Some of our best times involved talking about our mutual love of travel and our interest in the wider world. We were, neither of us, comfortable with most people, but we were both comfortable in most places.

Pierre Trudeau knew fully who he was. He had a core belief that his life would go well. This belief made him more comfortable than almost any other Canadian when something good happened to someone else. Pierre wanted everyone to do well – his children, his friends, and his family. In fact (and this could be the hard part) he expected us to. Of all the people I've ever known, he was the best one to bring good news to. He delighted in the accomplishments of those who mattered to him.

▶ KRISTIN BENNETT
Montreal teacher, artist, and friend of Trudeau's since 1968

Our friendship had its start back in 1968, when I was twenty-one years old. We met at the annual St. Mary's Ball in Montreal, a very grand and formal affair held yearly in November. Pierre was the guest of honour and, in addition, his niece was being "presented" that year. We were introduced by my twin sister, Barbara, whom Pierre knew, and he immediately asked me to dance.

This was the era of Trudeaumania, and Pierre looked every bit the dashing and sophisticated idol who had charmed the country so recently. I was flattered by his attentions and his suave dress in his tuxedo. He charmed me with his boyish smile and wouldn't let me go, saying, "Don't stop. Let's keep dancing." We were so intent on each other's sparkly eyes that no one dared cut in. I felt giddy and free as we danced and flirted. Finally someone intervened and we parted. My mother was furious. That night we both felt an immediate connection, which was to be the beginning of a very close friendship that spanned some three decades.

Kristin's portrait: On the rocks (with beard) at his lake north of Montreal in 1979.

Our personal lives diverged following our respective marriages and my move to Toronto. The year 1991 started very badly for me, and it was at this time that Pierre revealed his special qualities that remain so clear and bright in my mind. Two shattering events in my life managed to coincide, and Pierre was there for me when I most needed a friend. My father had been ill for some time, and the shock of his death in April was compounded by my husband leaving me the very week of the funeral. I called Pierre and left a message telling him of Dad's death. Pierre came to the wake and spent a couple of hours talking to me and sitting with the family.

By June, I was back in Montreal, but was still in shock and confusion. I phoned Pierre to tell him that my marriage was over and that I was devastated. He asked me what he could do. I replied, "Be a friend." And he was. The friendship took the form of lunches near his office, ski trips to the house up north, and dinners at my place. Pierre would gently remind me that it takes two years to get over a failed marriage.

Pierre was knowledgeable about good food and rare wines, but had absolutely no interest in preparing food. If a meal was not provided, he would eat spaghetti out of a can. One of my first visits to his Arthur Erickson–designed country house in the Laurentians was in 1991. I discovered to my horror that lunch was to be either canned ravioli or frozen hot dogs. His culinary skills apparently extended to the use of the microwave only! That was the first and last time we ate a meal from a can.

I developed a plan. Because I loved to cook and refused to eat canned spaghetti even on a hiking trip, I proposed a deal for our weekends up north. Pierre agreed that I would buy the groceries for the weekend, and he would reimburse me. I would cook all the meals, and for dinner he would supply one of the great red wines from his cellar. He loved the arrangement.

While I was preparing, Pierre would usually interrupt his reading and wander into the kitchen to see how things were going. "What can I do?" he would ask. At first I said nothing, but then over time we entertained each other with impromptu cooking lessons. I would show him how to do the basic kitchen manoeuvres, and he would have me in stitches trying to carry them out. For example, Pierre didn't have a lettuce dryer, so I taught him how to dry lettuce by spinning it in a dish-towel. He immediately discovered that this was best done outdoors!

Pierre would pick me up on Saturday morning to go up north and, in the back of the Jeep would be a dutifully packed cardboard box with the remains of the city kitchen: half a litre of milk, some tired vegetables, Saran-wrapped leftovers, and the remains of a loaf of bread. Pierre simply couldn't bear to throw things away. Our country weekends will always remain some of my fondest memories.

The last time I saw Pierre was at his office on June 30, 2000. It was obvious his health was declining. I was leaving the next day for a month of painting in Lunenberg, Nova Scotia, and, since he was expecting some people, I didn't stay long. I showed him my planned driving route on the map. He went through the route step by step to be sure that I was making the most of the trip. That was very Pierre, the details and the thought that he gave to everything he did. As I was leaving, he hugged me much longer than usual and said he wished that he was going with me. He gazed into my eyes for so long with that soft smile, and then I left. I knew I would never see him again. I knew he was saying goodbye.

▶ MARGOT KIDDER
Friend, actress, and political activist

People who had never been emotionally involved with Pierre, men in particular, always wanted to know what the deal was, how this slight and often outwardly aloof guy managed to keep rotating gaggles of women in a perpetual state of romantic willingness. He was written about like some sleazy Hollywood Don Juan, a Ryan O'Neal with taste, as if he toyed with women and then tossed them aside like used Kleenex, and the comments on his love life were rarely without the accompanying bitterness of envy.

He was not a Don Juan. Pierre was far too sensitive and conscientious to carelessly break hearts. I know morality is not much in fashion these days, but Pierre was someone who just could not give up the habit. And anyway, you always sensed with him that his own heart had been broken way, way back down the line by *someone* – a woman, his father perhaps, a cruel school chum – and he had vowed to not pass on his infection. But there is no question that many women, myself included, fell head over heels in love with him, and just plain stayed that way.

"It's just because he's the prime minister and women love power," said so many, with all the wisdom of second-rate pop-psychology manuals and the habitual chauvinism that denied a woman's ability to see past male surfaces.

That was not it. Oh sure, initially it was a thrill to be dating a prime minister, to be sitting kissing in the back of the bulletproof limousine, while the RCMP (with their ear wires) stared resolutely straight ahead in the front seat. And there's no question that it tickled the ego to be ushered into Sussex Drive as if you belonged there and have your suitcases taken up to your room (minutes, no doubt after another lady had just been ushered out, but you didn't know that until years later when you began comparing notes). Or to dance at a ball at the New York Public Library with the one Canadian export – that all of Manhattan admired – looking into *your* eyes and telling you that you were the most beautiful woman in the room. Or calling him direct in Ottawa and getting put right through.

And sure, it was perversely fun to sit next to him at a formal state dinner with everyone else kissing his ass and calling him "Mr. Prime Minister," when you got to hold his hand under the table, and lean your mouth to his ear, and just call him Pierre. Let's face it, there's nothing better than going to the prom with hands down the coolest guy in the school. It's like dressing in Armani.

But while being rich and famous and universally admired will definitely attract more members of the opposite sex than anyone can handle, it sure won't make them love you.

Almost all men who are truly successful with women share a common trait, and that is the unconscious ability to make women see the little boy who lives trapped under the layers of defences, because once a woman has seen that essence in a man she'll never get over him. And there are other men who make women fall in love with them because they exude the air of a protective and adored father, and they make you want to crumple up into their chests like some furry pet. Pierre, in spite of his best efforts to the contrary, had both these qualities.

Canadian Press, Peter Bregg

*Sharing a secret
with Margot Kidder.*

So one of the things that cinched it for Pierre with us ladies was learning that the prime minister, underneath all the impressive trappings of accomplishment, was the gentlest, sweetest little boy you'd ever known. When you realized this (as he eagerly handed you the simpleminded dinner of pork and beans and bacon out of a can that he'd cooked; or when he held you in his arms in the morning, beaming and enormously pleased with himself), it felt as if you knew a secret no one else knew, and in knowing it, you'd been anointed keeper of his flame. Even when he covered himself up in all his various useful disguises and jobs and sophistications, *you'd* remember who was in there.

There were times he made me annoyed. Such as having to play twenty questions, when he was grim and closed-lipped, in order to find out what had made him angry. Or having to run back into a fancy restaurant after a particularly wonderful meal on the pretext of having to go to the bathroom, so you could leave an extra ten bucks to compensate for his miserly tip; or watching him behave in a particularly snooty and dismissive manner to a brown-nosing lightweight. Or (and especially this "or") finally realizing that there was to be no going off into the monogamous sunset with this man, no white picket fence. In spite of all that, and in the face of all his social defences, you'd say to yourself, I know who's in there, I know who's in there, and you'd love him.

You slowly figured out that you weren't that one-in-a-million to Pierre as much as one of forty-in-a-million, or maybe forty-six or forty-seven, who knew? On the occasion of my first state dinner as his date, I looked out from the dais where I sat beside the foreign minister of Greece and counted three ex-girlfriends of Pierre's, sitting at the regular tables below us on the hotel ballroom floor. Instead of feeling smug and special for being the one and only high up there with the guests of honour, and not one of the plebe girlfriends down there in the cheap seats, I was washed in the bile of jealousy, and I fled the dinner with no explanation and ran back to my hotel room at the Four Seasons Hotel in Toronto and sobbed my eyes out. Pierre was mystified and the next day asked me why I'd run away and I lied and told him I'd got my period all over my pretty white dress. I don't think he believed me – I think he knew. But he never explained why he invited them; he knew he didn't have to, and it would have been dishonest to try.

Years later, whenever I saw Shirley MacLaine, she'd lean into me and ask, "How's our boy Pierre?" and I'd tell her whatever I knew and we'd smile. We're kind of a club, we ladies, *la crème de la crème* if you ask me. I don't know if he ever actually dumped any of his lovers – he never dumped me – he just stood back and let his arrangements morph into comfortable friendships that stood on more solid ground.

He was pretty goofy. One of the games he invented was Playing Indian. "Shall we play Indian?" he'd suggest on the weekend at Harrington Lake. You played Indian by skulking through the woods, trying not to alert your enemy as to your whereabouts by snapping twigs underfoot or breaking the branches of trees that hung over the paths. The RCMP, lurking at a discreet distance, would act as if they didn't notice that the prime minister was tiptoeing around with a girlfriend. They'd stand at attention in the woods pretending they weren't there, pretending they were trees.

His refusal to read the papers or watch the evening news was somewhat alarming, given that one always wants one's prime minister to know what is going on in the world, but he held newspapers and

most magazines (with the exception of *The Nation*) in the same contempt that most intellectual snobs hold the *National Enquirer*, and he
was not about to be seduced by the nightly current-events soap opera
that so many of the rest of us are addicted to. "I want an in-depth
account of what's going on," he'd say. "The media rarely tells the truth."
But then you'd find a briefing paper in his homework briefcase that
was a direct lift from a *New York Times* article of the day before.
"Pierre!" you'd say. "This isn't inside information for God's sake. I read
this yesterday morning over coffee." And he'd just shrug – or laugh, if
you'd managed to present your case disguised as a joke. Accusations he
hated; jokes he loved.

So you tried to make him laugh. This wasn't always easy, as there was
no formula to his sense of humour, not the old one-two-three punch that
defines the rhythm of most jokes, nor the ironic put-down; even the
absurdist paradox wasn't guaranteed to please. You never knew when
you'd be rewarded by a gentle burst of that somewhat surprised laughter.
He called me in New York several months after Gulf War One, to praise
me for an article I'd written on nationalism for the *The Nation* that he'd
felt was "particularly insightful." He always made a point of letting you
know when you'd done something genuinely deserving, just as he always
called if he learned you were in rough shape and needed reassuring.
That's just who he was. He was never *not* there, when it was important.

"Your ideas here are wonderful," he told me, "and so clearly presented."

I didn't know what to say. On the one hand, I lived for his approval,
it meant more to me than praise from anyone on the planet, and in that
respect he was "the good father," the one I'd not had in childhood. On
the other hand, this time his praise was somewhat embarrassing, seeing
as I'd plagiarized the entire article from one of his old speeches to the
United Nations that he'd sent me way back in 1980 or 1981.

"Gee. Thanks," I tentatively answered. If I stayed silent, he'd remain
convinced of my newfound brilliance; if I spoke up, I risked a tight-
lipped silence that would freeze my ear to the telephone receiver like a
tongue to a wrought-iron banister at twenty below in a Quebec winter.
And I was nervous that, instead of praise, I would get its opposite, blame.
Boy oh boy, was I torn.

"You don't remember hearing any of that before, huh?"

"Well, I am familiar with the ideas your argument is based on."

And then I went for it, I told him.

"Well, you should be. It's a direct lift from one of your speeches." The silence that followed scared me. I was in my child-seeking-validation mode and not at that moment confident about my standing with the man. But then it came: first the low cough of a back-of-the-throat chuckle, and then the delighted opening into a real honest-to-God laugh.

"I *thought* I recognized a lot of it!" And he laughed more, and whenever he laughed he relaxed, and we jabbered away for another good half-hour, and I was aware of the delicious weightlessness he was giving me. I never saw him let a man take the piss out of him, but with women it was different, he let us all the time, and I think he liked it.

He loved his own secret jokes, which were often based on a sly irreverence, and he got a kick out of letting you in on a few. During the last year of his time in office, Margaret Thatcher was to pay an official visit, and Pierre had a brooch made of rubies shaped like a maple leaf designed for her. It was a nice brooch, as ruby maple-leaf brooches go, tasteful and appropriate and all that. But he kept it for a time in a crumpled brown paper bag, like the kind you took your lunch to school in when you were a kid. It sat there in its bag like a slightly insulting lump, on top of his brown-paper-covered table in the dining room of his house on Pine Avenue, for quite some time, until it had to go to work.

"Mrs. Thatcher's present's over there," he said to more than a few people. "Take a look. Tell me what you think." Then he'd try to restrain his sneaking grin when they picked up the bag and tried to figure out if he was being disrespectful.

The arrogance was there, yes, but it wasn't the essence of his heart, it was simply an attitude, and at times an affectation. Once I asked him why a man of his intelligence would continue to believe in the Catholic Church. "I use it as a place of meditation," he said, "And I *do* believe. Well, I believe in most of it. I don't believe that I have to go through some priest in order to talk to God. I'm more than capable of talking to [God] directly all by myself." And that was that. End of discussion.

He saw the best in you and refused to see the worst. This was flattering and set the bar for your personal best somewhat higher than you cared it to be, but it could make things awkward, especially when it was a direct denial of objective reality. Sometimes I got drunk and far too physically enthusiastic, and he'd have to pick me off him like lint, but he never complained.

When I went crazy in the late spring of 1995 and was convinced that one of my ex-husbands was the head of the CIA and was trying to kill me, the only way I thought I could explain my situation to the police (who took me off in handcuffs to the loony bin), and to the growing gathering of onlookers, was to hand out Pierre's home phone number in Montreal to everyone, saying loudly, "Call *him*. He was once a prime minister and *he'll* know why the CIA's after me."

This was not a good idea. I realized that after I'd come down to earth. But in the ensuing months, whenever I tried to apologize to him – first over the phone, and later over lunch in an Italian restaurant in Montreal – he refused to listen to me, as if acknowledging my apology would be an acknowledgment of my occasional bouts with insanity, and that he would not do, as if by doing so he'd imply that he thought less of me than he did. I'm still a little annoyed about this: I was sorry, and I wanted him to know that. And I *was* crazy and I wanted him to love me anyway, but mostly I wanted him to respond to the apology, and tell me how many people had actually called him at home.

His love was elusive. I never heard him use the word about anyone except his ex-wife and his beloved sons, and I'm not sure he altogether trusted the emotion very much. It's as if he gave his love in such tiny, tasteful increments that you couldn't know how big his gift was until you added up the pieces after he was gone.

I still wake in the night, stranded in the darkness of half-finished dreams about him. It's odd that the dreams wake me, because they are (as they usually were during the twenty years that I knew him) the sort of dreams intended to soothe and calm, when your life feels full of bumps. Sometimes I write them down, so as to hold on to them a little longer before the warmth of them evaporates.

In my favourite dream, he had come back from the dead, all full of laughter and bonhomie, and he announced that one of the things he'd learned from being dead was that there was no point in living life all tensed up, and that this time round he was changing his point of view and was just going to have fun as often as he could. He was in his little Mercedes and wearing one of those ridiculous cravats of his, only this one had a long end on it, like a scarf of Isadora Duncan's in the 1920s, and his head was tossed back gaily, his left arm resting crooked on the outside of the car door. He let me snuggle against his bird chest and he drove us around, just laughing and laughing and laughing. He seemed so present and so alive, all of him – his impossibly fragile skin, like tissue paper on the frame of a Japanese lantern, his tiny feet like a child's, the absolute steadfastness of his friendship. Oh I was so lonely for him when I woke up.

I really, really loved the guy, and I miss him like crazy. Me, and forty other women – or maybe forty-six or forty-seven. Who knows? So much has happened since he died, and I need him to talk to. There's a big hole in my heart where he'd once been. Three years ago, I named my new puppy Pierre, and I snuggle him at night, but, let's face it, it isn't quite the same.

Chapter Thirteen

Canoe Gang

▶ ALASTAIR W. GILLESPIE
Cabinet minister, 1971–79

*M*uch has been written about Pierre's love of the outdoors – of his enjoyment of the quiet, the privacy, the tranquility of a calm lake in a canoe. The canoe also carried a subliminal message. The symbolism was right. What could be more Canadian? It represents the very essence of our existence, of discovery, of improvisation, the response to enormous challenges. His summer excursions in the Arctic provided both freedom and the challenge of danger – some of which was created by the inexperience of his companions.

Two to a canoe, one forward, one aft. Draw for partners. The pairing on this occasion, on the Coppermine River in 1966, had Pierre in a canoe with the then-retired headmaster of Trinity College School in Port Hope.

"I'll take the stern," said the somewhat imperious voice of the former headmaster. Pierre, a little unsure of his canoe-mate's prowess, made a bid for the same position. But the headmaster persisted. They were not far into the current before the guiding hand of the stern paddler failed. The fast whitewater current hit them broadside. Over they went, and so did all their belongings.

It was noted that, while both men reached shore safely, they did not land at the same place. It was also noted that, when they took to the

Paddling the stern, this time with Gerard Pelletier's son, Jean.

river again, they were occupying different canoes, and Pierre was in the stern of his.

▶ BECKY MASON
Canoeist, artist, and filmmaker, who grew up down the road from the prime minister's country residence at Harrington Lake, Quebec

I have fond memories of canoeing with my family when I was growing up on the shores of Meech Lake. On many occasions we had friends along to enjoy the thrill of whitewater paddling, and also to share the wilderness experience with us. One spring day in the late 1970s my dad (canoeist and author Bill Mason) declared that the water levels were up, the sun was shining, and it was perfect canoeing weather. All our scheduled tasks were gleefully put on hold, and it was decided that my dad, my brother Paul, our friend Terry Orlick, and I were going on a day run down the Picanoc River, near Kazabazua, Quebec. Dad phoned up his friend Pierre Trudeau and asked if he could break away too and go canoeing with us. Yes, Pierre said, he, Justin, and Sacha could come, so we all packed up our gear and headed out the door to meet at the put-in.

At the time, it seemed perfectly normal to me that the Prime Minster of Canada was coming over in his stretch limousine to shoot the Picanoc with us on the spur of the moment. And, because Pierre was the PM, the rule was that the RCMP had to follow him at all times. I had heard hilarious stories about some previous whitewater trips in which Dad and Pierre spent quite a bit of their time rescuing the RCMP (I guess their boot camp didn't include whitewater canoeing), because they usually flipped on the first rapid and spent much of the rest of the trip trying to keep their heads above water.

After a couple of these comical day trips, the head guys at the RCMP started to frown upon such excursions, but Pierre wasn't about to give up canoeing for a silly reason like security! So the RCMP and Pierre struck a deal this particular day. It was decided that we would run the Picanoc, and the officers would see us off at the put-in, then meet us at the bridge near the take-out at the end of the day.

We had a lovely day running the river, shooting some big waves, dodging rocks, and laughing about the near misses over lunch. It was hot and, to cool off, everyone went for a skinny dip. I was kind of shy about swimming with the guys, so I swam downriver.

We all had a great day, and as we drifted in our canoes toward the last bridge, where we were to finish, we expected to see the RCMP waiting for us. But no! There was no sign of them. It started to cloud over and get windy as we hauled our gear up the bank. We sat down and waited on the edge of the dirt road, hoping the RCMP would find us. Then the clouds burst and a pelting rain started soaking us through.

The take-out was fairly remote, and the only building nearby was a rundown old cottage. Pierre was getting mighty impatient about the RCMP losing him and was concerned about everyone getting soaking wet and cold. So we all trudged over to the cottage. I remember him knocking on the door and being greeted by a French-Canadian couple, their jaws dropping open in surprise as they realized the PM was standing on their doorstep! I think it was amazing they recognized him at all, because we looked like muddy drowned rats.

The tiny cabin was a mess, and already crammed with people, and it had only a couple of chairs. It did, however, have a sagging cot that our canoeing crew perched on, while Pierre got on the phone. For security reasons, Pierre had a code name, which was "Maple One," so we listened to him on the phone blasting the RCMP for losing Maple One. And Maple One – who, he reminded them, was with Maple Three, five-year-old Justin, and very tired Maple Four, three-year-old Sacha – was to be found *now*!

During the conversation Pierre discovered that the limo and RCMP truck had been stuck in the mud for hours at the put-in, but they had extracted themselves from the goo and now were waiting at the bridge and where were we? That phone line got quite a working over that day by Maple One. Dad, realizing that the RCMP must be at the wrong bridge, took off and hitchhiked to Gracefield. The rest of us all sat around in the steamy, mouldy cottage with the rain pounding down outside, hoping that Dad would soon find the police officers. We all started laughing at ourselves being in this predicament. It got worse though.

Through the paper-thin walls from the other room came the unmistakable sounds of an amorous couple enjoying themselves very thoroughly and intimately. We were all wondering if this surreal ending could get any stranger, when we heard the limousine tires on the gravel road, and we all leapt out of there. It was amusing to think our PM was stranded in such a situation while on a wholesome family canoe trip, and I still chuckle about our PM being so near a bedroom of the nation that day!

▶ PAUL MASON

In the spring of 1977, canoed the Picanoc River in western Quebec with one of his father's friends

The day I paddled in the bow of a canoe with Pierre Trudeau changed my life. It was the day I became aware that I *often* ended up having to paddle bow for one of Dad's friends during our spring whitewater day trips on the local rivers. I had learned to paddle whitewater in the bow of my dad's canoe during the filming of his *Path of the Paddle* series of instructional canoe films.

Later, when we began canoeing just for fun, I continued in the bow position, with Dad as the stern paddler. Then, one day, he had two friends who wanted to join us on a trip, but they were not skilled enough to paddle as a team. The solution was that one would paddle bow for Dad, and I would paddle bow for the other. The system worked well.

So it was no surprise to be paired with Pierre Trudeau (with me in the bow) for a run down the Picanoc River. While it had occurred to me that he was the Prime Minister of Canada, I also knew the river treats all paddlers equally, and we did too.

At one point, we approached the crux of a particular rapid that featured an intimidating hole, and I initiated the manoeuvre to avoid it. The stern didn't seem to follow my lead. That is when I yelled at the Prime Minister of Canada. He responded with the correct paddle stroke, and we made it through upright. Soon after that trip, I announced to Dad that I wanted to paddle with one of *my* friends instead of getting stuck with one of his, even if they were the prime minister.

I laugh about it now.

▶ TIM KOTCHEFF
Former vice-president of news for CTV and CBC-TV;
made three canoe trips with Trudeau between 1979 and 1996

I've always admired Pierre Trudeau from the very first day I met him at the Liberal leadership convention in 1968. Here was an unconventional individual who raised the bar dramatically for all aspiring leaders who dared to follow. He was flamboyant, fluently bilingual, exceedingly intelligent, and impishly irreverent. But did anyone really know Pierre Trudeau? Somehow I doubt it, because Pierre Trudeau was an intensely private person. But I was fortunate enough to get a personal glimpse of this Canadian icon on three separate canoe trips, the first in 1979.

My long-time friend Craig Oliver, CTV chief political correspondent, and I had been plying Canada's Arctic rivers since 1974. Over the years, we began to recruit other outdoor enthusiasts to join our annual summer pilgrimage to the far north, and our group eventually came to be known, jokingly, as the "Arctic and Rideau Canal Canoe Club." The title was not serious. But the trips were.

Planning, analyzing, readying the course.

With founders of the Arctic and Rideau Canal Canoe Club, Tim Kotcheff (left) and Craig Oliver. Pierre's T-shirt reads: "Blitz Canada 1979. This time no more Mr. Nice Guy."

© Tim Kotcheff

Just after the Liberals lost out to a minority Conservative government in 1979, Pierre Trudeau accepted an invitation to join our eight-man canoe team for an expedition down the Hanbury–Thelon rivers in the Northwest Territories. Joining Pierre, Craig, and myself would be Peter Stollery, John Gow, Jean Pelletier, John Godfrey, and David Silcox.

The Hanbury is a beautiful but fitfully rugged river that, in one instance, meanders through miles of sand dunes, and at another passes over a spectacular falls. At yet another, it cuts its way through an awesome canyon. Difficult rapids and dangerous rock gardens make passage down the Hanbury extremely hazardous.

But Dickson Canyon posed one of the greatest hurdles. Not only was it unnavigable, but bypassing it involved a brutal three-mile portage over rough terrain. Could we handle it? Better still, could sixty-year-old Pierre Trudeau handle it? Those thoughts would trouble us until the day the canyon stood in our way. In his more youthful days, Pierre had canoed the legendary Nahanni River, known to many as "the dangerous river." But that was then. This was now.

Our group assembled in Yellowknife in preparation for a Twin Otter charter flight to the headwaters of the Hanbury River, and met in a hotel restaurant to discuss arrangements for the morning lift-off. As we sat at a bare table, munching cold sandwiches and sipping warm beer, a mood of apprehension and even a little tension swept over us. Like any trip into the Arctic unknown, the emotional roller coaster begins early. And frankly, as silly as it seems, sitting beside a living legend like Pierre wasn't easy. People had packed the entranceway to the restaurant just to catch a glimpse of, or perhaps even to touch, this political celebrity. Someone sent over a bottle of wine, which was gratefully received. Others could be heard shouting his name. While we were intimidated, Pierre seemed totally unperturbed.

We flew out the next morning and, after several hours, landed in Sifton Lake, gateway to the fast-moving Hanbury River. The plan was to navigate the Hanbury, which converges with the Thelon River, pass through a game sanctuary named after the Thelon, and end up at the historic cabin where the legendary John Hornby and two companions starved to death in the late 1920s.

We had no intention of suffering a similar fate. We had enough food and drink to support a small army. We boasted that we operated the best restaurant north of the Arctic circle. About this there was no doubt. Amid the splendour of an Arctic sunset, what could be finer than a rum daiquiri, followed by smoked salmon, charbroiled lamb chops, saffron rice pilaf, and a glass of 1967 Château Lafitte? And, oh yes, a snifter of cognac and a high-class cigar to round out the evening. There are purists who will probably scoff at the mere thought of *haute cuisine* on the trail. If Pierre was such a purist, he never let on. In fact, he enjoyed his meals immensely and seemed quite impressed with their high quality. Initially, he said he didn't want any alcoholic beverages, but soon he, like the rest of us, would line up, cup in hand, for his daily ration of rum and wine.

We spent a couple of days at our landing site getting acclimatized. Pierre was now sporting a beard. It made him look older. I watched him fussing with his camp gear. He was clearly not himself. He seemed distant, aloof, and contemplative – perhaps still feeling the sting of rejection at the hands of a fickle electorate. Our first night was filled with small talk and not much else. A first night for any Arctic traveller can be unnerving. As the last echo of the departing charter plane fades into the distance, the vast, desolate sweep of the tundra offers precious little comfort. Fear of the unknown, self-doubt, and a sense of melancholy all begin to rise uncontrollably: there is no turning back.

It was time to get our sea legs ready for the challenge ahead. But we still harboured nagging doubts about Pierre. What would he be like on this long and difficult journey, an experience that can bring out either the best or the worst in people? How fit was he? Could he manage the dangerous rapids and portages? And what would happen, heaven forbid, if he . . . well . . . *drowned*? Someone joked that the final words of the headline would read "there were seven others on the trip." But, believe me, we were firmly resolved that nothing of the kind would ever happen on our watch. Seasoned Arctic travellers like us could never stand the humiliation of such a catastrophe.

Within a few days we got the answers to many of our questions. Pierre took his turn like everyone else with the camp chores: he was by far the best dish-washer, fire-maker, and camp organizer. He put some of us to shame. As for the whitewater, he never failed to meet a challenge but was

"By far the best fire-maker"
also carried the wood.

never reckless. He would examine each difficult rapid carefully, weigh the risks, and then take the plunge, moving his canoe gracefully and resolutely around rocks, ledges, and other obstacles. He often led the way. Not only was he fit, he turned out to be one of the best canoeists and sternsmen in the group. If anyone succumbed to the elements, it wouldn't be Pierre. He was just too savvy. For instance, on another trip with Pierre in 1995 on the Stikine River in British Columbia, I recall running a very dangerous rapid. Craig and I bucked five-foot standing waves, ran clumsily into a rocky outcropping, before threading a precipitous gap through a cliff wall into roiling water. Not a pretty manoeuvre on our part. After all parties, including Pierre, had negotiated these rapids safely using a smarter route, we were easy targets for criticism. Amidst the post-run heckling, on this trip Pierre gently reminded everyone that Craig and I had gone first, acknowledging that a lead canoe navigating a rapid faces the most danger and those that follow are then "schooled" on the correct route and strategy to employ. Pierre's comment put an end to the harping and I felt good for the rest of the day.

But back to the Hanbury. Pierre was a hard, steady paddler and often kept his canoe ahead of the pack. One might conclude that staying in front is where born leaders want to be. But seasoned Arctic travellers

© Tim Kotcheff

Happy and relaxed.

know it's the lead canoe that gets to see the most wildlife. Bears, caribou, and other animals have long disappeared by the time the other canoes catch up. Pierre always wanted to be the first to capture the beauty of such splendid virgin territory. I admired him for that.

After days of tricky rapids and heavy water, we beached our canoes to prepare for the arduous Dickson Canyon portage. We were still heavily laden. Pierre carried more than his share of the load, which included an eighteen-foot canoe. Try carrying one of those on your back for three miles over a terrain strewn with rock, bog, and bush, and you'll know what it's all about. We were impressed, to say the least.

By now Pierre had begun to open up, to relax. Gone was the tenseness, the grim determination. He was now . . . well, almost "one of the boys," and wonderful company. We were all relaxed, too. And there was some manly ribbing and joking along the way.

"What's the difference between ignorance and apathy?" someone pondered.

To which Trudeau quickly replied, "I don't know, and I don't give a damn." And then quickly rejoined, "What's the difference between fear and panic? Fear is when you learn for the first time you can't do it the second time. Panic is when you learn for the second time you can't do it the first time."

He was considerate, kind, and helpful. He surprised everyone with his reservoir of knowledge of the little things and the important things for survival in this remote and barren region of the Canadian North – about maps, weather conditions, plants, and wildlife – he knew, but he never presumed. Although we sensed he could never be our "buddy," he was the best companion you'd ever want on a hazardous trip like this.

Along the way a small private plane appeared out of the clouds. As it dipped to take a closer look at the group, someone wondered aloud why the plane had come. Trudeau quipped it was probably someone coming to tell us that the Joe Clark government had overthrown itself. (It did shortly after.)

I vividly recall one special day, a warm, sunny, lazy day, as we drifted aimlessly down a broad expanse of the Thelon, canoes lashed together, chatting amiably about this or that. For a moment we completely forgot that we were with one of this country's most dynamic leaders, a Canadian political trailblazer, who was destined to become a permanent part of our history. We were kindred spirits enjoying a perfect moment in a Canadian wonderland.

Someone once said that the Arctic is a lonely place, but the absence of human traces makes you feel like you understand it and that you can take your place in it. I have never returned from the Arctic without feeling renewed. That I have strayed but have now found my place. Every day is a challenge. Every day is a challenge met. What follows is a grand feeling of achievement and a sense of physical and mental renewal.

The Hanbury and the Arctic brought out some of the best qualities in Trudeau – his love of the outdoors, his personal courage, and an amiability not often seen by the public. I believe this Arctic adventure also served to revive his spirits, rekindle his physical and mental energy, and ultimately paved the way for his dramatic return to politics.

We reached the cabin where John Hornby and his companions had died in 1927, leaving a diary, a dramatic testament of their last horrible days. And there we stood before three simple wooden crosses that mark the site, and raised a toast in their memory. We also toasted the end of

our own historic journey. We had blazed our way through some har-
rowing rapids and exhausting portages. We had shared our meals and a
drink or two. We had bonded.

This Arctic journey had left me with a sense of exhilaration for
what had been achieved. But it also left me with a profound sense of
disappointment that these remarkable days on the Hanbury had in fact
come to an end.

There was another memorable moment at the end of our 1995 trip down
the Stikine River, which starts in northern British Columbia and ends in
Alaska. We were sitting at our final dinner in Terrace, British Columbia,
in the heart of the far west. As we rehashed the best and the worst times
of our trip, a rough-looking man stood up at the opposite end of the
restaurant and started moving menacingly toward our table. Things
grew tense.

But as he approached he held out his hand and said, "Mr. Trudeau,
I would like to shake your hand and thank you for the wonderful service
you have given this country." He then walked away. It was just a brief
moment but extraordinarily moving. It seemed to reflect the feelings of
so many people in every part of this great country.

Our final trip with Pierre was on the Petawawa River in 1996. He was
seventy-five and, while he was still in remarkable shape, he seemed a
little frail and distracted. The sparkle in his eyes had dimmed somewhat,
but the determination was still there. As we neared the top of a major set
of rapids, we drew our canoes to shore for a portage.

Pierre had stepped shakily out of his canoe into waist-high water
that threatened to sweep him away. He accidentally dropped his paddle,
and as he reached out for it, he faltered and at the last moment his canoe
partner grasped him by the arm, thereby preventing a serious mishap.
The contents of his canoe drifted down river, and it took us an hour or
so to gather up the soggy equipment. This was Pierre's last canoe trip. I
never saw him again.

▶ DAVID P. SILCOX
A canoe partner of Trudeau's

*W*e had had a long, strenuous day. The brisk west wind had stiffened considerably by mid-morning and made the crossing of Hoare Lake, an inescapable part of our route, a tense and dangerous one. Following that, we had to face the rough and lengthy portage around Dixon Canyon, a second brutal test, even if no one was likely to drown. Traversing the lake had begun with a nervous debate about whether to go around the perimeter (safely near the shore, but taking at least four hours and probably more), or to chance going straight across (about a mile in perhaps less than an hour, but at high risk). The waves were already ominously high for open canoes and were getting whiter and choppier while we fretted in a huddle on the windward shore. We were several hundred miles from anywhere on the Hanbury–Thelon river system in the Northwest Territories, and it was August 1979.

Each of us knew that, if a canoe capsized in the middle of the lake, it would be almost impossible to save anyone without imperilling everyone.

"What happens if one of our canoes capsizes?" was the unanswered question on everyone's mind. And then someone asked it. We all looked into the distance, or at our feet, or shuffled, or scratched ourselves. Trudeau answered the question.

"I guess we just sing louder and paddle harder," he said. And so, with a forced laugh, we got into our canoes. Although one canoe had to do some bailing, we all reached the far shore and headed on down the river.

We reached Dixon Canyon well past the normal dinner hour. The portage was over rocky terrain and early enough in the trip that the weight of food and fuel were still near the maximum. The freezer box that – as the self-appointed chef – I was experimenting with, while of modest dimensions (an eighteen-inch cube), was awkward to carry and an irritant to everyone when it was their turn to hump it. Nevertheless, I thought it, and the little box of spices I had carefully prepared, would greatly improve the boring and pedestrian meals we'd been subjected to on earlier trips.

We made camp on a rocky knoll overlooking the canyon. Everyone was hungry and on the verge of grumpy. While the "happy hour" of rum daiquiris was being served up by our chief bartender, Craig Oliver (Trudeau, who had said he didn't want any alcoholic drinks, was always in line with his cup), I got busy with my first "coup" in the kitchen. My ambition was to serve great one-pot main courses that had variety and nutrition, were not unduly heavy to carry, and were relatively quick to cook.

Over the fireplace, in the largest pot, I began my first creation. I started by heating the white wine that I had brought in my personal pack. As it was warming, Trudeau came over to ask what was for dinner. Like the others, he didn't want to have to wait too long to get at it, whatever it was.

"Cheese fondue," I answered cheerfully. He paused, thinking perhaps that I was pulling his leg, and then asked, as if he didn't know the answer, "Isn't it made with white wine?"

"That's what's in the pot," I said. "And a good wine too." I flashed the empty Meursault bottle at him.

"What kind of cheese do you have?" he asked next.

"I've got Emmenthal and Gruyère, of course," I replied, pointing these out to him on a plate. I hadn't really eaten either of these very often before this, so I was taking a recipe on faith. This seemed to satisfy him temporarily, yet, as he wandered off, I thought he was still skeptical, either believing the choice of dish inappropriate, or expecting that the result of my labours would be less than perfect.

A few minutes later he was back again, settling in near the fire, as if his presence could hurry things along.

"Hasn't cheese fondue traditionally been made with a bit of kirsch?" he asked, by now disguising his doubt with a smile. He didn't want to be *too* critical, lest his dinner be held hostage. By his tone he didn't want to be insulting either, but at the same time he seemed to want to be on the record that certain standards for cheese fondue were expected.

I reached into my little box of carefully measured spices and special ingredients (Cointreau for the mandarin oranges, for example) and held up a small vial of clear liquid as an answer. He smiled and conceded.

"And if you'd like a little freshly grated nutmeg to top it off, I have that too." At that point, he decided I was The Chef. Our subsequent meals, which featured such items as watercress and mulligatawny soups,

The best damn dishwasher in the North, even with his gold Rolex.

a memorable rabbit stew, great fish chowder, and Cherries Jubilee, I think, reinforced his decision.

Trudeau had been a national celebrity for more than a decade before I met him on our 1979 canoe trip, during the time the Liberal government was temporarily in opposition. His political philosophy and his personal life had been dissected so extensively that I thought I knew whom I was going to meet. The readiness for intellectual debate I expected, the sly irony and humour, and the daring man ready to run any rapid anyone else did, I expected too. But three things about him surprised me completely, and they became clear to me over the two weeks or so, every day and hour we spent together in the Arctic.

First, he was a perfectionist. This showed itself in myriad ways. He always did his very best, and he expected others to do the same. He packed his canoe very carefully, after bundling his own gear up meticulously. He wasn't fastidious or fussy about these things; he just wanted them to be right, and well and properly done. When it was his turn to wash up the dishes after dinner, he did it better than anyone else.

Once, when I was preparing dinner, he wandered behind me as I worked on the kitchen counter (an upturned canoe), and I heard him stop at the fireplace that someone else had just made and say "*Merde!*"

half in disbelief and half in disgust. As I heard rocks hitting rocks, I turned in time to see him kicking the whole rather awkward structure apart. He then proceeded to build a proper fireplace, and certainly a more practical and functional one, out of the same stones.

Second, he was shy and personal. The arrogance that has often been remarked about him, I attribute to his shyness – a combative overcompensation for wanting, really, to disguise his essentially gentle nature. Whenever any of our mutual friends were mentioned, his first question always was "How is he/she?" or "Is he well?" or "Is everyone in his family well?" or "How are he and his wife?" This concern for the personal well-being of colleagues, past and present, was an aspect of him I did not expect.

When he and I flew out together, in a little two-passenger Cessna, a four-hour flight from Hornby Point, we had a long chat about Margaret, from whom he was then separated. He was both worried about her and sad for her – a sort of melancholy sadness. Certainly there was no malice and no recrimination or resentment expressed, and I sensed that he would have done almost anything to help her.

Lastly, I didn't know about his immense reverence for and delight in being out in the wilderness. I knew that he canoed and liked camping but, given his highly keyed sensibilities, I was not prepared for the exultation he felt in being in that vast, unforgiving expanse of tundra.

Sometimes we talked about the profound sense of time's immensity that one feels so acutely there, where life is so transitory in the summer, where eons seem visible in the etched stone and the tenacious lichens, where change takes place over centuries, and "forever" seems like a real possibility. We were, we decided, the most transitory of travellers in a special time and place, children of a long-lived and implacable nature, both enthralled by and fearful of our awareness of our own brief lives.

This aspect of Trudeau was evident when we talked about our trips over lunches in later years. I've never seen it much referred to, yet I suspect that, like the religious side of his life that came to the fore upon his death, it was a larger part of his character and formed more of the basis of his view of the world than anyone can imagine.

▶ WALLY SCHABER

Canoe partner; also provided equipment and gear to Trudeau for over twenty-five years.

*I*n July of 1996, I was hired to guide and outfit a group of seven men who were as comfortable hiking up Parliament Hill as they were paddling down their chosen route, the Petawawa River in Algonquin Park. Among them were Craig Oliver, Tim Kotcheff, Peter Stollery, John Godfrey, and Ted Johnson. The guest of honour was the Right Honourable Pierre Elliott Trudeau.

For some thirty years of my life, this man had had a great influence on me, and suddenly I found myself overwhelmed with the togetherness as we shared a canoe and a tent for three days. I'd been guiding trips for twenty-five years, so the logistics of the trip didn't bother me, but the prospect of trying to make a good impression for seventy-two hours on someone you've admired all your life – that was another story.

The trip's beginning should have calmed my nerves. Pierre, Ted Johnson (our host, and Pierre's former executive assistant), and I were sitting at a picnic table near the park gate waiting for the rest of the party to arrive. Pierre carried the conversation and showed his experience as a wilderness canoeist, asking me good questions about our equipment and the river.

A large logging truck passed us as we were talking, then stopped, and backed up. A bush-hardened, tough, older guy got out of it and slowly walked toward us, staring at Pierre. No bodyguards were on the payroll here, and I looked at Ted, as if to say "*This* wasn't part of my job description." The logger stopped a foot away from Trudeau, who remained calm, and, after a long pause, the guy said, "I just want to shake your hand. . . . I've not always agreed with you, but I always liked your style." After the fellow left, happy with a handshake and a thank you, Pierre smiled and admitted that meetings like that didn't always go so well.

Pierre was seventy-five at the time we did this trip and, although he couldn't provide enough power for the perfect eddy turn, he still possessed the skills and agility of a good canoeist and athlete. He more than pulled his weight on the water, on the portage trail, and in the campsite. On the second night we were camped at the Notch and, while the others lounged and enjoyed some "Coffee-Mate," Pierre continued to clean up the camp with me. Finally, obviously happily exhausted with the day, he asked me, "Can I go to bed now?" Meaning, of course, was there anything else to be done. I'll always cherish the thought of one of Canada's greatest prime ministers asking my permission to go to bed.

The most dangerous set of rapids on our route between Lac Traverse and McManus Lake is Crooked Chute Rapids. They are a long set of Class I to II rapids that lead into a nasty Class VI chute. There are three take-out options, each of which shortens the portage by a third. I was weighing the pros and cons of cutting the portage short as we passed the first take-out. Pierre was pleased with our combined skills as we manoeuvred past the second take-out, but both of us were wet before the final option.

We'd put the canoe into a back-ferry position with the stern hugging the shore when a submerged rock broadsided the downstream end. I grabbed the most important things – Pierre, his pack, and my canoe. Anything else not tied down went over the chute. Pierre was cool and looked after his wet load without a complaint, while I sprinted down the trail with an empty canoe to rescue our floating gear. Another party had the salvage operation well in hand by the time I paddled up to the flotsam. But the moccasin telegraph had already sent word downriver that Pierre Trudeau was upstream, so I was forced to admit to all that I had dumped Pierre Elliott Trudeau, and had to suffer the deserved guffaws.

At lunch that day, while we dried out and ate, the men encouraged Pierre to tell the story of how the Liberals defeated Clark's government after only six months in office. It was obviously a story they all had heard before many times, not unlike a good locker-room tale or campfire story. Pierre was reluctant to lead the telling, but, as the tale stumbled along with colour commentary from the others, Pierre finally took over in that famous pose and classic monotone voice and told how they ordered every elected Liberal to fly, drive, or crawl into Parliament that night for a non-confidence vote on the budget, after they had calculated that a key number of Conservatives were too far away to make it in time. It was fascinating for me to sit back under the pines and listen to this moment in history being told as a campfire story by a living legend.

The final five miles of the Petawawa trip include a chain of lakes. The canoes got spread out, and I had Pierre all to myself. I wanted to tell him

about how, as an eighteen-year-old Ottawa teenager, I had shared the
thrill of the leadership convention of 1968, literally bumping into him in
the Château Laurier hospitality suite. I wanted to tell him that, as a university student, I had read his essay "Exhaustion and Fulfillment: The
Ascetic in a Canoe" (written when he was a student), and how it had
crystallized my philosophy that it is the *journey*, not the adrenalin
moment, that is the essence of the canoe.

I wanted to thank him for being such a committed supporter of
canoeing and conservation. His love of the canoe had turned many in
Ottawa on to canoe tripping for two decades, and that trend launched
my business. Finally, I wanted to thank him for making me proud to be
a Canadian, with him as our leader. But I didn't.

Instead I blurted out an abrupt "Slow down!"

We had been paddling at a very high stroke cadence for thirty
minutes. He thought the sternsman set the pace and I – lost in thoughts
about him – had instinctively matched his bowsman's pace. We enjoyed
a laugh, talked about past trips with mutual friends Bill Mason and Eric
Morse, and then, all of a sudden, it was over.

Canoes ground up on McManus Beach. I shook his hand and
thanked him, much like that truck driver, and wandered off to get the
vehicle.

It was Pierre's last wilderness trip. I hope he knows somehow that
this guide was proud to have shared a canoe, and a country, with him.

▶ TED JOHNSON
Executive assistant, 1980–84; canoe partner; and friend

*T*he essay he wrote in 1946, "Exhaustion and Fulfillment: The Ascetic in
a Canoe," captures Pierre's passion for canoeing. It was a lifelong affair,
and one he enjoyed sharing with his three sons and with friends.
Canoeing was one of the interests we had in common, and the subject of
many relaxed conversations when I could take off my executive-assistant
hat and "chew the fat," as he would say. While he liked flat-water paddling,

he really seemed to enjoy the excitement of descending a rapid. He did plenty of the former, including the long slog with three friends up the Ottawa River (against the current) on his Montreal to James Bay trip in his mid-twenties.

I became keenly aware of his interest in whitewater paddling – taking on rapids – in 1980 when, only a few months into my job as EA, I accompanied him on a military helicopter through the mountains of northern Norway, where we were visiting the Bardufos military base. As the helicopter passed over a fast-flowing mountain river, he pointed to a long boulder-strewn rapid and commented, "I think that one could be run on river-left." Over the four years that I worked for him, it became a sort of sport for us, on occasional flights over wild country: spot a rapid and figure out an imaginary route through it before it passed out of sight.

On the ground, he was quite prepared to paddle the real thing. He was in his mid-seventies when he agreed to join me and a group of six of his canoeing friends of long standing, on a ten-day descent of the Upper Stikine. The Stikine is a wild river, with frequent rapids, draining glorious, untouched mountain country around the Spatsizi Plateau in north-central British Columbia.

Pierre and I shared a canoe, alternating daily between paddling in the bow, which some (Pierre included) consider a bit of a joe-job, and the stern, where the action is. Our group was generally cautious, and we stopped to inspect most rapids from shore before running them. Early in the trip, on a day when it was Pierre's turn in the stern, he and I were caught on the "wrong" side of the river. The other three canoes had formed a consensus – communicated by hand signals over the roar of the river – that the better route through the whitewater was on the opposite side of the river, where they happened to be.

This provided Pierre with a powerful incentive to find a route down our side of the river. Regrettably, on inspection we couldn't find one – a ledge reaching well out into the river downstream from us was impassable – but Pierre came up with a route that took us far enough down our side to save face, before weaving a path across to the "right" side, to muted applause.

Ted Johnson explaining how they saved face.

Days of forty-mile paddles on the swift-moving river, hiking up to see the Spatsizi Plateau, camping among lodgepole pine at a rapid, and evening conversations around the campfire passed quickly.

Then the big test. It was my day in the stern when we came to the Beggerlay Canyon, with its reputation as the trickiest rapid on the route. The river makes a sharp left turn, splits around a rock the size of a truck, and thunders through a narrow cleft between yellow stone cliffs. At appropriate water levels, there is a route through it, but you have to hit it just right at the entrance to the rapid. I was not looking forward to this one, even to the point of checking the map ahead of time to see how long the portage around it would take.

We stopped to scout. Unfortunately, the water level was appropriate. Although the river is glacier-fed, it was a sunny day, so if we dumped, we could warm up and dry out fairly quickly. And anyway, Pierre was keen to give it a go.

We let the other three canoes go ahead. The first missed the entrance, swung into a large eddy, and careered nose-first into the cliff on the left. The expletives were audible above the roar of the rapid, but, undeterred, its crew turned and successfully negotiated the rest of the

Tim Kotcheff

Ted and Pierre not lost on the journey.

canyon. The next was slightly off the line, shipped a bit of water, but made it. The third hit the line perfectly and sailed through.

Our turn. Paddling out to mid-river, I thought I had us positioned pretty well, but it's one thing to inspect a rapid from a few feet above it on shore, and quite another to be down in it. Standing waves are much bigger when one is among them. As we hurtled ahead, it became apparent to me that I had missed the line by a good margin. In my imagination I could feel the coldness of the water, and, even worse, I imagined the headline that I was certain would appear if we kept going: "Former PM Trudeau and one other lost in rapid."

Fortunately we weren't in the thick of it yet, and I called for a "right-draw" from the surprised bowman. After we pulled out on gravel shore, it took some explaining from me to finally convince Pierre that there was an easy portage around the canyon, and that we shouldn't try again. Reluctantly, he agreed.

For our next trip together, roughly the same gang assembled for three days in midsummer to paddle the Petawawa River in Ontario's Algonquin Park. Pierre was then in his late seventies, in fine condition, and keen to be out in the wilds. I remember well his quiet frustration at how slow some of our number were to load our copious equipment into our canoes and get on the river. He travelled light – a minimum of gear in one well-travelled pack, a well-used paddle, and no camera. His memory served as his camera.

Once on the river, he loosened up, literally and figuratively. Canoes would come together and paddle side by side for a shared conversation, then drift apart for a few miles before someone would begin a story or toss out a controversial thought, and we'd bunch up again to chew the fat. It was the same in the evenings around the campfire – warm conversation followed by contemplative silences followed by more chat.

Friends ask, "What would Trudeau talk about?" The fact is, he listened more than he talked, though he'd join in, particularly when a topic was controversial. Inevitably we'd get on to politics and history. Thucydides, Rimbaud, and Robert Frost were occasionally referred to. And he was quick to correct the record if one of us made a half-baked assertion. Canoeing was itself a popular topic, and he enjoyed recounting stories of his James Bay trip, or the latest excursion with his good friends the Mason family in the Gatineau. And he would talk enthusiastically about his boys. The three of them were the centre of his universe.

But I think it's fair to say we were all particularly struck by his curiosity. He loved to ask questions on just about any topic under discussion and, with his razor-sharp intellect, he was able to come up with the tough, higher-order questions that would force us to think harder or (rare for our boisterous and opinionated gang) intimidate us into silence.

A canoe trip is a communal operation. The work is shared fairly equally, and Pierre went out of his way to do more than his bit. When it was his turn to wash the dishes by the shore of the river, the blackened cooking pots would come back as shiny as when they were new. (Some of us resented this, as we thought well-blackened pots were a badge of outdoor experience.) Indeed, on the Petawawa trip – where he was a good eighteen years older than the next-oldest participant – I found him carrying two full-sized packs across a long portage. I decided I had to do something.

"Pierre," I said, "I have to ask you to carry a lighter load; you're undermining the morale of the younger men on the expedition!"

When our canoes nosed up on the beach on McManus Lake at the end of the Petawawa trip, none of us knew it was the last time we would paddle together with Pierre. For each of us, the memories of our excursions with him are strong. The pleasure of tripping with this energetic, thoughtful, fascinating, generous, and considerate paddler was a privilege given to very few.

Two years later came the tragic news of the loss of his son Michel. Pierre was never the same again and, within a couple of years, we lost him. As I reflect on our canoe trips together I am reminded of the touching ending to the fine tribute to Pierre written by Lysianne Gagnon in *La Presse*: "and now he is out there paddling the River Styx, searching for his lost son."

Chapter Fourteen

Ami/Friend

▶ JACQUES HÉBERT
Close friend; travelling companion to China; senator, 1983–98

*T*rudeau and Pelletier. That was the meaning, *l'essence*, of friendship. Pierre was also my friend for over half a century, but their friendship was long-standing, wonderful, and cut short. I was simply a privileged witness. As fate would have it, the three of us met at about the same time at the end of the forties.

Some ten years later, way before the "three wise men," while Pelletier and Trudeau were editors-in-chief of *Cité libre*, which had become a monthly and whose managing editor I was, we often lunched together in a small and inexpensive Chinese restaurant to discuss the magazine's next issue, as well as to delight in each other's company.

Besides these lunches for three, there were those where only Trudeau and I would find ourselves in the same Chinese restaurant, which had no liquor licence. The chopsticks, if not the quality of the dishes, reminded us of our recent trip to China. Inevitably, we'd talk about Pelletier, our valued friend, at whose noble qualities of heart and mind we marvelled.

Pelletier and I would often lunch instead at Chez Pierre, a good French restaurant on Labelle Street, where the wines weren't too expensive. We had great fun, but, at some point, Trudeau's name would crop up in the conversation. At times, we'd kindly make fun of one of our friend's minor failings, as though trying to hide our great admiration and deep affection for this exceptional man whom no one suspected would change our country forever.

A free man, sure of himself, solid as an oak, Trudeau could make his way without anyone's help. And yet, in delicate situations, at the point of making a serious decision, he needed Pelletier, whose wisdom and compassion never failed. "Pelletier," he would say, "is a conscience . . ."

Following those tumultuous years in Ottawa, Trudeau was now living with his children in his beautiful house on Pine Avenue, and Pelletier in his on Elm Street, and we were able to resume the ritual of lunch for two or three, some washed down with red wine, others with green tea.

Being in public with Trudeau *was* an ordeal, even years after he'd left government. Each time – and we were used to it – Pelletier and I would take a blow to the ego. Each time, Pierre was the one who was recognized and congratulated, while the obscure senator and the barely less obscure former cabinet minister and former ambassador would sheepishly remain somewhat in the background.

One day, after telling Trudeau how highly he thought of him, an individual finally turned toward Pelletier and me.

"And who are you both?"

Without hesitation, I immediately replied, "Two bodyguards on loan from the RCMP."

Seated at our table, we almost always had as much fun as schoolboys, sharing as many memories "as if we'd been a thousand years old." But, when looking at the other two, each of us realized we were no longer twenty.

The first, Pelletier, was stricken by some terrible illness and had to give up our lunches for three. After having lunch for two, Trudeau and I sometimes went to see our friend in his hospital room, and then his home, where he was to die in bed, his soul at peace. Though we had expected it, Pelletier's death was a terrible blow to both of us. In all my life, I'd never seen Trudeau so distraught, sad, aged.

On the morning of June 27, 1997, we were at the Saint-Louis-de-Westmount Church for the funeral. Trudeau came up to me and hugged

Montreal Gazette

The two "bodyguards": Jacques Hébert (left) and Gerard Pelletier.

me very tightly (something he'd never done in our fifty-year friendship). It was not his style. In a broken voice, he whispered in my ear: "I've just lost a part of my soul."

The two of us had just understood that our lunches for three had come to an end, as had our everlasting youth. Lunches for two would never be the same again, darkened by Pelletier's death, and his good words, anecdotes, wisdom, his always-accurate analysis of things.

And his keen sense of friendship.

▌ PETER GREEN
Long-time friend, whose family spent most holidays with the
Trudeaus when the children were young

"Why are we in such a desperate haste to succeed, and in such desperate enterprises? If a man does not keep pace with his companions, perhaps it is because he hears a different drummer. Let him step to the music which he hears, however measured or far away."

With these immortal words of Henry David Thoreau, Pierre Trudeau addressed the cadets of Prospect College in Jamaica. The crowd of spectators was awed with the eloquence and the power of the words. There was no one to record what Pierre said, but everyone who was there will never forget the moment.

I had heard him speak on a number of occasions, but for me his most moving speech was in Edmonton, at the 1990 memorial service for my late wife, Mary-Jean Mitchell-Green, who died so tragically young at age thirty-eight. I had asked Pierre to speak, but he said it was too painful for him, as it brought back memories of the death of his father. My two sons, Andrew and Alexander, at ten and twelve, each read a lesson to a large gathering of a thousand people, and then Pierre followed with his lesson. To my surprise, he then started talking about Mary-Jean, how he had first met her when she was a twenty-three-year-old college student, and how she developed into the chairman of the family interests and one of the top corporate leaders in Canada. All were moved to tears, and Pierre's support and loyalty that day strengthened our long-standing friendship.

Pierre first came into our lives in January 1975, when, after meeting Prime Minister Michael Manley at a summit conference in Jamaica, he came to stay at "Prospect," the property of my father-in-law, Sir Harold Mitchell, in Ocho Rios. They had a great deal in common, as Sir Harold had been vice-chairman of the English Conservative Party in 1945, under Churchill. He was not only a politician but also an academic, a farmer, and a writer, and had business interests around the world, including in Canada.

This was the start of a long friendship, which grew stronger when my first son, Alexander, was born in 1978, and then Andrew in 1980, with Pierre becoming a godfather to Alexander. There was a two-year age difference between my sons and the Trudeau children, who became heroes and role models for Alexander and Andrew. Our families were to spend many holidays together, mostly in Jamaica, but also in Bermuda and Zermatt, Switzerland; and we visited the Trudeaus in Ottawa and Montreal.

There are many vivid memories ranging from chocolate fondue dripping over all of us at Sussex Drive to boating in Harrington Lake,

© Peter Green

© Peter Green

© Peter Green

*Our five sons (from left):
Andrew and Alexander
Green, Michel, Sacha,
and Justin.*

*Fishing in Bermuda with
muscle man Justin crewing.*

*From left: Lady Mitchell,
the Godfather with Alexander
Green, and Mary-Jean
Mitchell-Green, in 1978.*

where we all piled in a small over-loaded boat with Margaret several months pregnant. I often wondered, if the boat sank, whom I would try to save first, my new wife, the prime minister's wife, their young son, or my aging parents-in-law!

The Trudeaus were always highly competitive, and we used to have beach Olympics with all kinds of events with the younger children being given an advantage. After dinner we would sit in a beach hut and tell ghost stories and make all kinds of challenging word games.

Pierre would not stand any nonsense, and was a loving father but a firm disciplinarian. The boys had a mixed upbringing with Margaret and Pierre after they separated. In Montreal, they were allowed minimum television, either a soda *or* dessert, and a fixed bedtime; at Margaret's, they ate all kinds of fast food and watched as much television as they wanted. When they came to Bermuda, they would stay up all night watching videos.

Pierre, with his Jesuit upbringing, had high values for himself and his sons. When the kids used to fight, he did not interfere; it was the survival of the fittest. He was also very demanding – particularly on himself. We once climbed the four-thousand-foot Blue Mountain in Jamaica. It was more of a long trek, taking four hours up and four hours down. As some say, it is a mountain without a beginning or an end. We finally reached the summit at 5 p.m., only to find the view surrounded by mist, so we sat down to have a picnic. Pierre would neither eat nor drink, even when we returned to the base of the mountain. For three days afterwards Pierre went on a fast, and it always seemed to me that the climb itself was not a big enough challenge for him, much to the distress of Lady Mitchell, who had planned all the meals with care. One evening at dinner, Sacha was told to eat his beans (the boys always had to finish their meals) and Sacha responded that he was on a "bean fast."

One evening we went to a Chinese restaurant in Ocho Rios, where we usually had a quiet and early dinner with all the children, in a spectacular setting by a waterfall. Once, however, we were with the prime minister of the time, Edward Seaga, and all his family. Although the Trudeaus always attracted attention, we would quietly have our meal in the restaurant and enjoy the informality of the atmosphere. Mr. Seaga, however, planned something different and had arranged a private room

© Peter Green

This is how you ride a horse on the Jamaican beach, okay officer?

well away from everyone else, and we sat through every dish on the menu. Finally, with the kids getting more and more restless, Pierre suddenly got up at 9:30 p.m. and announced that his children had to go to bed. And we all left, leaving the prime minister and his group looking somewhat surprised.

When Pierre visited Jamaica as prime minister, he had one RCMP bodyguard, and made sure any Jamaican security police were kept well out of the way. This was in sharp contrast, we noticed, to Henry Kissinger, who came to visit us with eighty security people, a bulletproof car, frogmen from Guantanamo Bay, and armed guards with Uzi machine guns surrounding the house.

With Pierre it was very informal, but his demanding standards were shown one day when I brought a horse on the beach for the kids to ride. Pierre asked the Mountie to give a demonstration for the boys. The poor guy probably had not ridden for years, and stumbled around the beach on the long-suffering horse. Pierre, without saying a word, got on the horse bareback – in his swimming shorts – and gave a short demonstration of control and superb riding technique, much to the embarrassment of the Mountie.

It was always a joy to be with Margaret, and we all adored her. She was always fun and very loving and brought informality to Sussex Drive and official functions. Pierre and Margaret were very different, and it was sad when they broke up. Their age difference, and her impatience and boredom with officialdom, certainly did not help. But I always believed Pierre missed her and was distressed at not having a mother at home for his sons.

Pierre was never the same after the tragic death of Michel in November 1998. He, Justin, and Sacha came to visit us in Bermuda shortly after the memorial service. He had lost his spirit, and we used to go and look for him, only to find him gazing into the sea in deep thought.

When he died in 2000, I played my last role in his life by being a pallbearer at his funeral, where I said farewell to him. I had lost a good friend.

▶ JOE MacINNIS
*Physician-scientist, explorer, author, and friend, who first met
Trudeau in 1969; made more than fifty dives with him in
the Arctic, Caribbean, and Pacific oceans*

*O*ne day in the summer of 1970, I found myself sitting beside the Prime Minister of Canada on the edge of a work barge in Greater Lamashur Bay in the U.S. Virgin Islands. It was August and a fierce Caribbean sun burned down from an orange-white sky. Beneath the reach of blue water in front of us was the most ambitious undersea living experiment ever undertaken. Tektite Two was a five-million-dollar program supported by the United States government and a partnership of corporations and universities. Over a period of seven months, fifty-three scientists, in five-person teams, were spending two to four weeks in a large, four-room station at a depth of fifty feet.

Tektite Two had a dual mission. It was a long-duration study of the ocean and a preparation for distant journeys in space. Most of its participants were marine scientists, but one of them was a NASA human-factors engineer working on the design and efficiency of space stations. The Tektite scientists were spending as many as ten hours a day in the water trying to understanding the life on the Lamashur Bay reef and the great ocean beyond.

Pierre Trudeau was sitting in his swimming trunks and swim fins, his feet dangling over the edge of the barge, studying everything going on around him. I answered his questions as best I could. "What kinds of marine science are they doing down there?" "How do they train for this?" And then in a voice that was almost a whisper, "Are we going to be in anyone's way when we are at the station?"

As we spoke, a young man in khaki shorts walked up behind Pierre, lifted a large, rectangular breathing unit onto his back, and adjusted its shoulder straps. Trudeau looked into the young man's eyes. "It's heavier than I thought. Not something you'd like to carry over a two-mile portage."

The fifty-pound device was the most advanced undersea breathing unit ever built. Under its white fibreglass cover were control-and-delivery components similar to those used by the Apollo astronauts. With each breath the diver took, oxygen was added and carbon dioxide removed. There were no exhaust bubbles. If, however, its electronic heart failed, an unsuspecting diver might lose consciousness.

This morning, when we had arrived at Tektite Two's shore facility on St. John's Island, I thought we were going to make this dive wearing standard scuba gear. However, at the technical briefing, Dr. Jim Miller, the Navy psychologist in charge of the program, asked if we'd like to try the Mark One breathing system. Without hesitation, the man who had mastered the skills of skiing, swimming, and judo said, "Sure, why not?"

"Ready?" I asked.

"Let's take a look at what the Americans are doing with their tax-payers' money," he said with a smile. Then he carefully placed the breathing unit's rubber mouthpiece between his lips.

I slid into the water, turned, and faced him. Pressing his fins flat on the water to steady himself, he dropped in beside me. One safety diver and then a second, both wearing conventional scuba gear, moved quickly into position behind us. We exhaled and began to descend.

Our heads were barely below the surface of the sunlit water when we saw the station positioned on the sand next to a dark escarpment of coral. With its twin steel towers rising out of a large rectangular base, it had a starkly industrial look. Hose bundles holding air, water, and electricity snaked out from its base toward the shore, two hundred yards away.

Our first stop was the observation cupola, a circle of ten rectangular windows on top of one of the towers. When we arrived, Pierre placed his fingertips on one of the windows and drew himself closer to look down into the room below. He was breathing from deep inside his chest, as if doing a yoga exercise. I could almost feel his mind analyzing everything that lay in front of him.

Tektite Two was the Cadillac of undersea stations. The three adjoining rooms contained a well-equipped lab, five comfortable bunks, a heat-and-serve galley, a stereo system, and a fresh-water shower. On the far side of the control room, a young engineer was sitting at a desk, writing in a notebook.

I eased over to one side to get a better look at the world's youngest PM peering through the hemispheric window. His fins moved back and forth effortlessly. He leaned forward, scanning the contents of the control room, as if trying to understand the real meaning of the multi-million-dollar station, its scientists, and their research projects.

From our first conversation a year earlier, I knew I was talking to an inspiring human being, an athlete who made politics interesting, a politician who dared to ask questions that went beyond people's immediate concerns. Pierre was a statesman trying to shift the national conversation toward issues that would improve the relationships between humans, nature, and technology.

Pierre made certain he spent time each year in the wilderness. He was a born explorer, but an explorer with a purpose. He wanted to know how the natural world worked. He wanted to understand the relationships between the living forms of the earth and the human community, and how they might be more mutually beneficial.

As prime minister, there was a practical edge to his curiosity. He listened quietly as the major American oil companies discussed their plans for deepwater drilling off Canada's east and west coasts. He wondered aloud if it could be done safely. He'd heard the American claim that Canada's Northwest Passage was an international strait. When a huge oil tanker, the USS *Manhattan*, smashed its way through the full length of the ice-covered passage, Pierre was concerned that transporting mil- lions of gallons of oil out of the new fields north of Alaska could harm the very structure of the Arctic Ocean.

I looked carefully at the face of the man reflected in the curved window. Among his special gifts was a belief and determination that we were all connected to each other, responsible for one another and fully capable of figuring out how to fix seemingly insolvable problems. One of the best things about diving is that, after a while, nothing exists of the world except your thoughts about the ocean and the person you are with. Since your lives to some degree depend on each other, your thoughts usually turn to who the person really is. Pierre Trudeau was someone whose deep blue eyes and inquiring mind had their own unique depths.

He was not fearless, but had more grace under pressure than anyone I have ever met. He had also spent enough time underwater to know that a journey into the sea eventually becomes a journey into our inner selves. For me, it was an honour to share in a small part of that journey.

▶ JIMMY CARTER
President of the United States, 1977–81

*T*here are multiple entries in my personal White House diaries that refer to Pierre Trudeau, almost every one ending with "I like him very much," or words to that effect. My first visit with him was in January 1977, when I had been in office only a few days. It was a state visit, and his beautiful young wife, Margaret, came with him.

The subsequent big news story in the *Washington Post* the following day was that she had worn a very short skirt to a formal banquet. I agreed with Rosalynn and Pierre that it was very attractive. To ease any mutual discomfort, he and I agreed that we would approve of Margaret's dress if the Canadians would approve of our daughter, Amy, reading a book during the prime minister's official toast at the banquet.

Another interesting conversation occurred almost exactly a year later, when I called and wakened Pierre very early in the morning.

We had discovered several weeks earlier that a Soviet nuclear-powered satellite was having trouble, and Brezhnev and I agreed to share information, since it would be falling to earth. My message to Pierre was that the satellite was tumbling and would fall somewhere in Canada, hopefully just east of Great Slave Lake. He thanked me for calling him, said he would be sure to stay in Montreal, and would check to ensure that none of his cabinet members were fishing in the area. There was one whom he said he wouldn't warn, but he didn't name him.

▶ ALLAN J. MacEACHEN
MP, 1953–84; senator, 1984–91

*T*here were times when Mr. Trudeau's name and presence worked magic in my constituency. His August 1971 visit to my residence at Lake Ainslie with his wife, Margaret, was one such occasion, still recalled by my neighbours as memorable. That visit – as far as I was concerned – was the high point of the prime minister's tour of cultural events on Cape Breton Island, emphasizing in particular the contribution of the Acadians and the Highland Scots to its development. That emphasis took the prime minister to the thriving Acadian village of Cheticamp, and the Gaelic College at St. Ann's that commemorated the heroic settlements of the Reverend Norman MacLeod at St. Ann's Bay, Cape Breton, and Waipu, New Zealand.

At my place on Lake Ainslie on the day of the visit, we offered hospitality, music, and personal warmth. We were *not* to make an impression by style and high fashion. Pierre and Margaret Trudeau sensed that, and fitted into the atmosphere completely. We provided ample distractions against boredom, including lunch on the deck close to the lake.

But first there was Sunday Mass at Stella Maris Parish Church, Inverness, my home parish. Mr. Trudeau insisted there would be no press and no advance publicity. Politics and religion were not be mixed. His attendance at Mass was not to become a public spectacle and quasi-political event. However, the parish priest, Father Colonel MacLeod, who had been a classmate of mine at St. Francis Xavier University, had to be notified. We didn't want him to fall off the altar seeing, unexpectedly, the prime minister and Margaret among the worshippers. He was also pledged to discretion. But somehow there was a leak. Word got around, which meant there was an air of restrained excitement at the arrival of the guests. Things did not get out of hand, however. Regular attendees, in a low-key way, did greet the prime minister and Margaret to let them know the visit was full of excitement. After all, it *was* a first for Stella Maris.

The helicopter bearing the distinguished guests landed on my property shortly after noon, creating quite a stir. The visible contingent of security added to the fray. The usual peace of a summer Sunday at Lake Ainslie was totally shattered. I worried needlessly that my neighbours would resent this noisy and conspicuous intrusion. Happily, I heard no complaints.

On the contrary, local people were delighted at noticing that the prime minister and Margaret were taking a swim in the lake. Actually they were thrilled with Margaret. There was time for this relaxation before the noisy helicopter takeoff for the official event at the Gaelic College.

For preparing and serving lunch, I counted on Pearl Hunter, who ran my Ottawa office, and Joyce Fairbairn, then the legislative assistant to the prime minister, and now a member of the Senate of Canada. They got help from Joyce's husband, Mike Gillan, and my older brother, John, who was staying at Lake Ainslie for the summer on holiday from his duties as professor of English in the United States. (Since then both Mike and John have passed away.) During the preparation for the prime-ministerial visit, a strong friendship grew between Mike and John, fostered in part by a rising spirit of rebellion against the many demands being made on them, which included clearing brush on the property, and picking wild-flowers on the roadside for the luncheon table.

They believed Joyce – and I, in particular – had become "imperious" in issuing commands to perform various tasks. However, they both took silent revenge by helping themselves to the supplies in the bar. They had a grand time enjoying the liberties of the servant class, as they might sarcastically put it. Not wanting to be caught far from his supply lines, John stashed a glass wrapped in a napkin behind any suitable object on the mantelpiece, piano, and elsewhere that offered concealment and ease of access. Such was the tension created by the visit, particularly after I locked up the refreshments.

Considering the location of my house on both Lake Ainslie and Trout River, Joyce had decreed fish would be the main dish on the menu. Luckily, I possessed a large fresh salmon, given to me by a friend. However, my refrigeration failed. The night before the great event, Joyce discovered that the salmon could not be served and decreed a supply of fresh trout was urgently required. There was a moment of panic. The panic quickly turned into a minor triumph with the arrival of a supply of fresh trout, caught in the local streams by an angler friend who suddenly arrived on the scene with his morning catch in a large pail. Handing the pail to Joyce, he noted she must be the cook, brought in from Ottawa for the occasion.

Pierre and Margaret arrived on the grounds to the stirring music of the Inverness pipe band, a highly appropriate gesture, considering the area and the lineage of the guests. Pierre's mother was an Elliott, a clan from the Scottish border country. Nor was the significance lost on Margaret. Her father, Jimmy Sinclair, an outstanding colleague of mine in the House of Commons, born in Banff, Scotland, though never a stage Scot, was proud of his Scottish origins.

After lunch, we began changing to go into the lake (where local people with their binoculars were taking in the activities in their boats from afar). There was a good deal of confusion as we swimmers sought a room to make our changes of clothing. A slightly embarrassing moment arose when a male swimmer barged into a bedroom then occupied by Margaret. There was admiration all around at the speed of exit of the intruder. In the midst of the sunshine and laughter of the day, a high point was Margaret announcing – as she was being spun around in the water by Pierre – that she was to have her first child. Lake Ainslie was privileged to have the first public knowledge of this great event.

I wanted Mr. Trudeau to wear his kilt for his appearance at the Gaelic Mod. He had packed his Elliott tartan kilt, which he was entitled to wear.

A sporran-wearing MacEachen introducing the Trudeaus.

However he had failed to pack a sporran. Should he wear the kilt without the sporran? He asked my advice. Without fully considering the implications, I encouraged him to do so. The kilt was the appropriate garb for the occasion, I reasoned, and would please the crowd in attendance.

There is a reason why a sporran is worn with the kilt, as Mr. Trudeau acknowledged before the day finished. He received a wonderful reception – and more exposure than his communication adviser may have wanted.

Chapter Fifteen

Papa

▶ SHAUNA HARDY
Friend of Justin

A single question has been asked of me more times than I can count over the past twenty-seven years. It is a very simple question, to which there is obviously no simple answer.

"What was it like to be around Pierre Trudeau?"

There is the inevitable wide-eyed breathless pause by the questioner, and I am always left wondering how to respond. Although he was an integral part of my life, my insights do not pay tribute to his famous qualities. A five-year-old child cannot measure appreciation according to adult standards. Instead, my sleepy-eyed memories bear the innocent stamp of youth.

For over seven years, Pierre Trudeau didn't really have a first or last name. He bore a simple title: Justin's dad. His sternness made my knees shake. His ability to say the Lord's Prayer and a Hail Mary without a single hiccup left me awestruck. The fact that he was known to occasionally carry packages of licorice in his pocket made him magnetic.

Time spent in the company of Justin's dad was almost always defined by physical and mental challenges: show me what you have learned. Show me what you can do. Show me how you live.

One hot summer day up at Harrington Lake, he swam out to the floating dock and challenged six cocky preteens to a very simple exercise (or so it seemed). We were to push out from the dock and see how long we could stand on a thin Styrofoam surfboard. We all failed miserably. But when I close my eyes, I still see Justin's dad balanced between earth and sky on that slowly sinking piece of Styrofoam, his face a mixture of steely-eyed concentration and unabashed mirth. The air punctuated by the excited voices of children counting off second after unbelievable second. There was always an incredible intensity of feeling that he directed toward his sons, toward children in general. It radiated from him. It was what I loved most about him.

Of course, when that inevitable question is posed, these thoughts never leave my mouth. I prefer to sum up my experience in a single sentence. "He was the father of one of my best friends, and I liked him very much."

▶ BOUTROS BOUTROS-GHALI
Egyptian minister of foreign affairs, 1977–91;
UN secretary general, 1992–96

*N*othing is more delicate than giving words the redoubtable task of evoking the memory of a man, especially when that man is Pierre Elliott Trudeau, lawyer, law professor, intellectual, journalist, prime minister, statesman. Moreover, by themselves, those titles and occupations cannot express the boldness and freedom of thought, the courage and freedom of action, the dedication of a life to serving Canada and the universal ideals of justice, peace, and democracy.

I had the opportunity of meeting Pierre Elliott Trudeau on several occasions, of savouring his charisma, his intellectual agility, his impressive analytical skills, as well as his sensitivity to the problems of Third World countries. His keen perception of international issues, his openness to the world, the demanding view he had of his mission and of Canada's role in the international sphere led him to travel the world. I don't know why, but each time I think of Pierre Elliott Trudeau, in a conversation or during a trip, the vivid memory of our first meeting comes to mind.

It was during the seventies, in Egypt, where Mr. Trudeau had travelled on a working visit. As fate would have it, Senegal's president Léopold Sédar Senghor was staying in Cairo at the same time. So I had the completely spontaneous idea of trying to set up a meeting between President Sadat, President Senghor, and Mr. Trudeau. I still had to get my president to agree to this impromptu summit and to fit it into a tight schedule. Anwar Sadat was immediately taken with the idea and asked that I contact the other two eminent protagonists. Both agreed, and the meeting was scheduled for 12 p.m. that day.

I've always loathed improvisation, but this opportunity could not be missed. I barely had the time to inform the press, before leaving for President Sadat's villa in Giza. While I was speaking to him about some current files, Léopold Sédar Senghor arrived, followed shortly by Pierre Elliott Trudeau. The president's office had been informed too late about this meeting and didn't have time to provide an interpreter. So I had to translate from Arabic to French, and from French to Arabic, the words the three heads of state and government exchanged that morning on relations between Canada and Africa.

Once the photo session was over, Prime Minister Trudeau told President Sadat that he would like to introduce him to his young son Sacha, who was with him on this trip. President Sadat answered that he loved children and would be delighted to meet him. Sacha was just returning from the zoo, where he'd spent the morning.

"Sacha," said his father with solemnity, "I want to introduce you to two great and historically significant men, the President of Egypt and the President of Senegal."

The little boy then answered with the spontaneity that is the strength and grace of children:

"At the zoo, earlier today, I saw four giraffes, three elephants, and now I'm meeting two presidents."

Léopold Sédar Senghor burst out laughing, while Trudeau's cheeks flushed. For my part, I chose not to translate the message of Canada's young generation. And so, President Sadat, convinced that Sacha had given free rein to his admiration, leaned over toward him smiling and embraced him with affection.

I saw Pierre Elliott Trudeau to the door and he thanked me warmly, on his behalf and Sacha's, for this captivating meeting, before going back to presidents Sadat and Senghor, who'd continued their dialogue – or rather their monologues, since the interpreter I was had slipped away for a few moments.

It's that image of a loving and attentive father, of a profoundly humane man, who could, with the greatest ease, shift from the most serious subjects to the most immediate pleasures of life, that I will keep of my first meeting with Pierre Elliott Trudeau.

▶ EDWARD R. SCHREYER
Governor General, 1979–84; and premier of Manitoba, 1969–77

*A*mong my many fond memories of Pierre Elliott Trudeau, I remember him best (when we lived next door to each other) as a father. These memories provide an insight into his very human attitudes and interaction with a young and growing family.

*Attentive fathers: Ed Schreyer and Pierre chatting
in the Senate chamber before a Throne Speech.*

One summer Sunday, an operator of a children's games and rides phoned to ask whether he might drop off two go-cars. I thanked him and suggested he do so a few hours later that afternoon. I was quite sure that our two youngsters, Jason and Toban, would be delighted with the chance to drive motorized "Kiddy Cars" around the cricket pitch on Rideau Hall's sixty-acre spread.

I also phoned the prime minister at 24 Sussex across the road. He responded with genuine enthusiasm on behalf of his three boys *and* himself. Within minutes, we made a rendezvous. Soon the five boys were taking turns weaving about and doing figure-8s at top go-car speeds. The prime minister did his fair share of time at the steering wheel. All was great fun.

Then, there was a minor accident.

As one of the cars crossed over a pathway onto the lawn, the jolting of the little vehicle caused a fender to fall off. Pierre must have been concerned about the cost of repairs, and he began to mildly reprimand the young lad for driving too fast. Then the boy rounded on him and said, sounding exactly like Pierre, "I told you we shouldn't drive in that direction – but the trouble with you is that you never listen."

There was silence for a few moments and then everyone seemed to resume talking all at once.

Many regarded Prime Minister Trudeau, I am sure, as a man of towering intellectual aloofness and even of arrogance. While this was perhaps true at times, he was often considerate and capable of great sensitivity. His concern and caring solicitude for the three boys became widely known. It was, moreover, genuine. One such vignette, I recall, had to do with his desire that the boys have every practical encouragement and opportunity to be comfortably bilingual.

One evening when I was visiting him, one of the youngsters was sent down to say goodnight to his dad. As he was turning to take his leave, Pierre asked a parting question in French. The young lad answered in English. This repartee went through three cycles or more. Finally, in exasperation, young Sacha exclaimed, "For gosh sake, Dad! Give me a break!"

That left the two of us, minutes later, to compare notes on the complex maze of child rearing.

▶ KARMEL SCHREYER
Author and daughter of former governor general Edward R. Schreyer

When my father became Governor General of Canada in 1979, it meant moving into the imposing edifice of Rideau Hall, at Number One Sussex Drive in Ottawa. It was much more a government office building than a residence for a family of six and, with many other attendant "anomalies" – a greenhouse, footmen (and foot guards), a gas pump, a cricket pitch, a Queen's bedroom, and an RCMP detachment come to mind – it was an unusual place to live out one's teenage years. However, we had a very wonderful neighbour, which is a blessing no matter where one lives.

I remember when the time came for my family and me to make the move from Manitoba to Ottawa and Rideau Hall, Mr. Trudeau – in true Welcome Wagon fashion – picked us up at the airport to personally show us to our new home. We were all curled up together, my family and the prime minister, in the back of a limousine on a dull January day, and he pointed out the various sights: the Rideau Canal, the Château Laurier, Byward Market, sounding as excited as I felt at that moment.

Over the years, his family and mine engaged in the things good neighbours do. He brought his boys over for Easter dinner one year. And I think he and my mother exchanged more than a few recipes. When our place was being refurbished one summer, he invited us to use his Harrington Lake retreat. We were pleased to be invited to his boys' pool parties, and he offered my brothers and sister and me use of his pool at any time, although I don't remember being so brave as to take him up on the offer.

Mr. Trudeau even obliged us by appearing in a cameo role in a CBC Christmas special called "Christmas at Rideau Hall." In the show, Mr. Trudeau is putting a Christmas wreath on his front door, when an uncomprehending Charlie Farquharson happens by, asking for directions to our house. Mr. Trudeau points him across the way and wishes him a Merry Christmas. It was, to me, a very real interpretation of our neighbour.

On more than one occasion, my friends and I chanced to meet Mr. Trudeau on the grounds of Rideau Hall, where he would go for walks, and we would have a brief chat. I never got over the fact that he recognized

At Rideau Hall with Karmel.

me, just a shy teenager from across the street, but he always addressed me with a warm-hearted pleasant surprise, and he would quiz me about school, my marks, and my travels.

When I had the opportunity to speak with him at length, at certain functions such as awards dinners, he would often ask me how we were doing in "my dad's job." Of course, this question was common enough, but coming from him it was not simply a request for surface details – what kings and queens had I met recently – but more about feelings and coping. By then – and especially after understanding what an attentive, engaged father he was to his own sons – I knew that I could talk to him candidly, and I did.

Now, as a Hong Kong-based mother of two little girls, when I think back to my teenage years, what I feel strongly is that I was most fortunate to have known Mr. Trudeau personally. I am looking forward to telling my daughters about my favourite neighbour, Mr. Trudeau, who just happened to be the Prime Minister of Canada.

> HEATHER JOHNSTON

Wife of Donald, and friend of Trudeau's for over thirty years

*I*t was the summer of 1979. The Liberals were in opposition and Pierre was fairly recently separated from Margaret. My husband, Donald, invited him to come and visit us in Nova Scotia with the three boys. My family has a summer place on a point of land right on the ocean, idyllic for children. The boys at that time were, I think, three, five, and seven years old – comparable with our two younger girls.

"You taught me how to use the washing machine that summer," Pierre reminded me with a smile, years later. I have to admit, I was astonished that he had never before had occasion to use one. What did not surprise me, however, was his devotion as a father. I was extremely impressed with how consistent he was when dealing with his children. He was firm and loving. It was delightful to see how much he genuinely liked playing with all the children that summer – and there were many. Including nieces and nephews and friends, there were never fewer than ten children running about. Pierre would often jump in enthusiastically to participate in their rowdy games of Marco Polo. He also enjoyed gymnastics and building human pyramids with the kids on the lawn, and loved to play their favourite game with them: Kick the Can.

"Base-sticker, base-sticker," the kids would yell from their hiding places when Pierre was "it." His caution in not venturing too far from the can typified his competitive nature. He was always committed to winning, even if it was all in good fun. The children loved it, and he in turn often seemed to prefer the company of the young.

Another memory of Pierre from that summer concerns our daughter Rachel, who had a loose baby tooth that she was reluctant to have pulled out. Donald wanted to tie a thread around it and attach it to the doorknob and slam the door. Rachel wasn't so sure, and the father-daughter duo were at a standstill. Pierre, sympathizing with Rachel's reluctance, stepped in with his own solution. Asking simply to look at the tooth, he got Rachel to open her mouth, whereupon he deftly yanked it out with very little fuss. He wrote her a little note afterwards saying, "*Pour Rachel, avec mon bon souvenir et avec l'espoir qu'elle n'aura jamais une dent contre moi.*"

Barbara Collins

With the boys at Murder Point, the summer
he learned how to operate a washing machine.

My children especially remember the sand-castle contest that Pierre organized at the end of his visit that summer. Gathering all the kids on the beach, he carefully explained the rules and allotted areas to each child, timing the event and overseeing the elaborate constructions. Together, he and Donald acted as judges and were very sensitive about the winners and losers, offering each child a prize for obscure and specific categories. Possibly the reason that this event sticks out in the children's minds is because their prizes consisted of Mars bars, a decadent treat in our household.

All the children put on a play that summer. Drawing on the news of the day, they centred it on the theme of the Skylab falling on New York. If you recall, there was much hype and speculation in the press at that time as to where the Skylab would ultimately fall as it re-entered the atmosphere and broke up. Under the direction of my niece Susannah, then eleven, the children organized a play about it. Pierre was especially impressed with the topical nature of the play, but, like all the other adults, he was excluded from the rehearsals and had to wait until opening night to catch a glimpse of the performance.

The children took their parts very seriously, especially Michel, who was the youngest of the whole gang. They practised every day, and

Barbara Collins

Michel (third from left) practising his big line for the play.

opening night (which was actually at teatime) was exciting for everyone, for the adults were finally called in to be the audience. The performance was top quality, and although Pierre enjoyed seeing all of his boys acting, he got a particular kick out of watching Michel, since he was so little at the time.

Michel had a small but important part, which involved falling off a stool onto the stage. Michel loved the applause so much that after the play ended he proceeded to do it again, and again, repeating his one line "Oh, my God!" Pierre laughed and called him a ham.

▶ JANE FAULKNER
Family friend

When Pierre Trudeau was looking for a home in Montreal to raise the boys, he asked Margaret to look at a house on Pine Avenue. I was then living outside Montreal, and Margaret asked me to go along with her to look at the house. We ended up compiling a list of reasons why he should *not* buy it. One of the main reasons was that the house had marble floors throughout, with a circular marble staircase that descended from the main floor. Our concern was that three little boys running around and playing were likely to slip and hurt themselves on those unforgiving marble floors.

Years later when my husband, Hugh, and I had moved our family to India, Pierre came over for the 1984 Commonwealth Conference in New Delhi, bringing Justin with him. For the duration of the conference, Justin was to stay with us. When they arrived at Alirajpur House (where we lived), they had barely crossed the threshold, when Pierre's eyes travelled across our marble hallway, up a few marble stairs, to the marble reception rooms.

In a soft voice he remarked what a nice house we had, but were we not concerned for our children's safety on those slippery marble floors? Touché.

> JEFF GILLIN
Friend of Justin

I consider myself fortunate to have known Mr. Trudeau, but especially fortunate to have known him best during my childhood years. Justin and I attended preschool together, and Rockcliffe Public School until Grade 6. To me, Mr. Trudeau was above all else my best friend's dad – but a dad who happened to get us backstage after a concert, or to the front of the line before one. There were many outings to the National Arts Centre or the Ottawa Civic Centre for plays, concerts, circuses, or whatever else was worth seeing in town. These events always involved great seats and meeting the stars after the show.

The good times were just as much fun in less-public settings as well. I lived a short distance from 24 Sussex (four minutes by bike at age eight), and birthday parties there were a true delight. They always seemed to end up with several adults – including Mr. Trudeau – being thrown in the pool, fully clothed. Often this party game began with Mr. Trudeau pushing a Mountie in.

Looking back, what is most striking was the near constant access Justin, Sacha, and Michel had to their father. I spent a great deal of time with the three boys as a child, and never remember wondering where Mr. Trudeau was. He always seemed to be available to his sons, and from my perspective did all the things dads are supposed to do with their children – probably more. Whether it was in our occasional afternoon visit to his office on Parliament Hill, playing on the trampoline in the backyard, hiking in the woods at Harrington Lake, playing broomball games, trick-or-treating at Halloween, skiing, or going to church, he always seemed to be an active and enthusiastic participant in his boys' lives.

From my view, Mr. Trudeau's greatest success in life was as a father. Having grown up with his three sons, and knowing Justin and Sacha in later life, I have witnessed his love for – and devotion to – his children. Their strength of character and sincerity of heart is the true testament to this love and devotion.

One of my most vivid, and last, childhood memories of Mr. Trudeau involved his taking my mother's minivan for a test drive. It was just weeks before he was to leave office – and Ottawa – and he was trying to

Gillin Collection

With a shorter version of himself, Jeff Gillin, who wears a much fresher rose.

decide what vehicle would best meet the needs of his boys in their new life. He wanted something practical and safe to transport them on weekend trips from Montreal to the Laurentians in the years to come.

He showed up at my family's home one Saturday afternoon to borrow our brand-new Toyota minivan, one of the first in Canada. What I remember best from that afternoon was being buckled tightly in the back row and hearing Mr. Trudeau call out "Brace!" on several occasions, as he slammed on the brakes with full force, at varying degrees of speed. The brakes would squeal, the tires would leave long black streaks on the road, and pedestrians would stop and stare. To his credit, the RCMP member following within inches avoided rear-ending us on every occasion, despite the fact he did not seem to be given any warning of these sudden brake tests.

Rounding corners, Mr. Trudeau drove the standard-transmission van like a sports car, and I remember thinking at the time that at least two wheels must be off the ground during these manoeuvres. While I think he enjoyed the test drive, Mr. Trudeau eventually decided on a much larger – and far less trendy – truck that the family kept for many years.

▶ JEAN-SEBASTIEN BRASSARD
Friend of Sacha

I remember with fondness the first time I met Sacha's dad. Sacha and I were fifteen when we became close friends, and we would often have a snack at his place after school. We were then – and still are – very interested in poetry and classical literature, so my first contact with Mr. Trudeau was through his library. And what a library it was! Most of the books were originals, many of them from the beginning of the last century. I particularly remember a manuscript version of *Les Nourritures terrestres*, autographed and illustrated by André Gide himself. Other books were much older, such as the early impression of Machiavelli's *The Prince*. Yet most of the collection reflected the depth of Mr. Trudeau's humanism: Malraux, St.-Exupéry, Montherlant, etc.

What impressed me even more was the enthusiasm Mr. Trudeau displayed while discussing with me the ideas conveyed by these authors. He had that passion that captured the hearts of so many Canadians, including mine. Yet all the flamboyance and arrogance he displayed as a politician contrasted highly with the soft-spokenness and the humility he displayed as a private man.

I have to admit, I was quite proud and pleased when Mr. Trudeau expressed a certain disappointment to my mum that I had decided not to pursue an artistic career. This then prompted me to review my choices, and follow my dreams instead. So I decided to conquer America by foot, but, a few thousand miles down that road, my father's death brought me back to Montreal.

That summer Mr. Trudeau and Sacha had decided to take a road trip to New Orleans, with a slight detour into Kentucky to meet up with a mutual friend, Karim, for the Rainbow Gathering. Sach suggested I, and some other friends, join them.

Apparently his dad thought it was a great idea, because a few weeks later we were all snacking on tomato sandwiches next to the shores of Lake Ontario, at the beginning of our journey toward Daniel Boone National Forest. The trip itself was almost surreal. One can hardly imagine stopping for jumbo-sized soft drinks at Bob's Big Boy, accompanied by the father of modern Canadian foreign policy. Or trekking around a ghetto in Columbus, Ohio, looking for an ATM. But that was *nothing* compared to the fact that Pierre Elliott Trudeau was coming with us to the Rainbow Gathering!

To grasp what this means, you have to understand a Rainbow is an annual festival of thousands of Americans exercising their right to gather freely in national parks, outside the binding tenets of the legal system that is! It is quite an astounding (and relatively unknown) phenomenon, where accountants become witch doctors for a weekend. Or janitors become spiritual warriors in a drum circle. Beliefs of all kinds converge to create a completely self-sufficient community that includes its own system of barter and trade.

When we arrived, we met up with Karim (now a software engineer), who greeted us all with open arms – and a fully painted body. Leaving our car behind, we hiked a couple of miles down a dirt trail until we came to a clearing at the bottom of a ridge, where a ritual drum circle had been created around a bonfire pit. Seeing we had reached our destination, we all tumbled down the slope to join the drummers and dancers. But before the rest of us could get into the groove of things, Mr. Trudeau had already taken off his shirt and was engaged in a frantic tribal dance. We were all startled to see *he* was more comfortable with this than we were.

We spent the next few days dancing and singing, bartering and trading, or just sharing the simple pleasure of drinking tea in a makeshift coffee house, comforted by the warm embrace of the Kentucky skies, surrounded by freaks of all kinds.

I guess it was the spirit of that event that led us to organize a similar gathering for our own family of friends – one with better food and better drinks, but with the same wild sense of freedom and pluralism. Rainbow gatherings were celebrated until two years ago, when the Bush administration put an end to them. But every year, in the heart of the Ottawa Valley, a new season of life and hope is celebrated at our Summer Solstice Party. Not surprisingly, Pierre attended every single one of these celebrations.

▶ CHRIS INGVALDSON
Friend of Justin

I met Justin in September 1997, when we both studied at UBC's Faculty of Education. For the first few months we were both rather lukewarm toward each other, but after that we became fast friends. Justin, my wife, Pansy, and I ended up sharing a wonderful apartment at 12th and Granville in Vancouver, and during that time we became somewhat of a family. We had met Margaret and the rest of the Sinclair gang, and had visited Justin's grandmother's place several times for family meals. However, my relationship with Mr. Trudeau developed very slowly.

I first met him when he came out West to visit the site where Michel had died, and for one night he stayed with us. Justin introduced him to us when he arrived at the apartment, and he was very polite, thanking us for allowing him to stay over.

When my wife told Mr. Trudeau that she was bilingual, and that she'd gone to a French-immersion school – thanks to his government's policies – the two of them began chatting. This was wonderful except for the fact he didn't say a word to me! Throughout the remainder of the day, and the next morning, he didn't say anything to me. When Justin returned home from Nelson, I asked him if I'd done anything to offend his father; Justin said his father hadn't mentioned anything.

In June 2000, Justin and I drove back east to Montreal, and I stayed in their house for a little over a week. During that time, Mr. Trudeau was there – along with Gerry Wall, the caretaker. For the first few days the only words Mr. Trudeau said to me were "Hello," "Good Morning," and "Good night." Again, I wondered if I'd done anything wrong, and asked Justin, who said, "That's just the way my father is. Don't worry, he'll come around." Justin and I gallivanted around the city and had a ball.

I was told that I had free run of the house, but that I couldn't go into Mr. Trudeau's bedroom or office. No kidding!

On the fourth day of my visit, Gerry had the day off, and Justin had to go out for a while. That left Mr. Trudeau and me alone in the house. I was all set for another afternoon perusing the books in Mr. Trudeau's amazing library, but first, nature called. I had been in the bathroom for a few minutes when I heard a knock on the door.

Père et fils.

"Chris?"

"Uh . . . yes?" I replied, wondering what was up.

"It's Pierre Trudeau."

"Okay," I replied hesitantly.

"I'm going downstairs to watch TV now," he responded.

"All right," I said. Well, *that* was weird!

I went downstairs to find him sitting on the sofa, staring at the TV and channel-surfing.

"Anything you want to watch?" he asked.

"Not really."

And from that moment on, not only did Mr. Trudeau acknowledge my presence in his house, but he wanted to talk to me. We chatted at length about everything, from my family background, to my job and my aspirations. For the remainder of my visit, he acted like he was my friend's dad.

When it was time for me to return to Vancouver, Justin drove me to the airport. On the way, he said he had to make an important stop. We pulled up in front of a large office building downtown, and Justin told me to come with him. We were at his dad's office, and I assumed he needed to get something from his father, so I didn't say anything. We went into the office and Mr. Trudeau asked me to have a seat.

Then he did something that absolutely floored me: he signed a copy of *Memoirs*, writing me a small note. He said he knew what a great friend I had been to Justin, and *he* wanted to thank me.

I was almost brought to tears. In my house, when I was growing up, Mr. Trudeau was viewed as the worst thing ever to have happened to this country. However, Justin was my best friend and teaching colleague and – to be quite honest – I didn't care who his father was. So I never would have dreamed of asking Justin to get his dad to do something like that.

When Mr. Trudeau signed his book for me, I finally understood his silent behaviour toward me: he was being a father. He wanted to make sure I was Justin's friend, and that was why he took his time in accepting me.

In his book, he wrote: "Thanks for being my son's friend."

▶ BOOKER SIM
Friend of Sacha

*T*his is the story of how I came to know Pierre Trudeau. Who am I? No one really, but I've known Trudeau's middle son, Sacha, since we were five, and have thus known his family for twenty-five years.

I met Sacha at my father's second wedding. His new wife had worked for a spell at the PM's residence at 24 Sussex, and had come to know Pierre (who was not in attendance) and Margaret, who had brought sons Sacha, Justin, and Michel. At the reception, the Trudeau boys enlisted me into a rough-and-tumble game of "King of the Mountain." They thought nothing of getting grass stains on their suits. But I bowed out shortly into the game. "The suit's rented, man," I told them . . . or so the story goes.

I became schoolmates with Sacha a few years later (in Grade 2), and when Christmas rolled around, I was invited to Sacha's birthday party at 24 Sussex. My mum dropped me at the gate, and a serious-looking Mountie took me to the main entrance of the house and told me to go on in. But I didn't know where to go – and I heard only shouting. Thinking this was some sort of official parliamentary meeting, I stayed, paralyzed, in the palatial front hall. Finally, I got up the courage to investigate and found my classmates enjoying a spectacular magic show.

Sacha and I became very close as the years wore on. Ours was a prince-and-pauper story. I lived in a rundown downtown apartment with my hippie mother, whereas most of our classmates lived in large houses or mansions in Ottawa's fancy Rockcliffe Park. I soon learned to be self-conscious, even ashamed. But Sacha didn't care about my mother's hippie clothes, my long hair, or our quaint little pad. He was more interested in my formidable collection of toy guns. Beyond being upper class, Sacha had class.

Then there were the strange effects of Trudeaumania. The same parents who could be catty and cruel toward my mother would turn so very kind and gracious when in the presence of the Trudeaus. These were people my mum aptly called "Trudeaumaniacs."

Perhaps even my mother could be accused of being a Trudeaumaniac. If so, she was of a different sort. For her, Pierre Trudeau was not a symbol of the Establishment, but its opposite. She loved him for the same reasons John and Yoko did. The same reasons Marlon Brando and Leonard Cohen did. At the time, I didn't understand how my mother's contempt for Ottawa Establishment types didn't apply to the man who held the most Establishment job of them all: prime minister.

This paradox was to confuse me all the more when I actually came to meet Sacha's dad. At first, he was cold, distant, a titan of a figure. A Renaissance man, who seemed part of some Illuminati-billionaire-jet-set-Greek-god class of people. I imagined him riding horseback with the Queen, debating Aristotle with the Pope, sipping hundred-year-old vintages with the Rothschilds. Of a different class entirely from me and my mum.

But my later encounters with Pierre Trudeau turned out quite differently than I had imagined. I recall him taking Sacha and me and some of our friends to Harrington Lake to hunt for animal droppings, teaching us, as always, about the natural world, then rewarding us with chocolates. Then there was the time he appeared with a chocolate shaped like a champagne bottle at one of Sacha's birthday parties, doling out pieces of bittersweet Swiss chocolate to us kids in front of a three-storey Christmas tree. Children weren't a nuisance drawing him away from the Pope or the Queen or stately things. He seemed lost with us, part of our world.

Once he left office and moved Sacha and his brothers to Montreal, I would get to know him a little more with each weekend visit. At the grand dining-room table, lunches consisted of tinned soup, celery sticks, and conversation in French – with each grammatical error penalized by the loss of one of the Ronald Reagan jelly beans allotted for dessert. As an Anglo, this terrified me, but while his kids received reprimands for bad grammar, I was treated to small talk – in English.

"How is your mother?" he'd ask me. "I remember bumping into you as a baby once when I was walking home from work." Then he paused to reflect. "A big baby . . . but a baby nonetheless."

Never mind that it was my twenty-two-year-old stepmother he was referring to, or that I was at least five at the time – a big baby, indeed. I was astonished that, in a brain so filled with ancient wisdoms and government secrets, he'd found a place for a memory of me. And I didn't know the PM was even *allowed* to walk home from work!

But no matter how disarming he was, I was still terrified of him. Knowing this, Sacha once had me wait in the room adjoining his father's. Which I did, until the awkward moment when Mr. Trudeau discovered me. He wasn't angry, but genuinely perplexed as to how some kid got into his chambers. Sacha emerged soon after, deeply amused by how awkward we both felt.

As we grew into our teens, Sacha and I embarked on adventures together, adventures that Mr. Trudeau not only encouraged, but eventually even joined in. Sacha and I met in Paris to prepare for a hitchhiking trip across the same Saharan route used by the Paris–Dakar rally – until civil war in Algeria and Mali made the way impractical for a race. Most friends and family thought it too dangerous. The staff at the Canadian consulate in Morocco pretty much forbade us from going.

Mr. Trudeau, however, treated to us to a fine French meal and even finer stories. Over soup, he reminisced about his youthful days in Paris. With our entrees, he told us anecdotes from the G7 meeting at which Mitterrand and a newly elected Reagan had their infamous first meeting. Then over dessert, we shared a laugh at how the American Cold War cowboys had told Pierre they feared losing the South Pole to the Commies. His stories were light and playful – never grandiose. And after our delicious-yet-modest meal, Sacha and I were off for the adventure of our lives, no doubt leaving Pierre proud and worried in equal parts, though I saw no sign of any such emotions.

Five months later, Sacha and I returned from our pan-African odyssey. And soon after, he called me up to join him for another voyage, this one a road trip across the United States in his white Volvo "Moax" – with his father riding shotgun, poorly disguised in a white beard and fedora. So I took my place in Moax's back seat, next to two of Sacha's buddies. We made our way from one fast-food joint to next, keeping ourselves fuelled with inside jokes and loose debates. Mr. Trudeau joined in with a sincerity we younger "intellectuals" lacked.

At one point, Sacha was berating Philippe, one of my back-seat companions, for "selling out" to study finance. Phil was visibly distressed by Sacha's browbeating – until Pierre piped up.

"Listen, *jeune* Karamazov," he told his son, making reference to Sacha's hero of the day, the pretentious anti-hero of Dostoyevsky's *The Brothers Karamazov*. "Not everyone has the luxury of indulging themselves the way you do," or something to that effect. Sacha never shies from confrontation, but even then, he could only respond with a laugh.

We made it to our first destination: deep inside the Kentucky Hills for the Rainbow Festival, an annual celebration of peace, love, and nakedness that makes Woodstock look square. My friends and I were out of place – not real "Rainbows" – but Pierre fit in perfectly, tearing off his shirt on arrival, and rushing off to dance in the Dionysian drum circle, a hundred congas deep.

That night, after forgoing a dinner of nuts and lentils, Pierre plopped down in a random field, oblivious to the rocks, sticks, and naked hippies. On the road, food was a luxury for him, something replaceable by sleep. "*Qui dort, dine*," (basically, "if you sleep you don't need to eat") was one of his slogans oft quoted by Sacha (who, on the other hand, is not fond of missing meals).

The following day, we headed down to bathe in a nearby river. I was shy about the naked thing, but the cops had put an end to all such foolishness anyway by the time we got there. Luckily, Trudeau had his Canadian-flag Speedo handy and so could still take a cherished swim. Nobody recognized him the whole time we were at the festival. No Rainbows at least.

Fils et père, June 2000.

"Aren't you Pierre Trudeau?" asked a redneck cop on our way out of the festival, a hint of contempt in his voice.

"Yes."

"Weren't you prime minister of Canada?"

"You have a good memory. That was a long time ago."

And off we went.

Not all my Pierre Trudeau memories are happy ones. I won't talk about the much-publicized death of Pierre's beloved son Michel, except to say I'm sure most people were as touched as I was to see this giant of a man so hurt and so vulnerable.

In the years following Michel's death, even though Trudeau may have seemed tired and beaten at times, I can never recall him being cynical or bitter. When I was leaving for the former Yugoslavia with Sacha on another journey, Mr. Trudeau told me to "take good care of my son," looking me deep in the eyes for the first and last time.

His nonchalance toward Sacha's dangerous adventures had been an act. Of course he worried about his kids, but he knew they couldn't live their lives locked in some ivory tower. But, after Michel's death, Pierre couldn't hide his concern, his fear, his love, his disappointment, his frailty. He became ill.

On that same trip to Yugoslavia, Sacha met a special young lady, and upon his return to Canada, he knew he had to follow his heart back to the Balkans, even though his father was sick. So Sacha asked me to stay with his father for a few weeks, to cook for him and just keep him company. We'd dine on my mediocre meals (for which he always had compliments), then watch *BBC World News* for the latest scoop on the Balkans. And invariably, he'd express concern about Sacha, off in Milosevic's Serbia, where riots threatened to turn into civil war.

I became immeasurably fond of Pierre in those few weeks. I especially remember the time we walked to his friend Stratton's place for dinner. Just three bachelors talking about women, over bottles of Molson and a spaghetti dinner.

In the following months, as his father lay dying, Sacha would read him Herman Hesse's *Knulp*, the story of a childlike wanderer who touches the people he meets on his travels, and finally dies alone – but free and loved. With two loving sons, many friends, and millions of admirers, Trudeau was far from alone, but still I think he was much like this youthful wanderer.

When Sacha phoned to tell me his father had died, I couldn't believe it. This unique man, this man both titan and child, this man I was just getting to really know, was gone.

There is Pierre Elliott Trudeau the politician. For some, he is a hero. For others, a villain. And perhaps he is both. But to me, it is his childlike quality that marked me. But one thing remains from my youthful impression of him. He did belong to a special class. A class of one.

Chapter Sixteen

Memoirs

▶ JEFFREY GOODMAN

Senior communications adviser, 1980–83; president and CEO of
Goodman Communications; and Memoirs *book-tour director in 1993*

August 1993. Location: Montreal's Ritz-Carlton Hotel's Garden Restaurant.
Participants: Pierre Trudeau, Nancy Southam, Tom and Roberta Axworthy,
Jeffrey and Ruth Goodman.
Purpose: Social evening and preliminary discussion about the launch of
Trudeau's *Memoirs*.
Timing: The first night of the Progressive Conservative Party of Canada's
leadership convention and the farewell tribute to Prime Minister Brian
Mulroney, the party's outgoing leader.
Seating: As usual, Trudeau sat with his back to the entrance so as not to
be seen. He cherished his privacy. He also didn't want his dinner companions inconvenienced with people wishing him well or asking for
his autograph. It wasn't because he was imperious. It was simply an
evening out on the town as a private person – though for him that was
somewhat impossible.
Topics of Conversation: A multitude of things . . . Canadian politics,
international politics, baseball, family experiences. One brief topic in
particular.

"I understand the Conservatives are throwing quite a farewell bash for Mr. Mulroney tonight," I said. "And I understand that the video testimony is the video of videos."

"How much did his video cost?" asked Trudeau.

"I'm told it's about $300,000."

"How much did mine cost?" asked Trudeau.

"Seventy-five thousand dollars. There were a lot of volunteers. The production was at cost. A lot of people spent a lot of time doing it because they wanted to."

Trudeau looked at nobody in particular. But he had a contented smile. He liked the answer.

"But there's more than the video," I continued. "Apparently there's going to be a very, very special guest. And it is supposed to be a very big surprise. I wonder who it is?"

There was a pause at the table. We all put our knives and forks to the food and nobody looked up. No one wanted to say a word.

"Well – surprise – it's me!" said Trudeau.

Everyone, including Trudeau, broke into laughter. The next round of wine was poured.

*With Brian Mulroney (back to camera), and Jeanne and
Maurice Sauvé, sharing a big joke at Rideau Hall.*

Nancy Southam Collection

Avie's predecessor, Jack McClelland, negotiating the advance
with the author at a Great Literary Dinner Party in Montreal, 1986.

▶ AVIE BENNETT
Publisher and friend

*I*n 1993, Pierre Trudeau's *Memoirs* was published by McClelland &
Stewart, the company I then owned. I had many encounters with
Trudeau during the preparation and promotion of the book, but it was
one of our early meetings that I remember most vividly.

At that time, I was among the consortium that had bought the
Montreal Expos from the original owner, Charles Bronfman, in 1991. I
always looked forward to opening day in Montreal and enjoyed bringing
friends and writers to Olympic Stadium for the celebration, but it was
with certain trepidation that I approached my most notable author-to-be
in the spring of 1993 to accompany me. I was delighted when he accepted.

For philosophical as well as business reasons – after all, it was
important to impress upon him that we Canadian publishers were an
impecunious lot, and not given to extravagance – I did not hire a limousine to ferry us to and from the ballpark. Instead, I picked him up in a cab,
and we proceeded to Olympic Stadium through the heavy opening-day
traffic, experiencing all the frustrations of the ordinary fan (although

with the additional hazard of a cab driver who had a hard time keeping his eyes off the rear-view mirror).

As we walked through the crowds, both on the way to the owners' box for a pre-game meal and afterwards to our seats in the stands, I was moved by the warmth with which Trudeau was recognized by the fans. He had never struck me as a man who was particularly "of the people," but he was greeted with the kind of affection usually reserved for family and close friends, and enjoyed it more than I would have expected. This stood in marked contrast, I must say, to our reception in the owners' lounge.

Many of the ownership group shared strong separatist leanings, and while Trudeau was not my most controversial guest over the years (that distinction would have to go to Mordecai Richler the year that *Oh Canada! Oh Quebec!* was published), the temperature in the lounge dropped a noticeable degree or two upon our arrival.

It turned out to be a terrific afternoon. Trudeau surprised me by the breadth of his baseball knowledge. As he reminded me, his father had been one of the owners of the Montreal Royals, the Brooklyn Dodgers farm team on which Jackie Robinson first broke baseball's colour bar, and he had strong memories of games he attended when he was a boy. Like all good baseball fans, he insisted upon staying until the last out.

That was when the problems began.

In my egalitarian choice of our mode of travel, I had not given any thought to how we were going to get back downtown. As we left the stadium, it became obvious that there were no cabs to be had. We were carried along with the throng to the entrance to the Metro station.

"I don't suppose . . ." I began.

"Of course," Trudeau said, airily. "I use it all the time." Yeah right, I said to myself.

I lined up to buy two tokens, but one of the ticket-takers spotted my guest, and opened the gate and let us through for free. On the crowded train, the two of us strap-hanging with the rest of the fans, Trudeau struck up a conversation in French with a woman from Valleyfield, who was with her three children. Obviously delighted to meet him, she told Trudeau that she was a great Expos fan and never missed an opening day.

Thinking, as he later explained, that it would be quite a thrill for her, he introduced "my friend, one of the owners of the team."

I barely had time to reflect on his thoughtfulness in including me, when the Valleyfield woman turned and beamed at me.

"Oh, I am so pleased to meet you, Mr. Bronfman," she said.

▶ DOUG GIBSON
Publisher and editor

Shortly after the news of Pierre Trudeau's death was broadcast, I was sitting in the back of a cab in downtown Toronto. The cab driver and I shared our regrets about the news. The driver was a Greek who came to Canada as an adult in 1967, yet his English was good enough to summarize elegantly how he felt: "I grew with him."

Late in his life, I was fortunate enough to get to know Pierre Trudeau the author. At McClelland & Stewart we paid a great deal of money to publish his *Memoirs*, based on the 1993 TV series, but when the manuscript came in, bearing the company's hopes for a successful year, there were obvious problems with it. Our chairman, Avie Bennett, and I decided that it had to be reworked: in rough terms, made chronological rather than thematic. We flew to Montreal, and Avie, who knew him, introduced me.

We sat in his prow-shaped office, jutting out high above the St. Lawrence River, with the snow starting to fall down past the deep windows, and, after the usual courtesies, Trudeau asked us what brought us to visit him. Avie turned the conversation over to me, and I started to explain why the book had to be rewritten.

Did Trudeau listen and then say, "Sure, whatever makes sense to you"? No. He leaned forward, the eyes narrowed in that look we all remember, and he started to make objections.

"But what about this?" "But if we did this, what would happen to that?" On and on, a tough, unyielding barrage of questions. Had I considered this? How would I handle that? Obviously, I'd thought this through very carefully, so I was able to answer all his questions, while Avie watched like a fascinated tennis-match spectator.

If I'd ever said, "Of course, Mr. Trudeau, if you don't like it, we don't need to do this," I'd have been lost. Because he was grilling me to be sure I knew what I was doing. And in the end he leaned back, changed his tone, and said, "Fine, your plan makes sense. Let's do it your way." And thereafter, with *Memoirs* and the other three Trudeau books we published, we had a terrific working relationship, marked by his professionalism in getting proofs back to me exactly when he'd promised, every time.

There's a lesson here, I suggest, about Canadian politics. A prime minister runs up against people with all sorts of ideas, some of them excellent, some totally crazy. One way to spot the ones who do know what they're talking about is to grill them aggressively, and I can tell you, he was very, very good at it.

When the book was launched in Toronto (I'd been among the throngs at the televised launch in Ottawa, and then had seen the dangerously surging crowds at the Ritz-Carlton in Montreal behaving with un-Canadian enthusiasm), we had to rope off sections to deal with the 1,200 people clustered in the huge hotel convention room on the waterfront. It was a very big deal, and I'd brought my fifteen-year-old daughter and a cousin in town from Edmonton, and we'd taken a place on the TV camera island ten feet above the crowd.

When Trudeau began to speak, the huge crowed chanted, "Trudeau! Trudeau!" (even "Four more years!") and it was all very exciting. Then, after the usual "It's-very-nice-to-be-in-Toronto" stuff, he talked about his book and about working with Avie Bennett (on stage with him) and the others at M&S. And then Trudeau said, "But the man whom I especially want to thank, the one who pulled this together, is my good friend at McClelland & Stewart" – and I smiled modestly – and then he said, "my good friend *Fred* Gibson." And then he looked stricken and said, "Ah, Bob Gibson? Don Gibson?" Avie Bennett stepped forward and whispered into his ear. Trudeau said: "Doug Gibson. If he's here tonight, he'll never work with me again."

(This problem with names was not reserved exclusively for me. Barney Danson, who went on to long service in his cabinet, recalls a meeting in his riding where the PM came and delivered a barn-burner that ended with him urging the crowd to vote for, well, someone with the same number of syllables in his name as Mr. Danson.)

I had my revenge at dinner that night – and this, of course, was shortly after Mr. Mulroney's term in office – when Trudeau and I crossed paths while changing tables and he apologized for getting my name wrong. "That's all right, Brian," I said, "I do it all the time."

Happily, we did work together again, and McClelland & Stewart went on to publish *The Essential Trudeau* (with Ron Graham), as well as *The Canadian Way* (with Ivan Head), and *Against the Current*, on which Trudeau worked with his old comrade Gérard Pelletier.

I remember a lunch at the Beaver Club in Montreal with those two old veterans at a time when provocations in Paris by Quebec's delegates (*plus ça change*) were once again causing trouble for Ottawa. Trudeau and Pelletier, once his ambassador to France, were mesmerizing as they described, with weary irritation, every possible move on the diplomatic chessboard.

My most amusing, strictly literary, memory is of an argument about poetry with Trudeau. Toward the end of *Memoirs* he quotes the Rimbaud poem "Ma Bohème." The English translation, it seemed to me, could be slightly improved with a metrical twist of my devising. By speaker phone, with Avie Bennett as referee, Trudeau sprayed spondees and declaimed dactyls as he demonstrated the rhythms of the original French, then the very different rhythms of the two English versions, expressing a strong preference for the original one. I was hopelessly outgunned, in two languages. We did it his way.

In later years, when I was in Montreal and had time to spare, I would call and, if it was convenient, drop in for a visit to his law office on René Lévesque Boulevard. Once, when he was in his mid-seventies, he took me to lunch. Instead of making for the nearest corner crossing, he set off straight across the wide boulevard named after his old rival. When the light changed and a mass of cars hurtled toward us, he called out "Run!" with great cheerfulness, and sprinted to the other side through what seemed to be an unbroken stream of whizzing, honking metal.

As a non-Montrealer I remember thinking that, although the company was good, this was a really stupid way to die (immortalized on a Trivial Pursuit card as "the man killed along with . . ."). I also remember being surprised to live to tell the tale. And as we walked to lunch, my pulse slowly subsiding, I noticed how, with nods, smiles, nudges, and turning heads, his fellow Montrealers reacted with pleasure to his presence among them. In our conversations, his own pleasure was greatest when the talk turned to the boys, and his face would light up as he spoke about his three sons.

Today, a signed photograph from Trudeau hangs on my wall. It speaks of "the best of memories." For me, that certainly is true. Perhaps my taxi driver friend put it best for all of us: "We grew with him."

▶ JEFFREY GOODMAN
Senior communications adviser, 1980–83; president and CEO of
Goodman Communications; and Memoirs *book-tour director in 1993*

He was reluctant. And a bit snarly too at the beginning. But that didn't stop the book tour for *Memoirs*.

He wasn't overly pleased with the television documentary, and he was less than satisfied with the book. In fact, he spent the entire tour denying that he was the author, something that was technically true. He also wasn't relishing the idea of being in public again. There was even some doubt and a momentary lapse of self-confidence.

"I don't know why we're doing this," he said. "I haven't been prime minister for a long time and I'm not sure if anybody really cares what I have to say anymore."

But he had made a commitment to the publisher, and commitments were always met. He was satisfied with and approved the six-city, two-week tour in the fall of 1993. There would be no private receptions or book signings at retail outlets. It would be a combination of news conferences, interviews, Q & A sessions with Canadian youth, and public receptions. Tickets for the public receptions were sold for more than the cost of the book, but proceeds went to favourite causes and institutions – the Liberal Party of Canada, literacy, and Canada Parks and Wilderness. And the launch of the tour would be to sign his "deed of gift," handing over the papers and correspondence from his sixteen years as Liberal prime minister to the National Archives of Canada.

The first day included pre-taped, in-depth interviews in his hometown of Montreal with CBC, CTV, Radio-Canada, and TVA, and a photo shoot that was arranged at the last minute with *Maclean's*. He wasn't happy with one of the interviewers, but didn't show it. However, his penchant for punctuality remained steadfast. When dinner that night went later than anticipated, a number of "untempered" comments flew on the drive home.

Each city was to provide many memories and highlights. In Ottawa the next day, the ceremony at the National Archives of Canada provided him an opportunity to renew acquaintances with long-time political friends, share the stage with Jean Chrétien at his first official function as prime minister, and deliver a philosophical speech about history and how it is interpreted or misinterpreted. The news conference afterwards also provided an opportunity to butt heads with the national press corps. The fire had returned. To the claim that his ideas were "old ideas" his retort was "Old ideas are better than no ideas."

The following day, back in Montreal, a reception with fellow Liberals followed a news conference, and he invited those so loyal to him over the years to join him on stage. But the highlight was more personal. As he signed books, his eyes lit up and he smiled warmly when Justin entered the room and their eyes met.

On the third day in Toronto, he was into it. However, on the flight from Montreal to Toronto, he read an editorial in the *Globe and Mail* lambasting him for being so full of self-praise in the cutlines that accompanied the pictures (particularly the ones with John and Yoko Lennon, and Jacquie Desmarais with Mila Mulroney). He quietly chuckled at the jibes in the editorial, agreeing with it.

There *was* a problem and a mistake with the cutlines. Not only had he not written them, he hadn't even seen them before they were published. He consulted a copy of the book. He checked out the preface, which he had written himself. Then he checked out the final chapter, entitled "The Photographs: A Publisher's Note." He pointed out that there was a contradiction in the two explanations about his own involvement in the cutlines.

Swarmed by autograph-seeking fans.

I saw what he meant. "Well, Pierre, books are produced by people and people aren't flawless," I said. He found the comment bordering on profound, but I had a sense he wasn't prepared to let it go.

Later that evening, at a reception for ABC Literacy, he was mobbed by people wanting an autograph and hoping to shake his hand. Trudeau-mania was back once again. He received numerous ovations. The crowd was thrilled listening to his remarks and being in his presence. During his remarks, he decided to make a point to the publisher, but in such a subtle manner only a few would understand. He got his first name wrong a few times when thanking him. He referred to him as Fred, Bob, Don.

"I guess he won't want to be my publisher again," he ended. He then gave me a sidelong glance with a sly smile. The mistake wasn't accidental. The point had been made.

The crowd of twelve hundred was so eager to get close to him as he left the ballroom that the Emergency Task Force had to be called in to ensure there was order and he got out safely.

The fifth day, the following Tuesday in Vancouver, began with the Q & A session at the University of British Columbia. He found the questions challenging and invigorating. But there was that penchant for punctuality again. He was not pleased that he had to wait for the six-minute newscast by Don Newman of CBC Newsworld to end, before taking the stage in front of a live television audience. Some of the staff received his words of displeasure.

"You told me it was beginning at eleven o'clock," he said to Gene Diamond, one of my vice-presidents. Gene explained to him about the six minutes of news before the live broadcast began. Trudeau threatened to go up on stage anyway. Gene managed to convince him otherwise. "It was the longest six minutes of my life," Gene said afterwards.

In Edmonton the next day, at a media session with no cameras, he was thoughtful and elaborate in his responses. But he was still feisty. When his red rose arrived a minute after the media session began, he put it on carefully and remarked, "Now I'm dressed." Later that day, one of his visions was realized first-hand, when he attended a Q & A session with French immersion students at a junior high school in his "beloved Edmonton," a city that never voted for him.

The long flight to Halifax followed, and he arrived late at night. He didn't like early-morning public engagements, but it was more important that Atlantic Canadians knew he appreciated their support. Plus, he had caught on to the fact that Halifax was not originally on the initial draft for the tour, and he had had that changed. "I guess the publisher didn't realize that people in Atlantic Canada can read English" is how he began his remarks.

All along the way, he was discreet, not wishing to be noticed at airports, on planes, in hotel lobbies, nor did he want any RCMP security. Yet when someone recognized him and approached him, he was always gracious, signing autographs and chatting warmly with whomever, whenever.

The tour ended at Dorval Airport. He was tired but pleased. Everything he said on the book tour had a purpose and a meaning. Everything he didn't say was also for a reason, because he didn't want to directly offend or embarrass anyone (well, except maybe his book publisher).

Canadians everywhere had received him warmly, listened intently to his words, thoughts, and beliefs. They appreciated his brief return to public life. He appreciated their response and reception.

"Thank you. It was interesting and enjoyable," he said, while shaking hands goodbye at the airport. He turned around and walked alone through the terminal that would one day bear his name, back to his private life. Mission accomplished.

▶ CHARLES PACHTER
Toronto-based artist, whose images of the Canadian flag and the
Queen sitting on a moose are well-known Canadian icons

*T*he first time I met Pierre Elliott Trudeau was at a small dinner party near Pine Avenue in Montreal in October 1988. I had just opened an exhibition of new paintings in the Citadel Hotel near the Place des Arts. The other dinner guests were engaged in a heated discussion about the Meech Lake Accord. As I slowly sipped a very good wine, I suddenly found myself asking Pierre Trudeau what had become of my flag painting, which the Liberals had given him on his retirement in 1984.

He looked straight at me, then said, "Would you like to see it?" "Sure," I said glibly, not thinking much of it.

"Then come with me!" he replied, getting up from the table, as the other guests looked at us, slightly astonished.

"We're going to see my painting," Trudeau announced, putting his napkin down.

I followed him dutifully out the door into the night. We walked down the street to his landmark art deco house, a block away from the dinner party. We went in, descended a grand staircase, and there was my "Painted Flag" hanging over the entrance to his library. He told me how much it meant to him, and said, "You're the artist, so you have a right to know where your painting is hanging." I was amazed at this kindness.

He then gave me a tour of the house, which he obviously enjoyed doing. Somewhat flustered, I thanked him sincerely. As we walked back to the dinner party, I thought to myself, what a generous gesture, and what a class act. I never forgot it.

A few years later, I stood patiently in line among his fans in Toronto's Metro Hall when Mr. Trudeau arrived to sign his recently published *Memoirs*. I noticed that he seemed somewhat frailer and more distanced from the crowd. As I inched along the line to shake his hand, I briefly got the chance to say hello. I re-introduced myself. He looked at me quizzically, trying to place the name and the face. A few seconds passed. He looked searchingly at me. Then his eyes lit up, and as he grasped my hand warmly, he whispered, "My flag!" and beamed.

I will cherish his memory.

Chapter Seventeen

Back Home

▶ GERRY WALL
Caretaker and driver at 1418 Pine Avenue, 1994–2000

One morning Mr. Trudeau came upstairs early. Even though he usually walked back and forth to work, he said, "This morning, Mr. Wall, I will be needing a ride to work, because I must make a stop on the way." Later, as we were driving downtown, he explained to me that he must stop on rue St-Denis to find a gift for the wedding of a friend's daughter.

Seeing as there was no parking near the shop, he directed me a little farther down the street, where we were able to park. Under normal circumstances, I would have stayed in the car while Mr. Trudeau ran his errands, but that morning, Mr. Trudeau requested that I accompany him.

As we were walking to the shop, I noticed many people staring at us. I turned to Mr. Trudeau and said, "Mr. Trudeau, I bet I know what all these people are thinking."

He looked at me and said, "What is it they are thinking?"

I answered, "I wonder who that guy is with Gerry Wall!"

Mr. Trudeau laughed and said, "I'll remember that one, Mr. Wall!"

Happily back home.

▶ ROY ROMANOW
Saskatchewan premier, 1991–2001, and Healthcare Commissioner,
2001–2002, who first knew and worked with Trudeau in the late 1970s
and early 1980s during the Constitutional and patriation talks

*O*n an early summer day in 1995, Pierre Trudeau and I met at the Mount
Royal Club in Montreal for a chance to renew our acquaintance. My
experience had always been that the mercurial public persona of Trudeau

– aloof, intellectually rigid, and stubborn – often gave way to a more gentle man in the softer protocol of private conversation. As I climbed the stairs of the elite club, a place where an immigrant's son from the west side of Saskatoon never expected to be invited, I was preparing myself for a courteous, informative, and stimulating social luncheon.

Upon being ushered into a small second-storey private dining room (where Trudeau, naturally, was already waiting for me), I immediately felt welcomed, and I enjoyed, for a moment, the former prime minister's unconditional warmth as he stood to greet me. Barely seated, I heard these words:

"Well, Roy, I guess we socialists have lost the fight."

What? *We socialists?* Did I hear correctly, here in this fancy bastion of capitalism? From a former Liberal prime minister, whom – though progressive in his social policies – certainly didn't conform to the tenets of socialism as I saw them. Was he kidding or being genuine and, if so, what particular *fight* was it that *we* socialists had lost anyway? And how?

So we got into his opening line, big time, dissecting it through most of our main courses. Trudeau argued that the fight to fundamentally transform the goals and principles of capitalism had been lost to the globalization of trade and capital, and the explosion of new technologies. The capacity to widely disseminate American economic and social values, he claimed, had taken the steam out of the engines of traditional social democratic theory.

He noted that former British prime minister James Callaghan had – in a recent conversation – disagreed with him. Callaghan had argued that capital had most recently been "democratized," and that the growth of workers' pension plans (for example) resulted in more discrete economic investments that were more mindful of broader social purposes.

After I interjected to express my optimism at Callaghan's point of view, citing the investment activity of the Ontario Teachers' Pension Plan (for one), Trudeau went right back to his thesis. His reply was that, even if capital had been democratized, the rules and the culture surrounding its investment were now firmly dictated by the marketplace, with social structures (and those who advocated them) reduced to mitigating the worst influences of an otherwise unbridled market economy.

Leaving the Mount Royal Club, I was puzzled, as I am to this day, by what this exchange told me about the alignment of the man's character and ideology. Clearly, he saw himself in the mold of a social democrat, and yet, for years I saw him wear the garb of a Liberal PM with apparent natural flair. His affinity for individual rights led him to pursue social change through the enhancement of these rights, but it did not describe the totality of his personal and private contradictions.

My lunch with Pierre reminded me that true intellectuals do not allow themselves to be easily poured into political molds, and perhaps, over time, develop a deep attachment to the very *doubts* that propel them to seek answers to political and philosophical questions in the first place. In this sense, he was a man without answers, and lived to teach all Canadians the value of reason, deliberation, and doubt.

As for his socialist sympathies, who can really say? Perhaps they remain just that – sympathies. I've carried the memory of my lunch with Pierre for many years now, and, like most Canadians, my fond impressions of Trudeau go beyond his politics to the heart of his character and his indelible and lasting impressions on our country.

▶ JEAN-PAUL MURRAY
Jean-Paul Murray is the former managing editor of Cité libre,
and continues to be a member of its board

*P*ierre Elliott Trudeau was like Cyrano against a hundred men – always ready to fight the good fight, no matter the outcome. Few individuals have struck me so much by their presence, intellect, or capacity to inspire.

Though I've shaken hands or made contact with the last six prime ministers, the one I knew best and got closest to was Pierre Trudeau. The first time I saw him in person was on June 14, 1984, at the Ottawa Congress Centre, while he was giving his last speech as prime minister. Reciting Rimbaud's poem "My Bohemian Life," he immediately carried his audience off into the dream state created by all great speeches, and captured it with his vision of a future Canada:

Such splendid loves I dreamed of . . . and we will dream some more. Our faith in the people is great. Our courage is strong and our dreams for this beautiful country will never die.

He had me, and the audience, in his hands, but it would be several years later that I'd get to meet him in Ottawa, during the launch of his book *Towards a Just Society*. I'd decided to go over to the Parliamentary Press Gallery to cheer him on and maybe get an autograph. As I approached the building, I ran into him and we struck up a conversation. He signed my dog-eared copy of his book *Federalism and the French Canadians*, commended my love for both official languages, and went off to set someone's record straight.

Little did I know I'd meet him again and get to work with him a year or so later to revive *Cité libre*, the magazine he'd founded with Gérard Pelletier in 1950 to fight obscurantism in Duplessis's Quebec. At the launch of the magazine's first issue in Montreal's Chapel historique du bon Pasteur in June 1991, two or three people approached me, saying, "Trudeau wants to talk to you about your article." I shrugged this off in disbelief and ignored their entreaties until *Cité libre* president Michel Dupuy came over, grabbed me by the arm, and led me to Trudeau. "That's exactly the kind of article I want to see in *Cité libre*! I liked the way you argued that every society needs checks and balances to avoid inertia, sclerosis, and ultimate collapse into a sorry state of decline . . ."

And from then on, thanks to *Cité libre* and Jacques Hébert, I got to meet, phone, and break bread with Pierre Trudeau on numerous occasions, most often at Montreal's famous Maison Egg Roll Restaurant.

At one point, in 1997, I got the zany idea of making him a canoe paddle, something I'd learned to do a few years earlier. While sitting beside him at the Maison Egg Roll one night, I asked whether he'd mind my doing so.

"Only if you accept a copy of my latest book *Against the Current*," was his reply. So I hand-carved the paddle out of American black walnut, the true wood of kings if there ever were such a thing.

Once the paddle was finished, a meeting was scheduled at which I'd present it to him. It was to be on a July day in 1997 at his office. On the appointed day, he greeted me warmly, and I gave him the paddle, which he eyed for straightness and handled for balance. We talked about the many qualities of walnut, and I told him the wood for the paddle came from the Ohio Valley, whose deep, rich loam is famous for producing sturdy trees and fine lumber. He answered that, while he was prime minister, he loved to hike from his Harrington Lake residence to a nearby walnut grove to meditate and watch the deer eat walnuts.

My last encounter with Pierre Trudeau was in June 2000, at the Maison Egg Roll during a *Cité libre* conference celebrating the magazine's fiftieth anniversary. At one point in the evening, Jacques Hébert came over to me, saying, "You have to say hi to Trudeau." So I went over and greeted the "Chief" with some reserve. Though he was very frail, he fixed his steely blue gaze on me and said, "Thanks for the paddle! Have a good life!" They were the last words I ever heard him speak.

▶ JERRY LEVITAN
Toronto writer, musician, actor, and lawyer, who first met
Trudeau in 1984

I was going through the upheaval of a divorce in the fall of 1995, and sitting miserably alone in my apartment, when the phone rang. It was Pierre Trudeau. He had heard from a mutual friend of my predicament and wanted to cheer me up. "People told me it takes twelve months to feel human again after a separation," he said. "They were wrong. I think it to be more like two years."

I had known him for some eleven years by then, during which we visited once or twice a year, corresponded, and talked on the phone. But this was the first time he had called me at home. "It's good of you to call, Mr. Trudeau," I said.

"Jerry, we're friends. Call me Pierre." He knew how important that gesture would be to me. His kindness overwhelmed me.

"I'm in a bad way, Pierre," I said.

"It will pass," he told me. "The Portuguese have a good expression.

'The worst thing about the future is that it is uncertain.' It's the uncertainty that makes the mind spiral, but it will pass."

He then invited me to come to Montreal and to bring my kids. He suggested the Friday before the referendum. There would be a large pro-Canada rally that day and he had been asked by Chrétien's office to keep a low profile.

"They are afraid I will cause an insurrection," he mused.

So, on that historic Friday, I took my children, Daniel, Rebecca, and Joanna (then fifteen, eleven, and nine), to spend the afternoon with Pierre Elliott Trudeau.

Usually, Trudeau's secretary would greet visitors at the reception area of his office. This time Pierre came out himself to meet and welcome my children and escort them into his office. The office had paintings and pictures of his boys, many books piled in stacks behind his desk, an inviting couch, and the Albert Einstein Peace Award on the wall. His attention was focused on my kids. He asked each of them where they went to school and what their interests were.

He then took them to the window that overlooked Montreal. Joanna pointed down and asked him why there were so many buses in a parking lot. Some had Canadian flags on the roofs and looked like a cluster of toys.

"Those are people who love Canada," he said softly, while resting a hand on each of my daughters' shoulders.

We then went down to a small food court in his building. Chinese food. Burgers. Souvlaki. He told me he thought the children would prefer that to a restaurant. Besides, he said, it would be difficult to wander the streets given the massive rally that was forming in front of his office building on René-Lévesque Boulevard.

We talked about the upcoming referendum. He thought it would be dangerously close. Mistakes had been made, he said, but he was hopeful the federalists would win. He regretted, as always, the timidity of the federalists, and he commented on that with a pained expression on his face. Daniel asked him about the Bosnian crisis, and Trudeau gave him a concise historical perspective over the course of two or three minutes and concluded it by telling Rebecca that he was going to "steal" one of her fries.

When lunch was over, he walked us to the elevator, where we rode to the lobby. Some people came up to talk to him and asked for his autograph. He was polite, signed his name, but told them, "You have to excuse me, I am with some friends." The front of the building was all glass, and the crowd walking toward the rally was impressive. The Canadian flag was everywhere. People were proud and determined. Pierre took us to the revolving door. He said goodbye to each of my children, and then to me.

We could hear speeches in the distance. I was standing next to the greatest Canadian orator of my generation, and he was muted, in self-exile, in a glass cage. I thanked him for his time and for his generosity. He waved us off and smiled, and we wandered into the flow of the crowd. I looked back, and saw Pierre Trudeau watching the passing crowds, alone, deep in thought, and hurting. Of all the photos, films, and videos I had seen of this man I so admired, I had never before seen that anguished expression.

▶ ROY ROMANOW
Saskatchewan premier, 1991–2001, and Healthcare Commissioner,
2001–2002, who first knew and worked with Trudeau in the late 1970s
and early 1980s during the Constitutional and patriation talks

*T*hree years or so before his passing, I had the opportunity to visit Pierre Trudeau in his downtown Montreal office. His invitation afforded my small travelling staff, and me, a brief break in our hectic circuit of political meetings and speaking engagements. It was with no small degree of anticipation that we rode the elevator up into the highest echelons of the cityscape to pay a visit to the great man.

It had been a couple of years since I had last seen Trudeau, and, at the time he looked very much the feisty PM of old, but as he cordially opened his door to me that afternoon, the image I had been keeping in my mind was shattered. I was stunned. He was a shadow of the man who so vigorously defended his concept of Canada during those 1981–82 constitutional battles. I saw before me a frail and snowy figure.

Smiling, welcoming me in, bidding me to indulge in the incredible view of the city, Pierre Trudeau was now as thin as a rose stem, his suit jacket hung like a robe over his shoulders, his blue eyes burned deep and steady in the sculpture of his hollow cheeks.

His office, glass on three sides, jutted out and away from the building, giving the illusion of a birdcage hanging in the air. Polite conversation quickly turned political, against the panoramic backdrop of the Montreal skyline.

Trudeau's bitter distaste for the Quebec separatist movement hadn't softened over time, perhaps renewing itself in the years following the 1995 referendum. From his refuge in the city that voted No, it was clear that he still struggled with the unanswered political questions surrounding Quebec secession.

In what manner should a simple vote determine the fate of a country? To what extent should the fate of the greater Canadian polity be considered? Should a prime minister preside over the dissolution of the federation?

Trudeau's hope was that those who believe strongly in Canada would stand vigilantly against separation and offer satisfactory answers to these questions.

"Roy," he said, "we've ceded too much of the argument to the separatists in the misplaced hope that appeasement would eventually lead to an end of the demand for separation. We're behind in this debate, and you – and every other committed Canadian – must not back down an inch on the vision of a united Canada, and the mechanics to ensure its continued survival." That the debate be conducted passionately was as important to the statesman now as keeping the country in one piece (an interesting contradiction in light of his oft-stated motto of "reason over passion").

He insisted on escorting me down a winding flight of stairs to the floor below, where my advisers were waiting patiently in the hopes that they would have the opportunity to meet him. With his tie charmingly askew, Pierre greeted every one of our delegation with grace and warmth. When one of our members (who was born and raised in Montreal) teased him, in French, about having met Mr. Trudeau in his student days "from the other side of the protest line," Pierre's response was, "Exactly where you should have been as a young student." And when assured that my colleague was not there as a separatist, but as a protester against some of the Trudeau government's policies, he endorsed peaceful dissent even more emphatically.

It was late in the afternoon, and I thanked him for his hospitality, remarking on behalf of the whole group how much we all appreciated a bit of time with someone "destined to be in the history books."

Pierre smiled wryly, and before he turned to ascend the stairs back to his office, replied to the small audience, "I'll only be happy if you're all there with me."

▶ B.W. POWE
Writer, teacher, author

*H*e still comes through in my notebooks.

Memory: piecing together fragments, growing the present from seeds, restoring voices to echoes and fading whispers, finding traces, following tracks or pathways of dormant patterns in the mind. He is still there, Pierre, speaking up from the words I had written down.

I went away from our lunches, and wrote down what he said, putting those encounters on paper. So I could – over the years – find him again, mentor and friend, visionary and hard-nosed politician, riven personality and complex soul, now myth and existential person, historical portrait, and controversial, impelling presence. Few have stopped remembering him. Canada made Trudeau, and he helped to make Canada what it is now, and will surely be. In my notes I find myself continuing to chart ways round him, and toward him.

1987: In his office, at Heenan Blaikie, on de Maisonneuve.
I had brought books: *The Glenn Gould Reader*; Elias Canetti's *The Conscience of Words* and *Crowds and Power*. He loved receiving books, and since he insisted on paying for lunch, I always brought a book for him, something I (somewhat slyly) knew he would read closely and would

want to talk about on other occasions. I handed him this passage I had
typed up from Erich Fromm's *The Anatomy of Human Destructiveness*.

> Reason is more than intelligence; it develops only when the brain
> and the heart are united, when feeling and thinking are integrated,
> and when both are rational. . . . The loss of the ability to think in
> terms of constructive visions is in itself a severe threat to survival.

He was startled and pleased by the Fromm quotation.

"This is fascinating. Exactly what I've tried to express for years.
Reason shaping, controlling passion. Not thinking without passion. The
press hasn't often understood this. I like this very much. May I keep it?"

Of course, I told him.

"Reason and passion together. This is what I meant. The uniting of
mind and heart. A rational person has all this in balance."

1989: At a Chinese restaurant around the corner from his office.
"When I was young, twenty-two or twenty-three, it was liberty that
obsessed me. Liberty was all that I thought about. There was, of course,
at that time, in Quebec, an authoritarian mood. From the authoritarian
church, the corrupt provincial government, to the nets of institutions.
There was a lot to want to throw off.

"But when I entered politics, I changed my mind. I began to feel that
equality was one of the most important factors in that revolutionary
trinity of liberty, equality, fraternity. Equality over the liberty to do anything you wanted. Equality to restore balance to the system."

He said this, speaking quietly, during the burn – and afterburn – of
the Reagan–Bush, Thatcher, and Mulroney neo-conservative policies.
Though he made no direct reference to them, I knew where he was firing
his words.

"I've begun to realize how inequality – I mean, specifically, inequality of opportunity – can be the source of injustice. For if liberty only
applies to the privileged and strong, then their expression of liberty can
be oppressive. Who else right now can afford to be free except for the
rich? Liberty means for some the right to do anything you want. But
where does this leave others who are scrambling to survive?"

Typically, when he spoke in that way, there was a great concentration in his stare. He glared into you. He made slicing gestures with his hands. Yet his voice remained quiet, the tone steady.

"What if it's only the wealthy who have liberty? The underprivileged, the weak, the desperate, the sick, the elderly, may need equality in society in order to establish just patterns. Take the current regimes. They give more power to the rich, and liberty to the rich through tax breaks, but what happens to the less privileged?

"Liberty is still essential to me. But equality of opportunity must be the essence of a just society. This means a constant balancing, a constant process of understanding the limits of liberty. Because if liberty is not for everyone – an equality of liberty, if you like – then liberty too can become a tyranny."

1990. At the same restaurant.

We were discussing Joseph de Maistre, the dark apostate of the Enlightenment, the thinker who countered the idealism of Voltaire and Rousseau.

"A strange man for you to be reading."

Pierre talked in an almost paternal way. "*Les Soirées de Saint-Petersburg*. I read it so many years ago. A fascinating mind – the true opponent of what all the agents of reason stood for."

I told Trudeau how profoundly disturbing I found the thought of this philosopher I took to be the model for Dostoyevsky's Grand Inquisitor. After some exchanges on the Enlightenment, I told him that I'd found a curious omission, a gap in de Maistre's thinking.

"Which is?" He was quick to pounce in any debate.

"The omission of love, the other force in history. De Maistre exalts authority and order and sacrifice, and the power of the irrational over the rational, yet I don't find him acknowledging the mysterious energy in the cosmos, which is love. De Maistre's arguments resemble the Grand Inquisitor's in *The Brothers Karamazov*. Was Dostoyevsky thinking of de Maistre when he wrote that section of his novel?"

"I don't know, but it's a good hypothesis. What was the answer given by Christ to the Grand Inquisitor? I've forgotten it."

"Christ doesn't answer. He walks across the floor, and embraces the Grand Inquisitor, then kisses him on the cheek. The other unanswerable factors in history, in time: love, forgiveness, charity, embracing the other."

He sat forward at those words. This was his response, uttered in a slower and more methodical manner than I'd ever heard from him before:

"Perhaps more strongly still, people are driven by a sense of justice, fairness, and balance. Where does the striving for justice come from? If we can't get people to love one another – at least not now – or even to like one another, then we can try to guide them toward being more just. To allow ourselves a greater sense of justice, of fairness. I believe it can be justice that determines the relations between people. I find it difficult to dismiss justice in history, that movement toward justice. The entire Enlightenment program thrived on the sense that we must find a fair arrangement in law and wealth. Against hate, violence, greed, opposition, we can see justice emerging as a singular force, perhaps the one rational element in history."

"Do you think the ideal of justice derives from feeling or intellect?"

"From both. We can feel when processes are unjust. We know it too. And if, as de Maistre says, there are evils in society that social contracts can't remedy or restrain, or indeed change at all, then why are there also the presences of reason, goodness, and justice too? These are more than delusions."

He had spoken passionately. And I had wanted to pursue this line of thought, when we were interrupted by the waiter who served us our meals.

Return to another meal in 1987.
After we'd eaten, and talked, we went out to the lobby of the Queen Elizabeth Hotel. People recognized him and called out his name.

Sometimes they simply said, "Pierre." While Trudeau sat down on a chair to pull on his boots – the snow was still deep in the streets – three businessmen wearing Stetsons ambled by. One looked in our direction.

"Hey, look guys, it's Pierre."

The three sidled up.

"Pierre! We miss you," one said.

Trudeau promptly stood up to shake their hands.

"Then you couldn't possibly be from the West," he said, nodding at their impressive Stetsons.

"But we are!" Another man laughed. "We're from Saskatchewan. None of us ever voted for you. But we miss you anyway!"

The two others nodded and laughed again, and all shook his hand once more, and said goodbye.

This is how I remember him: how people waved to him in the street, calling his name, more often than not using his first name, calling out in that strangely possessive way. And I remember how they often stopped to say, "Prime Minister," then said goodbye in the way that I keep saying goodbye to him, a farewell that holds him in memory, and in the imagination, where he never leaves, and where he never stops asking primary questions and speaking of time struggling toward the recognition and implementation of justice.

▶ GERRY WALL
Caretaker and driver at 1418 Pine Avenue, 1994–2000

I remember getting to work one morning around 6:30 and I met Mr. Trudeau in the kitchen. He wasn't usually up that early. Also, he was holding a mop – and looking very tired. I said, "Sir, what is wrong?"

He replied, "We had a water leak last night and the boys were all out."

I was more than a little stunned and confused.

"But, sir, why didn't you call me?"

"Mr. Wall, I know that your father-in-law is very ill, and I didn't want to scare you in the middle of the night." (My father-in-law had worked for Mr. Trudeau before I took over.)

Two hours later, when Mr. Trudeau was lying in bed resting from his exhausting night, the plumber was fixing the leak, and Sacha had just arrived home, the telephone rang. It was my mother-in-law telling me that my father-in-law had died. It was Valentine's Day, 1995.

Mr. Trudeau would sometimes come to my home and have a quiet meal, which my wife, Marlene, would prepare with care (and lots of stress). I remember he liked Chinese fondue with lots of sauces, homemade bread,

A backyard barbecue at Gerry Wall's with (left to right)
Mme Gagné, Sacha, Gerry, and Justin.

and baked potatoes (not all in the same meal!). He was always down to earth with my family and made them very comfortable.

I remember one time we had Mr. Trudeau, Sacha, Justin, and Mrs. Gagne (my mother-in-law) for a barbecue in our backyard. As we were sitting talking and having a drink, Mr. Trudeau noticed an older man in our neighbour's yard. Mr. Trudeau went over to him and had a conversation as if they were old friends. This was the type of person Mr. Trudeau was, easy to please, down to earth, enjoying the simple things of life.

▶ TED JOHNSON

Executive assistant, 1980–84; canoe partner; and friend

Pierre's love for the outdoors and for swimming are well known. His close friend, the lawyer and poet Frank Scott, accompanied him in the 1950s on an excursion down the Mackenzie River on the summer supply barge, and composed several poems capturing vignettes of the experience.

The best-known of these is "Fort Smith," which tells of Pierre taking a dip in the icy waters of the fast-flowing Mackenzie.

Humbly speaking, I think I can go one better.

A couple of years after he had retired as prime minister, a friend of mine at First Air – the airline serving the Canadian Arctic – invited Pierre, his sons, and a few friends on a summer excursion to Greenland. Some would hesitate to accept an opportunity to visit one of the more forbidding and isolated – not to mention cold – environments on Earth. Pierre and Justin jumped at it. My wife, Sharon, and I had the good fortune to be included, and we enjoyed trips by small boat among icebergs up spectacular glacier-lined fjords, hiking among reindeer across miles of tundra, and camping at the head of an inlet well above the Arctic Circle, many miles from the nearest fishing settlement.

One morning – I think it was our last day in camp – I was getting some fresh air when an apparition appeared. It was Pierre, dressed only in a bathing suit and hiking boots, with a towel over his shoulders, heading deliberately down the steep path to the ocean. Many of us would stop and contemplate the water. Perhaps dabble a toe. Not Pierre! His technique was to kick off his boots and jump right in. I suspect he had been testing the temperature of the water for several days without telling anyone of his scheme. In any case, he was in the freezing cold water for a good minute.

The thing about this solo expression of freedom (or craziness, depending how you felt about the water temperature) was that he seemed to be doing this for himself. I don't think he saw me. This was the same Pierre about whom Frank Scott wrote a poem some thirty-five years earlier on the Mackenzie.

This time it was a solitary challenge, without anyone writing a poem about it.

▶ JEAN MacMILLAN SOUTHAM
British Columbian; philanthropist

*I*t was in the late 1960s that my husband, Gordon, and I first met Pierre at our home in Vancouver. He apparently wanted somewhere to swim.

His British Columbia "people" or "handlers," or whatever you're supposed to call them, had asked us if the prime minister might have the use of our indoor swimming pool, one afternoon, while he was on a visit here. Gordon and I probably discussed the request over a martini that evening. We didn't see anything wrong with it (the swimming pool proposal, I mean).

So Pierre came and swam lengths in the pool for about half an hour, and then – while we walked him around the back garden – his eyes lit upon the trampoline, which he used with great flair, front flips included. Pierre was perfectly charming, and attractive, and I probably began my lifelong crush on him that very afternoon, even though I voted Conservative.

Gordon, a Liberal voter, was a great Trudeau supporter through all five of those elections. He never minded how I felt about Pierre. On his desk *still* (Gordon died in mid-October 1998) is a large colour photograph of Pierre and me, taken in the early 1970s. I don't know where the picture was taken; none of my family can remember. Oddly, it looks like some bar. Pierre is smiling and I am standing next to him, smiling and staring at him. No, that's wrong. My eyes are glued to him, locked on him. I really loved Pierre. He was so good-looking.

Jeannie Southam gazing at the man she loved.

In a biography of my father, H.R. MacMillan, there is a letter Daddy wrote to his friend, R.S. McLaughlin, after meeting Pierre for the first time, a few weeks before the 1968 leadership convention. Daddy was a pretty good judge of character, but he was slightly off in his assessment of Pierre. Here is what he wrote:

> I had a chance last Sunday to be one of a small number of people who spent a couple of hours with Trudeau in the sitting room of his hotel. I had never seen him before. He did not make any speeches but in a gathering of about 20 people he answered questions and conversed about his political views. I was very favourably impressed by him. I do not expect that he will win the leadership of the Liberal Party in April, but I would expect that later, when he has had more experience, he would make a great leader.

In November 1998, I was in the East visiting my daughter Nancy. We had just lost Gordon a month before and I didn't know what to do with myself. And then the terrible news came about Pierre's youngest son being killed in that avalanche. A few days before Michel's memorial service, Nancy and I had Pierre over for lunch at the Fire Station. They insisted on eating raw fish – *sushi* or something – while I stuck to a nice cooked piece of salmon.

Pierre was subdued, understandably, but I made him laugh. We were talking about how it was interesting whom you heard from, when a family member dies. I thought Pierre might be interested to know that I had heard from Prince Philip.

"After Gordon died, I got a telegram from Prince Philip," I said.

"Well," he said, "I got one from the Queen!"

About a year and a half later, in June 2000, I was in Montreal again, and Pierre came to the Fire Station one afternoon. We drank champagne and ate too many chocolate biscuits. We talked about C.D. Howe, my war years in Halifax, and what it was like growing up in Vancouver in the 1920s. We compared notes on the countries we had visited, and Pierre was particularly impressed with the 1939 trip I took around the world with my father, to Japan, China, India, Egypt, and several European countries. He was amazed (who wouldn't be now) when I told him about staying with the Maharajah of Gwalior, who had an enormous garage full of the latest British cars – Bentleys, Rolls-Royces – cars like that, each in three different colours: grey, navy, and black. Then we had a long conversation about riding elephants in India.

I don't know why, but Pierre always enjoyed my stories, and he always laughed out loud at them. Nancy was there that afternoon, but I remember at some point she got up and started to walk quietly out of the living room. Both Pierre and I wondered where she was going.

"I'm not going anywhere," she announced. "I'm just overwhelmed by your conversation and laughter. You both are having so much fun, I thought I'd just leave you two alone together for a while." That seemed fair enough to us.

"But we'll need some more champagne in a minute," I said. Pierre giggled.

I remember looking at him (I always *loved* looking at Pierre), and thinking to myself how weak and thin he was. Even though I'd been warned, it was still a shock to see him like this, almost pale and old – certainly not the memory I had of him. He looked like a Douglas fir without branches. He made some reference to not "feeling all that strong," but I let it go. We talked, again, about loss and death, and faith, and he asked me for advice, since he knew I had lost both my sons in sudden and tragic circumstances.

Pierre stayed a long time, a couple of hours anyway. He seemed hesitant to leave. When he did get up to go, I offered to walk him home. He thanked me and said, "It's okay, I can manage. It's all down-hill from here anyway."

I was struck by that remark, and have never forgotten it, even though I knew he was referring to the short walk to his house. So we kissed and hugged each other goodbye, and off he went. I went to the window that overlooks the sidewalk. I wanted to watch him go, to wave to him, knowing in my heart I would never see him again. I wanted to wave at him because I *really* loved Pierre.

When I looked out the window he was already standing there, looking up. And he waved back.

▶ LEONARD COHEN

Musician, author, poet

He was kind and powerful. He asked me to read him a poem. And then he asked me for another. And another. This was on the roof of Nancy's house, which she called The Firestation. Nancy gave us lunch, and then I read some more. Later many sorrows befell them both.

Death of a Lady's Man

Chapter Eighteen

Michel

▶ GERRY WALL
Caretaker and driver at 1418 Pine Avenue, 1994–2000

When I started to work for Mr. Trudeau he said to me, "Gerry, be careful with the boys. There are only two cars available, and there are three boys, so don't get in the middle of it." It was great advice! But I do remember Justin, Sacha, and Michel were all very good to me. Justin was at McGill University studying teaching; Sacha was into philosophy; and Michel was still at Brébeuf College, and every morning they would all talk about different things. Michel would then take the bus off to school.

As the years went by, Justin and Sacha went their different ways, toward their various interests and projects. Then I remember Michel coming home one day with a dog. It was just a pup, half black lab and half German Shepherd. But I'm afraid of dogs. Michel told me the puppy's name was Makwa, a Native word for bear. Okay, I thought to myself, but I was terrified to find out that this puppy would get bigger.

Then, a year later, I was introduced to this big baby black bear named Makwa. Needless to say, I was wondering if I was going to quit my job. But Michel had a way of calming you down. He was very easy-going.

"Don't worry, Gerry. He won't eat you."

So every morning, I would take Makwa for a stroll in the park.

Michel on the balcony of 1418 Pine Avenue.

I will always remember the last time I saw Michel. Don't we all. I had helped him to get his equipment together, and to tie his bike onto his Ford Bronco. He was heading out West, he didn't know for how long.

"Gerry," he said when the truck was all packed up, "thank you very much for everything you do for my dad.

"It makes me feel much more at ease, when I'm not around."

Then he and the baby bear headed out West.

▶ JOYCE FAIRBAIRN
Senior legislative adviser, 1970–84; communications adviser, 1982–84; and long-time friend

On November 13, 1998, Canadians across the land listened to newscasts with shock, hope, and prayers as they learned that Michel, the youngest son of former prime minister Pierre Trudeau and Margaret had been caught in an avalanche while skiing with friends in British Columbia's Kokanee Provincial Park. Two of them had been swept into the lake, and Miche was missing.

I received the news when I arrived at the Macdonald Hotel in Edmonton, where the prime minister's switchboard in Ottawa had tracked me down, and asked if I would help them handle calls from old friends and colleagues of Pierre's with whom they were not familiar. I have never received such an unexpected, devastating message. The search continued through the weekend, but it became clear that, while Miche's friend Andrew Bednarz had managed to get out of the icy waters of Kokanee Lake, Miche had not.

Even after a friendship of more than thirty years, I could not begin to imagine the anguish Pierre was feeling. To him his children were simply indispensable – the centre of his life and the source of his greatest pride and love.

The next week friends gathered from around the country to attend Miche's memorial service in Montreal. While the depth of the loss for Pierre and Margaret and Justin and Sacha was clearly overwhelming, each one of them was as strong as a rock. Part of that strength came from the group of young people, friends of all the boys, who were helping at the church and gathered like a protective shield around the family at the front.

Those young friends were particularly protective of Andrew, who, in a state of almost uncontrollable grief, had come with his parents from British Columbia. They were strangers in this crowd, and I had been asked to look out for them by an old parliamentary friend and cabinet colleague of Pierre's, Dr. Stanley Haidasz, who had called from Toronto to say the Bednarz family felt strongly that being part of the farewell would help Andrew work through his sorrow.

When the service was over there was a gathering at the Mount Royal Club for old friends of all the family. When Pierre arrived, he was engulfed by the group, each wanting to have a private word with him. He could hardly move an inch. Ted Johnson, his former executive assistant, and I tried to clear a path, but without much success. I asked Pierre if he wanted to go it alone, and he suggested it would be helpful if I stuck with him, and he gently moved around the room.

He wanted to have a word with the young people, particularly Miche's friends. Given the amount of pressure and sadness he was under, he moved ahead with great patience and kindness, which switched briefly to a broad smile when his young daughter, Sarah, dashed across the room to give him a hug.

During a bit of a break, Mr. and Mrs. Bednarz took me aside and asked if I thought it would be all right if they had a few words with Miche's father. They clearly were under a great deal of stress themselves, as parents whose own son had managed to survive the avalanche. I said I would do my best to make that happen. Pierre responded to them with warmth and understanding. As he moved on, they said that Andrew wanted to meet his friend's father, but was too distraught to do it alone.

The crowd had grown, and Margaret, Justin, and Sacha were also moving about, showing their appreciation for the affection and goodwill of all the old friends. I was keeping an eye out for Andrew, and I could see him standing over by a wall, looking truly miserable from the sadness and the pressure of the day. I told him I had spoken with his parents and would be happy to bring Mr. Trudeau over. He responded that, while he very much wanted to talk to him, he was having difficulty in trying to find the right words to say. I told him not to worry; it would be fine.

By this time, Pierre had been moving slowly through the rooms for a considerable period of time – for much longer than he had intended to stay. He was getting weary and asked me to stick with him and head toward the door. I pointed to Andrew and said the young man needed help in getting through all this and wanted at least to shake his hand. Pierre immediately nodded and smiled. I moved back a bit so they could talk, but close enough that I could join in if there were difficult moments.

After they had shaken hands and exchanged a few awkward words, Pierre opened up with a smile: "Now, I understand why Miche was up there in those mountains. Tell me, what made *you* choose to go and live in that beautiful place?"

Well, Andrew talked about his love of life outdoors, the challenges, and the sheer enjoyment of that area. He talked about his friendship with Miche, or Mike as he was called out West, and the strong attachment Mike had had for his beloved dog, Makwa, who was best friends with Andrew's girlfriend's dog. He hoped he would be able to help Makwa now that his master was gone, and Pierre thought that was a good idea. Pierre flowed right along and gave a message both of comfort to Andrew and of encouragement to move on, to follow his instincts the way Miche had been following his own in the search for the best way to live his life.

It was a short interlude that ended with smiles and warmth and, I think, perhaps a new level of comfort for Andrew at that truly tragic time. In those moments of quiet connection, a devoted father had lightened some of the heavy load for one fine young man, while his own heart was breaking over the loss of his youngest son. Through all the years I had known Pierre I never admired him more, nor felt so proud.

▶ ANDREW BEDNARZ
Friend of Michel

*M*ike and I met at Taylor Statton Camp when we were about fifteen, on a canoe trip, in Quetico Park near Thunder Bay. Later on, we became camp counsellors there together. I used to visit Mike in Montreal, and that was when I first met his dad. We didn't talk that much, we'd say hello and everything, and then Mike and I would go out on the town.

When I moved to Whistler in 1996, Mike came out and we roomed together until he went to Halifax to attend Dalhousie University. I remember once Pierre came out to ski at Whistler. That was my first introduction to sushi, since Mike and his dad loved to order it. I guess my clearest impression of Pierre then was that I liked his clothes, his wardrobe in general. It was an indication he was his own person. That was always my favourite thing, seeing what he was wearing. The Trudeaus were all like that – they didn't care what people thought about how they looked.

After that, Mike moved to Rossland, and he called me up in Whistler and said that Rossland was a good place to live, and work, and ski, and that I ought to come out there, so I did. That was in the spring of 1998.

Mike never really talked much about his dad. Obviously we all knew about him and who he was, but Mike didn't want to make a big deal about it. He was pretty quiet about stuff like that.

Michel Trudeau

Tie-dyed and overalled.

After the accident, the three of us (Jeff Butcher, Brad Hamacher, and I) were stuck there for the night in a small outhouse by the lake, along with the two dogs, Makwa, Mike's dog, and my girlfriend's dog, Tyra. It was pretty cramped quarters. The three of us were flown out the next morning, but we had to leave the dogs behind, because there wasn't enough room in the helicopter, so we put them in the outhouse, with some of their rations from our trip, telling them we'd be back for them soon. I guess it was the next day, I don't remember now, that John Tweedy, a senior guy in avalanche control who worked for Search and Rescue, picked the dogs up. He found them in a snow cave they had dug just near the outhouse. Tyra was pretty excited, but Makwa was really shaken up from the accident. I have Makwa now, and I notice still that, once in a while, he has these moments – when he doesn't have much energy, or he gets all quiet – and I'm sure he's thinking about Mike.

I went back up to the site to help the Search and Rescue people in trying to locate Mike's body. I had to help them with the "last-seen point." I remember Mike's brother Sacha coming out there, a few days later, to help as well. That was pretty tough, as I felt responsible for the accident, being the most experienced person of all of us in backcountry

*Andrew and Justin at
Michel's memorial service.*

Canadian Press, Ryan Remiorz

travel. Looking back now, there were signs I could have read, but I try to
remember what the Search and Rescue guys said to me, that they had
seen a lot more experienced people do much worse things.

I went to Mike's memorial service in Montreal, but I don't remember much of it. I was pretty messed up. All I remember is walking into
the church and somebody asking my name, and I started to cry. At the
reception after, at the Mount Royal Club, somebody brought Pierre over.
It was a short visit; we were both obviously feeling pretty bad. I didn't
know what to say, because I was feeling pretty awful for him. I don't
remember what we talked about; mostly I was just thinking about Mike.
I remember looking into Pierre's eyes, knowing what he was going
through. There weren't any words to say that would help. Silence seemed
better . . . it was more about that than words.

The last time I saw Pierre was about a year later, when he and Justin
went to Lake Kokanee. Mike's backpack had surfaced in the lake, and I
guess then there was some possibility of finding his body. But the pack
was all they found. Once again, words between Pierre and me were
pretty brief. He had a quick look at the pack. As you might imagine, that
was not at all easy for him. I just tried to offer him support.

Showing the boys the sites and sights of Greece.

▶ RALPH COLEMAN
Assistant press secretary and chief advanceman, 1974–79;
press secretary, 1980–84

*P*ierre Trudeau relished his role as father. On official travels he often took one son or all three with him, and Canadians grew accustomed to seeing photos of the prime minister and his sons in exotic locales around the world, as well as here at home.

One of the most memorable moments for me was a domestic trip in the late 1970s. The prime minister was attending the opening of a summer exposition at the old Expo 67 site in Montreal, with his three boys in tow. His host was the colourful mayor of Montreal, Jean Drapeau.

While touring the site with the mayor – and despite the distractions of the media, the public, and the entourage of staff and RCMP security – the prime minister was constantly interacting with the boys. As each vied for his attention, the prime minister would listen attentively and respond in a way that would answer their questions. Watching this *père et fils* interplay, I noticed that one of his favourite words of praise was "Bravo." So, throughout the tour, I often heard: "Bravo, Justin," or "Bravo, Sacha," or "Bravo, Michel."

The tour was followed by a large official luncheon hosted by Mayor Drapeau. The mayor, the PM and his boys, and other official guests were seated together at one table. Before the food was served, the mayor gave the obligatory speech of welcome to the prime minister and asked him to address the invited guests.

The prime minister dutifully gave his speech to officially open the exposition. Now, this was *not* a speech that was destined to go down in the history books as great or memorable, such as the ones he gave during the 1980 referendum. I cannot remember even one word or phrase from this speech, for it was one of many such routine events that a prime minister is called upon to do. However, it impressed one bright young mind in the room.

When the speech was over, there was, of course, a round of enthusiastic applause from the invited guests. In these situations, of which I have seen many, there is always that momentary silence following

Canadian Press

Bravo Papa!

the applause, during which people turn their attention away from the speaker and are about to resume their table conversations. The silence lasts only about one or two seconds. But in this case, it was clearly long enough for young Michel, who was about four years old, to shout out loud enough for the entire room to hear.

"Bravo, Papa!"

Chapter Nineteen

Gloaming

▶ ALLAN J. MACEACHEN

MP, 1953–84; senator, 1984–91

*P*rime Minister Chrétien held a dinner in October 1999 at 24 Sussex to celebrate Mr. Trudeau's eightieth birthday. I had two conversations with Trudeau that night, and they proved to be among my last. The main receiving room was crowded on my arrival, so I had to make my way through a throng of his former associates, consisting really of his core political friends, in order to greet the guest of honour.

Expressing his welcome, he said to me: "Thank you for making the effort." At times, after he left office, he seemed truly puzzled that his friends would make the effort, for example, of going from Ottawa to Montreal to seek him out. This attitude was probably a sign of both detachment and humility.

At dinner, I was seated between Mr. Trudeau's son Sacha and Keith Davey, an old friend who was clearly showing the signs of illness by asking my help in identifying friends, and by his confusion in the details of his career in the Senate. Keith's waning powers and Mr. Trudeau's fragile presence made the atmosphere, for me, less than fully celebratory.

I had been asked to say the "proverbial few words" in taking note of Mr. Trudeau's outstanding career, and in expressing the appreciation of the assembled guests for the association and friendship they had enjoyed with him. In putting substance into my remarks, and linking

Allan watching his old friend pin the rose.

Mr. Trudeau with significant events and the accomplishments of his career, I selected for special attention the Charter of Rights and the defeat of the Clark government in 1979. Mr. Trudeau, I thought, needed to be brought out of his quiet and reflective mood that evening.

With respect to the Charter, Mr. Trudeau had consulted closely with the national Liberal caucus in the complicated process leading to the final enactment. He knew the support of caucus was critical. What is not generally understood and appreciated is that the national caucus insisted on – and gave the final push for – the inclusion of the Charter in the final package. It is not generally recalled that the cabinet did its work from a series of options, beginning with the patriation of the Constitution as the bedrock requirement, and escalating upwards in ambition to the Charter of Rights.

The attainment of the bedrock requirement would constitute a considerable achievement, and Mr. Trudeau, if necessary, would have settled for this bedrock. However, the inclusion of the Charter in the constitutional package was put before caucus for consideration. To thunderous applause, the Honourable Hazen Argue summed up the sentiment of that historic caucus by declaiming: "Let us go first class." Going first class meant including the Charter in the constitutional package. As I recounted this exciting episode from the Trudeau past, it brought a glow of energy to the face of Mr. Trudeau.

The night of the defeat of the Clark government was my second recollection. The political context was troubled and uncertain. The House of Commons itself was a scene of high tension facing a no-confidence vote on a Liberal motion on the John Crosbie budget. If it carried, the resignation of the government and a general election would follow. The stakes were high; the implications were momentous. The general air of nervousness and excitement increased, as members filled their seats, particularly as the clock moved to the time of the vote. No one was certain of the outcome. Some expected (even some Liberals hoped) that at the last minute the Liberal leadership would back off to a point. At least, it would not bring down the government.

All eyes were sizing up Mr. Trudeau, then the Leader of Her Majesty's Loyal Opposition. I was his desk-mate. Speculation was rife that, at the last minute, we would come up with an ingenious parliamentary man-oeuvre to take members away from the precipice staring them in the face. In the circumstances, this was not an unreasonable expectation, in view of the announced resignation of Mr. Trudeau as leader of the Liberal Party. The party was preparing for a leadership convention, and potential leadership candidates were assessing their prospects. It was natural enough to assume that no party would precipitate an election at such a time, and then scramble to organize a leadership convention in the relatively short period before the inevitable election.

Mr. Trudeau himself had given no assurance he would re-consider his resignation – the matter had not been discussed with him – and these considerations weighed heavily on the minds of Liberal members poised to vote. Mr. Trudeau did nothing to alleviate such concerns. He made no commitments. The closest he came – and that was not very close – to the subject was an oblique reference to "duty."

Alert and cool, he took a keen interest in the voting, as each member's name was called. He was delighted and impressed that every Liberal member showed up for the vote. He himself had taken no steps to influence Liberal members; in fact, he had made himself scarce all day.

When the Speaker announced the result of the vote, he kept his eyes fastened on Joe Clark. By this time Mr. Trudeau was clearly excited, moving around in his seat, and he kept saying: "Look at Joe's face! Look at Joe's face." At that moment, Trudeau's focus was not on the political. It was on the drama of Joe's personal predicament.

At the birthday dinner, I chided Mr. Trudeau on this reaction, saying to him, "Instead of getting a comment of political significance worthy of a statesman like Disraeli or Gladstone, all I got was a reflection on Joe's face!"

Mr. Trudeau's reply was brief. He thanked the prime minister and the guests, but he did not pick up on any of the themes of the evening.

However, at the end of the evening we had a deeply personal conversation. That was rare for us. He brought up his failing memory.

"You know, Allan, I cannot recall those events like you," he said.

That, from a person who previously showed a splendid recall of events. When I asked him about the state of his health, he replied, referring to the death of his son: "I have had a hard time. I believe I am getting better."

A readiness to mention any failing was not usual for Mr. Trudeau. I took it as a reflection of the depth of his suffering, and a readiness to accept what lay ahead.

▶ JACQUES HÉBERT
Close friend; travelling companion to China; and senator, 1983–98

*L*ast winter I was asked by a close friend of Pierre's if – during his last year, his last months – he ever talked to me about the fact he was dying. Decidedly no, I answered.

In over fifty years, the recollection of my encounters with this exceptional friend evoked nothing but happy moments. Above all: he liked to laugh, and I liked to laugh, and so . . . we laughed a great deal together. Our long lives, of course, were marked by a few tragic moments, even enormous sorrows that all the resources of an old friendship couldn't dispel. But, no, I said, Pierre never spoke to me about his death, even as its shadow already lurked in his gaze, which grew increasingly serene as his life was drawing to a close.

Jean-Marc Carisse

With Roméo LeBlanc and Jacques Hébert
at his 80th birthday party at Sussex Drive.

Then, suddenly, I remembered our last lunch, in June 2000, at the Chrysanthème, a Chinese restaurant on Crescent Street. I was about to begin a three-month trip aboard a van through the ten provinces and northern territories to promote Katimavik, a national youth program that never would have seen the light of day without Trudeau.

What amused Trudeau, the Spartan, in particular, was that I'd be roughing it: three months of driving and camping.

I was far from suspecting that this Chinese meal would be our last in a string of several hundred. As always, the General Tao chicken and Szechwan shrimp reminded us for the umpteenth time of the outrageous jokes we had played on each other during our trip to China, some forty years before. And *still* we laughed over them.

When we were done at the Chrysanthème, as usual, I saw him back to Heenan Blaikie, to the elevator leading to his office. This time, however, he insisted I go up with him.

"I have a small document I want to give you," he said, quietly.

We went into his office and he handed it to me. I began reading it. It was a photocopy of Teilhard de Chardin's beautiful prayer: "When the signs of age begin to mark my body (and still more when they touch my mind); when the illness that is to diminish me or carry me off . . ."

He interrupted me.

"You can read it later . . . at home. And since you're abandoning me for three months, allow me to walk you to the subway."

All of this was unusual, so out of the ordinary. He knew he was going to die soon; he knew I knew: then why talk about it. Still, the Teilhard de Chardin "document" was a clear allusion.

Standing by the stairs leading to the subway, he gave me a prolonged handshake, and left me with these rather strange words – at least coming from him – "Oh, how I envy you."

While I was on the road, I'd call him on a cell phone now and again, ostensibly to give him news of the trip, but mostly to reassure myself about the state of his health. We joked, as was our habit. A little less, perhaps, during our last phone conversation at the end of August.

"I see the summer's done you good. Your voice is stronger. You're doing better!" I half-heartedly blurted out.

Following a few seconds' silence, he answered in a voice that was calm and already frail.

"No, Jacques, I'm not doing better."

For the first time, I realized his days were numbered. When I was in Winnipeg, a few weeks later at a press conference on Katimavik, a reporter arrived with news that was shaking the entire country: Pierre Trudeau was at "death's door." From that point on, it was impossible for me to talk about Katimavik or anything else. The media only wanted to hear about one subject from me. All the questions related to my friend, the former prime minister.

So I decided to head back to Montreal by the shortest route. My mission was drawing to a close in any event, and if the speculations concerning Pierre Trudeau's health were the least bit accurate, I didn't want to waste a single minute, in the hope of seeing him one last time.

When I reached Montreal, on September 10, if memory serves, I contacted Sacha. He confirmed that his father had taken a turn for the worse. Mostly bedridden, he was seeing only members of his immediate family. I didn't insist.

The next day, Sacha called me back.

"My father says he wants to see you. Try to come over at about 4:00 p.m. That's the time of the day when he's up and sitting in a chair."

So I went over to Pine Avenue, my heart sinking, with a few of his favourite chocolate bars, which rekindled fond memories for us.

In that final conversation, we talked about his children, about Michel in particular, about the immeasurable beauty of the Canada he loved so much, about Katimavik and Canada World Youth . . . which filled him with *almost* as much pride as his own children.

Despite everything that last afternoon, when we were both trying to be strong for each other, through those moments of intense emotion, chewing our chocolate, we managed to laugh a little.

Perhaps that was the secret to our friendship that lasted over half a century: our ability to laugh with each other, even *that* afternoon. As I look back now on that last encounter, it was Pierre's generosity in sharing joy that remained, always, so strong.

▶ PETER MANSBRIDGE
CBC-TV correspondent, 1968–present

*I*t was an amazing scene. One you'd never expect to see in Ottawa.

There, late on a fall Saturday night, old people and young – elderly moving their walkers, youngsters being guided in their strollers – lined up around the walkways of Parliament Hill. They'd been arriving for hours and were quite happily prepared to wait for hours more for their moment – a moment in front of the casket, lying peacefully at the end of the Centre Block's Hall of Honour, draped in a Canadian flag and adorned with a single red rose.

But in those hours of slow movement outside, some remarkable conversations were taking place and, as I walked along the lines, I heard some of them. While the vast majority of the thousands and thousands who'd come to pay their respects were the so-called ordinary Canadians, people witnessing a moment in their country's history, many were also

*Former governor general Ray Hnatyshyn accompanied
by his wife, Gerda, arrive to pay their respects.*

men and women who were connected to that history. There were partisan admirers of course, who had flown or driven from across the country, but partisan opponents too – the men and women who had spent their political careers trying to break through the mystique that surrounded the most charismatic Canadian politician of our times.

There they stood, some silently, others exchanging the great stories of political battles past. With grudging admiration they conceded how, deep down, they'd more than just respected their opponent; they'd been honoured to do battle with him. They talked of how his arrival in Ottawa had brought fresh, dynamic energy to a place stodgy with old ideas; and how his (at times) controversial moves had forced them to work harder, and longer, and with more imagination, to counter and then propose bright alternatives.

And perhaps most often they'd talk about how, when he'd enter a crowded room, his eyes would mesmerize supporters and critics alike, and how it would feel as if the oxygen had been sucked out of the place from all the energy he consumed. There was a lot of heady talk that night from people who'd loved him and some who had, at times, actually despised him – but all of them felt he'd defined the most exciting and engaging time of their lives.

A few days later, a few hours after the train that took him away through the splendour of the Ottawa Valley's spectacular late-season colours, I found all of what had happened that weekend, from the emotion of tears and laughter to the memories of times past, captured in a single tangible object.

When the casket had been removed from the Hall of Honour, that single rose – the last one he'd wear in the building where he had made rose-wearing his daily ritual – had been left on a nearby chair. As no one else was picking it up, a close colleague of mine did, and he gave one of its petals to me. That single petal is now pressed and framed, and waiting for my son, whose mother had been one of those pushing a stroller for hours along Parliament's walkways. It's waiting for him to be old enough to understand and appreciate that unique time in Canadian history, which it will always represent.

▶ UNSIGNED

*I*n August 2000, Pierre Elliott Trudeau was dying. For this most public of men it was to be a very private process. For all Canadians, the end was to be a very public one. A few friends or faithful retainers (because no matter how much you became the former, you always considered yourself the latter), came together that month in an effort to take some of the load off his family, and to begin to plan for a possible funeral that would give all Canadians an opportunity to honour his memory while respecting his and the family's wishes for privacy during the difficult final weeks of his life.

Pierre Trudeau was first and foremost a Canadian, but also very much a strong Quebecker, with deep roots in the province, particularly in Montreal and in the Laurentian mountains, where he maintained a property and to which he returned frequently while prime minister. Unlike many of his predecessors, Ottawa never became his permanent residence. Immediately on retirement he returned to Montreal, where he was to be seen daily, walking to work no matter what the weather. Any funeral arrangements had to include an opportunity for Canadians, in general, but also Quebeckers and Montrealers, an opportunity to pay their respects and say goodbye.

The natural reluctance of Justin and Sacha to consider these issues while their father was dying, and their desire to keep his condition private, meant that the organization of this relatively complex set of events had to be done in a very short time frame and involve very few people.

He had been seriously ill once before, in January 2000. Despite freezing weather, the media immediately surrounded the hospital where he was recovering from pneumonia. But a press release from his family describing his condition and asking for privacy was immediately respected.

A similar press release on a warm day in early September 2000, following a tip from Ottawa to his family that a television network was about to announce his hitherto secret failing health, met with an entirely different and utterly inconsiderate response. An undignified stakeout began around his house, involving camera crews, satellite trucks, and dozens of reporters. One television network erected a live camera on a telescoping pole that peered permanently into a third-floor window.

Friends and family were impeded in coming and going. Even some of the journalists involved were embarrassed at their own behaviour, and after a day or so, the siege was lifted when the family issued a second press release saying they would inform the media if his condition worsened.

Pierre Trudeau died September 28, 2000. The initial small group of four who met to work out a State Funeral was expanded, and started to meet almost continuously, beginning the next day, with the full involvement of the boys. There was rapid agreement on the program: his lying in state in Ottawa in order for all Canadians to pay their respects, his casket brought home to Montreal by train, accompanied by some of his old Quebec friends; the lying in state at the Hôtel de Ville for Quebeckers and Montrealers to say goodbye, followed by a State Funeral at Notre Dame Basilica; and finally, a private burial in the family tomb at St-Remi-de-Napierville, a small town on the south shore of the St. Lawrence River and the original home of the Trudeau family.

This program, the organization of the church service, and the selection of the pallbearers, was approved by Justin and Sacha, within twenty-four hours of their father's death. For the last time, Pierre Trudeau inspired everyone to work beyond his or her limits and, with the help of an outstanding team from the Department of Canadian Heritage, the program came together flawlessly.

However, the question for all of us was, how would the Canadian people, generally, and Quebeckers specifically, respond to the death of someone who had been absent from public life for over sixteen years? From the long lines on Parliament Hill, to the school children lining the tracks in Eastern Ontario and Western Quebec, to the crowds that met his casket when it arrived in Montreal, to the line-up to say goodbye at City Hall, to those who stood patiently outside the Cathedral during the funeral service, and finally, to the millions of Canadians who followed the events across the country on television, the response was dignified, emotional, and massive.

At the request of the family, the location of the burial was kept confidential and the attendance at the graveside restricted to family members. But as the cortège approached St-Remi-de-Napierville, the local villagers stood quietly in the streets and on their porches. They knew Pierre Trudeau was finally coming home.

Leaving Parliament Hill for the last time.

Acknowledgments

Nobody can put a book like this together without a staff of two or three dedicated and focused people to keep on top of phone messages, addresses, e-mails, general correspondence, including envelope stamping, and finding correct zip codes, or returning hundreds of messages. Not to mention regularly smoothing and consoling some very hefty egos associated with a project of this magnitude.

But I had no staff or secretary. Well, I did have Michele Sansoucy, Pierre's long-time secretary, come in for a few hours to help write some letters and fix up a messy (but amazing) address book. The first time she was here, a particularly cold January afternoon, I was having a horrid time trying to keep about ten ideas in my head (two of them non-book-related), and returning from lunch with a potential contributor, I drove my vehicle into the icy driveway and promptly creamed the whole left side of Michele's car. She took it all quite cheerfully, saying something like, well, let's get back to this list, and by the way your phone has been ringing off the hook. Thank you, Michele, for your sense of humour and perspective.

Gathering the master list of names, contacts, leads, and unlisted phone numbers was one grand deep-sea fishing expedition. It took me five months. Along the way, I relied heavily on a group of friends for advice, direction, and counsel. In no particular order, I am humbly grateful to Ivan Head, Ted Johnson, Bob Murdoch, Joyce Fairbairn, Jacques Hébert, Jim Coutts, Marc Lalonde, Roger Rolland, Lowell Murray, Leonard Cohen, Shelley Ambrose, Ron Graham, Arthur Erickson, Marie-Hélène Fox, Rick Kohler, Louise Duhamel, Gerry Wall, Kelley Lynch, Isabel Fonseca, and Laurence Freeman. Without them, this book would easily be only fifty-six pages long.

Pat Kennedy (formerly of McClelland & Stewart) helped straighten and tighten the manuscript.

To all the contributors, those here and those that I didn't include in the book, I am honoured to have worked with you.

I want to publicly thank the biggest fan of this long, long journey, my mother, Jeannie M. Southam, who for over two years allowed "The Pierre Book" to come first.

Lastly, I want to thank Gerald H. Johnson, my fiancé (who had to live through the last nightmarish year of finishing the book), for his patience, his faith, and his love.

Index

Boldface page numbers indicate a contributed piece.